Miles to Go

Also by Daniel Patrick Moynihan

Pandaemonium: Ethnicity in International Politics

On the Law of Nations

Came the Revolution: Argument in the Reagan Era

Family and Nation

Loyalties

Counting Our Blessings: Reflections on the Future of America

A Dangerous Place

Ethnicity: Theory and Experience (Editor, with Nathan Glazer)

Coping: Essays on the Practice of Government

The Politics of a Guaranteed Income

On Equality of Educational Opportunity (Editor, with Frederick Mosteller)

On Understanding Poverty: Perspectives from the Social Sciences (Editor)

Toward a National Urban Policy (Editor)

Maximum Feasible Misunderstandings: Community Action in the War on Poverty

The Defenses of Freedom: The Public Papers of Arthur J. Goldberg (Editor)

Beyond the Melting Pot: The Negroes, Puerto Ricans, Jews, Italians, and Irish in New York City (With Nathan Glazer)

MILES TO GO

A Personal History of Social Policy

◆

DANIEL PATRICK MOYNIHAN

HARVARD UNIVERSITY PRESS
Cambridge, Massachusetts
London, England
1996

Library of Congress Cataloging-in-Publication Data

Moynihan, Daniel P. (Daniel Patrick), 1927–
Miles to go : a personal history of social policy /
Daniel Patrick Moynihan.
p.   cm.
Includes bibliographical references and index.
ISBN 0-674-57440-0 (hardcover)
1. Social policy. 2. United States—Social policy.
3. United States—Social conditions—1980–   I. Title.
HN28.M69 1997
361.6'1—7dc20   96-8291

For Margaret Bright

Acknowledgments

The Congressional Research Service of the Library of Congress has been indefatigable in shoring up the arguments that follow. As a member of the Joint Committee on the Library I have endeavored to show my gratitude, and can report that with the end of the 104th Congress in prospect, the Library has not yet been privatized. Adam Levine made wondrous work of the opportunities the Library presented. Eleanor Suntum was prodigious, as ever.

Contents

Introduction

In the summer of 1987 I was in Moscow on a mission of possible importance. Our small party was received with courtesy and a measure of ceremony. One morning we visited the Lenin Mausoleum, laid a wreath at the Tomb of the Unknown Soldier, and thereafter were shown through Lenin's apartments in the Kremlin. Behind the desk in his working office was a small bookshelf with several rows of works in English and French. These, one had to suppose, had been selected for the impression they would make on visitors in, let us say, the 1930s. It was, even so, a bit of a start to see books by three authors I had met in my own lifetime: Bertrand Russell, G. D. H. Cole, and an American whose name has fled. That afternoon we met with "Alternative Member of the Politburo Yeltsin." Our Ambassador, Jack F. Matlock, Jr., later recalled, "As the conversation began, Senator Moynihan attempted to establish a little rapport by mentioning that they had visited Lenin's apartment and office and he had noticed some books in Lenin's library by people with whom he was familiar, and he named them . . . This drew a total blank from Yeltsin, whereupon Senator Moynihan explained that he was simply trying to point out that the intellectual traditions of our systems do have some points where they touch.

Well, it was pretty clear that Yeltsin had not read the books in Lenin's library; as a matter of fact, I doubt that he had read a book since the technical manuals he was forced to read in the construction institute which he attended. But it was a noble effort."[1] What Yeltsin really wanted to know from me was how in the hell he was supposed to run Moscow with 1929 rent controls. So that is what it had come to; banality, indeed!

The scene recurred to me as I contemplated the ruin of the 1994 Congressional elections. The Soviet system had collapsed—something I claim to have foreseen and in about the time frame in which it did occur. But what of the seeming collapse of everything at home! Nothing so momentous, to be sure, but I had expected the Soviet implosion; the Congressional debacle of 1994 came as a complete surprise.

Something *had* happened. A roiling discontent with government had in 1992 overturned a first-term Republican president, bringing forth the first significant third-party challenge since the beginning of the century. We had now seemingly rejected a first-term Democratic president who had won by default as much as anything but had set out to govern as if he had a mandate for all manner of governing. The reader will take my mood.

Then there was the matter of my own 1994 campaign. Elections are binary affairs, or are seen as such. One person wins; the other loses. Margins don't much matter, or aren't much noticed. Withal, my contests in New York had been singular. In 1982 I broke the state record for the largest margin of victory in a Senate race. Then in 1988 I broke the national record also, with a margin of 2,172,865. (The previous record in a contested race, at 1,611,968, was set in California in 1980.) I had run up the largest *vote* of any Senate race in New York, greater than Kennedy, Javits, Wagner. With 67.0 percent of the total vote cast (excluding blank and void ballots), I had achieved the highest percentage of any modern candidate for Senate *or* Governor. (Rockefeller in 1958 had stunned the state with a 54.7 percent margin.) I became one of five persons to have carried New York City by more than one million votes—a few more than Franklin D. Roosevelt in 1936, somewhat fewer than Lyndon B. Johnson in 1964.

The 1988 election had been a broad-based victory. From the eighteenth century on, our politics has been divided between the great city and the rest of the state. In 1949 Herbert H. Lehman was elected to the Senate carrying 5 of our 62 counties; in 1988 I carried 61. That was a presidential year, and the ticket-splitting was unprecedented. In the village of New Square in Rockland County, where Orthodox Jewish voters live frugal lives, George Bush won by a margin of 773 to 9. I came in at 756 to 21. Across the Hudson River in Westchester County, the conspicuously affluent township of Lewisboro recorded a 59.1 percent margin for Bush, 58 percent for Moynihan. In the more diverse precincts of Staten Island, the Vice President won 61.8 percent of the vote, the now-senior Senator 63.1 percent.

Among ethnic, racial, and religious groups the outcome was similarly striking. An NBC News and *Wall Street Journal* exit poll of 2,528 voters on election day showed us with 94 percent of black voters, 91 percent of Jewish, 90 percent of "Reagan Democrats." That, along with 75 percent of "Less than High School Graduates" and 79 percent of "More than College" about wraps it up. Well, one last return just in: I carried Dutchess County, seat of the Roosevelts. In four presidential contests, FDR never did.

In 1989 I went back to Washington, where George Bush, a good friend for the longest while, had been elected President and where the Senate had returned to what was judged to be its normal Democratic majority. I was now the first New Yorker since Robert F. Wagner to serve in the majority with 12 years' Senate experience. My revered Jacob K. Javits served 24 years in the Senate, but never a day in the majority. It followed I would become chairman of the Committee on Environment and Public Works, again the first committee chairman from New York since Wagner.

By 1991 Robert A. Roe in the House and I had put together the Intermodal Surface Transportation Efficiency Act (ICE-TEA, as it would be known). It was just exactly 30 years since I had written for the *Reporter* magazine a long cover story, "New Roads and Urban Chaos," which argued that the Interstate and Defense Highway program—conceived in the General Motors Futurama exhibit in 1939 (I had *seen* it), authorized by Roosevelt, begun as the New York State Thruway by Governor Thomas E. Dewey, and launched nationwide by President Dwight D. Eisenhower—was going to devastate American cities. Interstate highways were too big to fit; they would smash up everything; jobs would flee. Now the Interstate system was at last finished. Roe and I decided it was time to redress the balance in favor of transit and rail. A *Washington Post* commentary called it "the first advance in thinking about transportation in 35 years, a near revolutionary change," adding, "for which Sen. Daniel Patrick Moynihan deserves most of the credit." In a moment of audacity, I even got $5 billion to repay New York for the Thruway which runs the breadth of the state on the old Erie Canal route.

1993: The First of the Clinton Years

Then came the presidency of William J. Clinton. Senator Lloyd Bentsen of Texas became Secretary of the Treasury and I, in turn, Chairman of the Senate Finance Committee. Now this *was* something. Starting back in 1977, I had produced an annual accounting of the flow of federal funds between New York State and the federal government.[2] New York's "balance of payments" was devastatingly unbalanced, and more devastating still was our seeming incapacity to grasp this. Federal money was seen as a free good, and—especially for liberals—the more, well, the merrier. The thought that the federal budget was, in fact, a debilitating exaction—and not by accident, for the New Dealers conceived it that way—was beyond our political reach.[3]

In the course of the next century, the United States will have to address the constitutional problem of "equal Suffrage in the Senate" (Article V), but for this century the next best thing for a large state is to have a chairman of the Committee on Finance, a position last held by a New Yorker in 1851. From its creation in 1815 the

Finance Committee, along with Ways and Means in the House of Representatives, has raised the revenues of the federal government mostly, at first, through tariffs. Its consequence grew legendary. Thus, Ambrose Bierce in *The Devil's Dictionary* (1906): "*Quorum,* n. A sufficient number of members of a deliberative body to have their own way and their own way of having it. In the United States Senate a quorum consists of the chairman of the Committee on Finance and a messenger from the White House."

The Sixteenth Amendment, ratified in 1913, added the income tax to the Committee's jurisdiction. Then social insurance was added under the New Deal. This appears to have been a pragmatic accommodation suggested to Frances Perkins, Roosevelt's Secretary of Labor, by Supreme Court Justice Harlan Fiske Stone. At a garden party in Washington in 1934 she described her great hopes for a Social Security Act, but feared they would be dashed when the great men of the Court declared it, as they surely would declare it, unconstitutional. Mr. Justice Stone leaned over and whispered, "The taxing power, my dear. All you need is the taxing power." (Perkins, who had handled Big Tim Sullivan in the New York State Assembly, had not the least difficulty with a mere Supreme Court Justice.)

Thus, while lore attributes the Social Security Act to Wagner, and indeed he was there on August 14, 1935, when the bill was signed, the man standing immediately to Roosevelt's right in the official photograph was Representative Robert Lee Doughton, of Allegheny County, North Carolina, Chairman of the House Committee on Ways and Means. Social Security was a *tax,* and of course revenue bills must originate in the House. Inevitably this produced a degree of tension, notably in the Senate. The enthusiasts for social insurance and income maintenance programs tended to be concentrated in the Labor Committee (most recently, the Committee on Labor and Human Resources), but the jurisdiction implacably resided in the Finance Committee. Some years ago, a new member asked then-Chairman Russell B. Long of Louisiana what was the Finance Committee's jurisdiction. "Just about everything," the Chairman replied.[4] On May 31, 1993, *Time* would record me as one of "the ten most powerful people in Washington." Well, not exactly. Republicans had picked up one Senate seat in the 1992 election, making for a 56–44 party split. This, in turn, meant that the Finance Committee would be divided 11–9. *That,* in turn, meant that when there was a partisan division, every Democrat had to vote with the chairman for the chairman to prevail. (Tie votes fail.) This, in effect, gave each of the remaining ten Democrats a veto over the Committee's actions. Each of us, then, was one of "the ten most powerful people in Washington."

A presidential candidate wins, and the opposing party is effectively excluded from presidential matters for the next four years. By contrast, in the Senate a party can win a majority, organize the body, and need minority votes the very next week. To complicate matters, this is not true in the House, where the majority, if united, can rule in a House of Commons mode. In any event, these facts of the Congress rarely impress themselves on Presidents. Woodrow Wilson, having published fifteen editions of *Congressional Government* ("I know not how better to describe our form of government in a single phrase than by calling it a government by the chairmen of the Standing Committees of the Congress"), proved utterly unable to understand that if Henry Cabot Lodge, chairman of the Committee on Foreign Relations, determined there had to be certain reservations to the Covenant of the League of Nations, there had to be such, else the United States would not join. Wilson was the last President to have been elected by a margin as small as William J. Clinton's 43 percent. But not unlike Wilson, the margin seemed to argue for adventure rather than caution.

I set to work, abetted by a fine Committee staff now headed by Lawrence O'Donnell, Jr., who carried out his mission with a combination of intellect and brawn that only someone out of the street corners of Irish Dorchester by way of Harvard College could conceive, much less carry off. The recession that undid the presidency of George Bush still lingered. On February 24, 1993, the Committee reported out the Emergency Unemployment Compensation Act (S.382), which passed the full Senate 66–33 on March 3. Take particular note: when there is a true majority, Congress can act in a matter of hours. (A second extension of emergency benefits passed the Senate on October 28 by a 76–20 margin and became law November 23.) Soon we were bumping up against the debt ceiling again. On April 2, the Committee passed out a bill to increase the limit from $4,145 trillion to $4,370 trillion. This passed the Senate three days later and became law on April 6. This got us through until the following fall, by which time I had put through the Senate an increase that would get us through the end of 1995.

The President's authority to negotiate the Uruguay Round trade agreement, the largest of the postwar era, which is to say, the largest ever, expired June 1, 1993. I managed an extension to December 15, which passed the Senate 76–16. The negotiations had been dragging on for ten years, the consequence of having moved from issues of tariffs on *things*—iron, steel—which had been the subject of Cordell Hull's original reciprocal trade agreements, to the more complex and now more central issues of trade in services—banking, intellectual property protection, patents, dispute settlements, and the like. I had worked on these matters since the Long-Term Cotton Textile Agreement reached in Geneva in 1962, which in turn set the Kennedy Round going. It was for me an affair of the heart, especially the establishment of the World Trade Organization.

The postwar economic planners of the United States and Britain had three new institutions in mind: the International Bank for Reconstruction and Development (the World Bank), the International Monetary Fund, and an International Trade Organization. The last not least, for if one were to list a half-dozen events that led to the Second World War, surely one would be the Smoot-Hawley tariff of 1930, the former being Reed Smoot of Utah, chairman of the Committee on Finance. It cost him his seat, but his ghost lingered on, and in 1947 the Finance Committee declined to endorse an International Trade Organization. Now, near to half a century later, the Committee caught up with history.

I got the final measure through on December 1, 1994, by a 76–24 vote. The ranking member, Bob Packwood of Oregon, and I thereupon wrote the President asking that we try to have the new

organization located in Washington, reasoning that Geneva, where
the General Agreement on Tariffs and Trade had settled, was too
far from us and too close to the impenetrable bureaucracy of the
European Community in Brussels. (We never did get a reply.)

Few realized it, which may be just as well, but this was vast
legislation. Elements included: clarification of the relationship of
the new Agreement to state and federal law; provisions requiring
notification and consultation regarding WTO dispute settlement
proceedings; extensive changes to the antidumping and counter-
vailing duty laws; renewal of the "Super 301" statute aimed at unfair
trade practices; amendments to the 1930 Tariff Act, providing
remedies to imports infringing U.S. intellectual property rights, to
conform with GATT rules. The implementing legislation also contained financing provisions (to offset the cost of reduced federal
tariffs) which included major reforms to the laws protecting workers' pensions—the so-called Retirement Protection Act of 1993.
This in turn contained major reforms to the funding requirements
for private employer pension plans, to better insure workers' retirement security, and provided for more effective oversight of employer plans by the Pension Benefit Guaranty Corporation. More,
it was bipartisan. I had been on the Finance Committee some
sixteen years before heading it. There had been four chairmen, two
from each party. The Committee was often split, but rarely along
party lines. An economist would probably reason that there was too
much to be gained by cooperation to make partisan division
sufficiently rewarding.

Now, however, came the budget, *the* great measure of Clinton's
first year. It was surely political, how could it not be, but the politics,
or so it seemed to me, were not at all understood on the Democratic
side, and perhaps only dimly so among Republicans. This was a
matter of large consequence from a particular perspective. Toward
the close of the 1970s, settling into the Senate, I had begun to
sense a stirring among a new group of conservatives. Even as the
pieties of the balanced budget persisted—FDR had, after all, attacked Herbert Hoover's deficits and promised to end them at

once—certain Republicans had commenced to treat deficits as something rather to be encouraged. But not in the now-classical Keynesian mode that informed, say, the economists of the Nixon administration. This new inclination to enlarge the debt had nothing to do with managing the economy; the issue was the size and reach of government. Of a sudden, Republicans on the Finance Committee were proposing tax cuts quite unrelated to any business cycle. They had an idea, and a big one. By the close of the Carter administration, it was plain enough that the Democratic party had nothing much to offer by way of ideas about whatever it was that troubled us. But Democrats quite failed to see that the Republicans did. They had become a party of ideas. I wrote of this in the *New York Times* in July 1980:

▼

Psychologists call it role reversal. As a Democrat, I call it terrifying. And to miss it is to miss what could be the onset of the transformation of American politics. Not by chance, but by dint of sustained and often complex argument, there is a movement to turn Republicans into Populists, a party of the People arrayed against a Democratic Party of the State. This is the clue to the across-the-board Republican tax-cut proposal now being offered more or less daily in the Senate by Dole of Kansas, Armstrong of Colorado, and their increasingly confident cohorts.

It happens that just now they are "right." The economy is in a steep recession, facing a huge tax increase (Social Security payments, combined with the "bracket creep") next year. Certainly a $30 billion cut in 1981 taxes is in order, and ought to be agreed on quickly . . .

But these same Republicans were calling for tax cuts in 1978 and 1979 when clearly they were "wrong"—by, that is, established standards of fiscal policy. The point is that these are no longer men of that Establishment. The process of change has been unremarkable enough. After a half century of more or less unavailing opposition (Republicans have controlled the Congress only four years since 1930), it was possible to agree that new ideas were necessary.

Observe Bill Brock, chairman of the Republican National Committee, announcing the appearance, in 1978, of *Commonsense: A Republican Journal of Thought and Opinion*.

> We must not forget that the last great partisan coalition of American politics was built on ideas. These were no less forceful and appealing, if also debatable, for all their identification with a political party. The notion of an activist federal government, with an obligation to use its centralized power "to meet new social problems with new social controls," was a new idea in the 1930s. But it took hold, built a durable coalition, became the foundation for decades of programmatic public policy, and tended to capture the terms of the political debate.
>
> As an idea, it had consequences. Only lately have these come to be generally understood as having mixed implications for the nation and for individuals in it. Accordingly, the Republican Party finds itself in opposition, at this writing, not only to a majority party that controls the machineries of government, but to the force of certain such ideas. It is our continuing obligation, therefore . . . to articulate our own.

This journal has been faithful to its promise. The material is first-rate. We Democrats have nothing approaching it. Of a sudden, the GOP has become a party of ideas. The Republicans' dominant idea, at least for the moment, seems to be that the social controls of modern government have became tyrannical or, at the very least, exorbitantly expensive. This oppression—so the strategic analysis goes—is made possible by taxation, such that cutting taxes becomes an objective in its own right, business cycles notwithstanding.

▲

Within six months of the date of that article, Ronald Reagan would be President and the strategy to "starve the beast" would be put in place by a formidable group of presidential aides who knew just what they were about.[5] I could follow this, withal dimly, and set about warning fellow Democrats. They are creating a fiscal crisis, I would argue. Why would anyone do that? was the general response. In his fine study, *Sleepwalking through History: America in the Reagan Years,* Haynes Johnson writes, "Moynihan was the first to charge that the Reagan administration 'consciously and deliberately brought about' higher deficits to force congressional domestic cuts. Moynihan was denounced and then proven correct—except that cuts to achieve balanced budgets were never made, and deficits ballooned ever higher."

By 1993 the deficit, with the accompanying debt service, was doing the job that had been expected from the tax cuts. Government was approaching paralysis. In 1982, for the first time in history, the federal government was forced to close, howsoever briefly, for lack of funds; by the end of 1995, this would have occurred twelve times. Plain prudence argued that this condition had to be reversed.

President Clinton proposed to do just that, asking for $500 billion in deficit reduction over five years, divided roughly equally between tax increases and spending cuts. The Finance Committee would handle most of it. Republican members promptly opted out, leaving it to the eleven Democrats to enact, *inter alia*, the largest tax increase in history. Which we did. Just. The bill was reported out of committee on June 18, 1993, 11–9, and on August 6, 1993, passed the full Senate 51–50, with the Vice President casting the deciding vote. Four days later the President signed the bill in a ceremony on the South Lawn of the White House. I ought to have noticed I was the only Senator present.

Very well, it *was* the largest tax increase in our history (probably in all history). Back in the Kennedy years in the Department of Labor, a thoughtful economist had concluded, as regards the New Economics, that we had shown we could *cut* taxes but we had yet to show we could *raise* them. Now, finally, we had done so. Further, in the arcane ways that markets are said to interpret and anticipate events, it now appeared we were serious about the deficit. Whereupon the "deficit premium" on interest rates—the extra charge for the risk that we would monetize the debt through inflation—fell off sharply. With the consequent decline in the cost of debt service, we ended up having saved an additional $100 billion, for an overall deficit reduction of $600 billion. In time the idea that inflation was a fixed condition began to recede, more perhaps the effect of global markets than of the American political economy, but we had even so done something significant.

We had shown we could raise taxes; cutting them had been the easy part of countercyclical economics as bequeathed from the 1930s. Martin Feldstein, Chairman of the President's Council of Economic Advisers (1982–1984) and professor of economics at Harvard, would argue that this actually slowed growth, but in the first three years of the Clinton presidency the United States created some eight million new jobs, while employment in Japan scarcely moved and actually fell in Germany. Who knows but that the eight million might have been nine million? We had done what it was thought could not be done; on occasion this is good for government.

There were other useful things in the mammoth bill, the Omnibus Budget Reconciliation Act of 1993. I was able to expand the Earned Income Tax Credit, a tax cut for families with incomes of $30,000 or less; to manage a permanent extension of the Low-Income Housing Credit, a longed-for alternative to public housing which seemed to be working well; and to reinstate the tax deduction for gifts of appreciated property to colleges, museums, and other nonprofit institutions.

The Finance Committee portion of OBRA '93 was not without its embarrassments. At the insistence of the new White House, we found $2.5 billion for nine "Empowerment Zones" and 95 "Enterprise Communities." This was a recurrent urban planning enthusiasm going at least as far back as the community action programs of the 1960s War on Poverty, through Model Cities, and into the present.[6] Wage credits, tax deductions, and HUD grants would make the urban desert bloom. New York—Harlem—would get one, as would Chicago, Atlanta, Detroit, and Philadelphia-Camden. But this being Congress, a representative body, there would also be a Kentucky Highlands Empowerment Zone, a Mid-Delta Mississippi, and a Rio Grande Valley. Of the Enterprise Communities, 65 would be located in urban areas, 30 in rural areas. The usual.

Nor was that the end of it. The administration's proposal had all manner of '60s enthusiasms tucked in here and there, notably immunization. In talking with the new White House staff, counting word for word, make that hour for hour, the issue of the deficit rarely arose. The *big* issue was finding $3 billion to provide universal free immunization for infants and children. Dan Rostenkowski on the House Committee on Ways and Means and I were puzzled. New York and Chicago *had* free immunization—had had for most of the century. What *was* this? It was, in painful truth, another mode in which to avoid the facts of family life in the ghetto. Ominously, the plan provided that the free vaccines would be distributed across the nation from a single warehouse in New Jersey. But there was no arguing with them; we found the money.

I was, in truth, an untroubled loyalist. I had roundly supported the U.S.-Canada free trade agreement of 1988. Mexico, however, was another matter. It was, to my thinking, a one-party state, a Marxist party to boot, now seemingly entering into the final stages of corruption and piecemeal collapse that such regimes seem to undergo. Putting aside any question of political science uniformities, I simply did not want American businessmen or union leaders appealing to Mexican judges in the pay of the Party of the Institutionalized Revolution, continuously in power since 1927. I had voted against giving fast-track authority to President Bush, who, of course, got the authority he'd asked for anyway. Now his successor sent us a final agreement. I dutifully enough held hearings, got my argument into the record, and saw the bill out of the Committee by a voice vote. On the floor I asked Senator Baucus of Montana, chairman of the subcommittee on International Trade, to manage the bill, which passed 61–38 on November 30. That close a vote might have suggested a measure of caution for the future. (Some while after the event Bruce Ackerman and David Golove would publish *Is NAFTA Constitutional?* contending that it is a treaty, not a trade agreement, and accordingly, subject to the treaty clause of Article II, Section 2.) No matter, the President ended his first year in office with yet another success.

1994: Health Care Reform

Then came health care. The administration was persuaded the time had now come for this last, culminating measure of social insurance—an achievement that had eluded Truman, Nixon, all manner of Presidents previous. Polls proved it; election results showed it. It had been thought a bill would be ready in short order. As it happened, it took a year. The bill I introduced just as Congress was adjourning in the fall of 1993 was not, in fact, the final bill; but we got it on record that there was a bill during the First Session of the 103rd Congress. Already, on September 30, I had opened hearings with the First Lady, Hillary Rodham Clinton—the first of thirty-one full-committee sessions. We needed them, leastwise I needed them, as I knew little of the subject. At best I knew two things.

First, the United States had probably the best, and certainly the most expensive, health care system on earth. The great infectious diseases of the past were just that: gone. This was mostly the triumph of sanitary engineering, nutrition, and housing. As Lewis Thomas would note, medicine had been marginal in that transformation, but now was coming into its own. It had taken the whole of the nineteenth century to get doctors to stop harming their patients. Which was something. But now the advent of antibiotics made significant cures possible. Inquire of a professor of medicine: In what decade of the twentieth century was the random patient with the random ailment encountering the random doctor better off for the treatment received? The response rarely varies: Somewhere in the 1930s, perhaps a bit later. Bear in mind that Franklin D. Roosevelt, as President of the United States, was treated for poliomyelitis by seating him in natural springs with faintly sulfuric aromas. A Roman magistrate would have been similarly doctored. As governor of New York, Roosevelt had caused to be built the great complex of thermal baths at Saratoga, north of Albany, for just such purposes. Into the Harriman years the state provided page-long analyses of the mineral contents of the waters of the various springs, suggesting subcutaneous absorption of miracle-cure potential. But following the Second World War medicine entered a great age of discovery. By contrast with physics in the early part of the century, which had been almost entirely a European science, medical science was notably an American field, much of it centered in New York City.

As results improved, effort increased. Expenditure flowed to medicine much as it would to any newly discovered, rewarding activity. In an article in *Science* in 1980, Thomas began: "The health-care system of this country is a staggering enterprise, in any sense of the adjective. Whatever the failures of distribution and lack of coordination, it is the gigantic scale and scope of the total collective effort that first catches the breath, and its cost. The dollar figures are almost beyond grasping. They vary from year to year, always upward, ranging from something like $10 billion in 1950 to an estimated $200 billion in 1979, with much more to come in the years just ahead, whenever a national health-insurance program is installed. The official guess is that we are now investing around 8 percent of the GNP in health: it could soon rise to 10 or 12 percent."[/]

By 1994 it had in fact risen to 15.1 percent, with a "Congressional Budget Office baseline" projecting a rise to 18.9 percent by the year 2000, a rate of increase just perceptibly slowing from 9.4 percent per year to 8.0 percent, which is to say, doubling every eight or nine years. From something like $10 billion in 1980, health expenditures were projected to rise to $1,631 billion 20 years later.

Now then, how were Americans taking all this good fortune? Not well, leastwise not well from Thomas's point of view. To the contrary, he wrote: "We are, in real life, a reasonably healthy people. Far from being ineptly put together, we are amazingly tough, durable organisms, full of health, ready for most contingencies. The new danger to our well-being, if we continue to listen to all the talk, is in becoming a nation of healthy hypochondriacs, living gingerly, worrying ourselves half to death. Tennis has become more than the national sport; it is a rigorous discipline, a form of collective physiotherapy. Jogging is done by swarms of people, out onto the streets each day in underpants, moving in a stolid sort of rapid trudge, hoping by this to stay alive. Bicycles are cures. Meditation may be good for the soul but it is even better for the blood pressure. As a people, we have become obsessed with health." This obsession had come to Washington; no doubt.

A second thing I can be said to have known as this (high) drama commenced is that health care costs to government were indeed out of control. As I will remark in a moment, health care costs overall were stabilizing, but where government provided care as a free good, demand was effectively limitless. Nothing new there; but a hugely important distinction which the administration planners couldn't or wouldn't make, insisting that the particular was the general. For indeed the particular, that is to say, the federal programs, had become unsustainable and seemed to validate the rhetoric of crisis. In the eight years of Ronald Reagan, Medicaid spending doubled from $14.5 billion to $30.5 billion. In the four years of George Bush, it doubled again to $67.8 billion. Our staff at this time was graced with the presence of Jack Fowle, a geneticist on leave from the Environmental Protection Agency, who conceived this as a geometric progression and demonstrated that, at that rate, on December 29, 1996, the cost of Medicaid would double in *one day.*

I had no difficulty diagnosing this as Baumol's disease. William Baumol, sometime President of the American Economic Association, was a friend of many years. Although early on he had settled in Princeton, he and his vibrant wife, Hilda, remained devoted to the New York opera of their youth. At about the time, 1962, that Arthur J. Goldberg, as Secretary of Labor, was asked to arbitrate a strike of the Metropolitan Opera orchestra, Baumol began to ask himself *why* it seemed always to be on strike. A question an economist might well pose, and one of some personal interest. In association with William G. Bowen, he came up with the idea of the "cost disease" of personal services, which in time economists would call Baumol's disease. The number of players, the number of instruments, the amount of time it took to "produce" a Mozart quartet in the eighteenth century will not have changed one whit two centuries later. To play the "Minute Waltz" in 50 seconds leaves something to be desired. True of first violinists, kindergarten teachers, beat cops, sculptors, and so through a great repertoire of occupations.

At one of the Committee hearings, three eminent medical deans had finished testifying. I faced them and asked what could they do about Baumol's disease? Troubled looks. (Can I have missed that lecture?) Chairman: "Montefiore Hospital was founded in New York City in the 1880s. At that time, how long did it take for a professor of medicine to make his morning rounds, and how many interns would he take along with him?" Dean: "Oh, about an hour; say 12 interns." Chairman: "And today?" Dean: "Got it!" (Not for nothing Dean.)

Back in 1962 Secretary Goldberg had determined that with the best will in the world, the opera trustees just couldn't find any more money. He awarded the orchestra a token raise and asked me to draft a proposal for a national response. This portion of his findings was reprinted in the *New York Times,* which hailed it as a State of the Union message on the arts. It was time for federal aid. The Secretary's arbitration award sct going the events that would lead to the National Endowment for the Arts, and also the Endowment for the Humanities. I was involved in all this; got onto Baumol who explained it; and in time produced my own corollary: Activities with Baumol's disease migrate to the public sector. It follows that it will be the undoing of modern government if too much migration is allowed. And so I approached universal health care with caution.

This, I should own, was also in measure a response to the presentation of the new administration. Health care spending had gone from $10 billion to $2 trillion in a quarter century. Four-fifths and more of the population had health care insurance. Biomedical research and the like were roaring ahead. Yet all this was presented in a rhetoric of crisis, deprivation, suffering. The language of protest.

As hearings commenced, I learned a third thing. Cost increases were beginning to abate. This was the central insight of Paul M. Ellwood, Jr., who had been leading a national conversation on the subject for some years. Managed care was coming, for all the reasons touched on above. The administration rejected this proposition, but the Finance Committee hearings rather confirmed it.* On April 28, 1994, Monsignor Charles J. Fahey of Fordham University appeared as a witness on behalf of the Catholic Health Association of the United States. "We want to alert the committee that the not-for-profit mission in health care is being seriously threatened by the increasing commercial environment in which we find ourselves operating; a real commodification of health care." Here was the Catholic tradition in its now established way cautioning against the unforgiving strictures of the market, cautioning that what had once been a vocation was becoming a business.

As indeed it was. In the summer of 1995, the Health Care Financing Administration of the U.S. Department of Health and Human Services recorded that in 1994 National Health Expenditures as a Percent of Gross Domestic Product had been 13.9 percent, not the 15.1 percent that had served as the base of the administration's cost projections. Further, there had been no increase from 1993. We were being asked to stop everything to cope with a crisis that was seemingly resolving itself.

Not without other consequences, as Robert K. Merton taught us a half-century ago. Monsignor Fahey's testimony brought immediately to mind an earlier comment by Dr. Raymond G. Schultze, head of the teaching hospital for the medical school at the University of California at Los Angeles. In Southern California, there was now a "spot market" for bone marrow transplants. Yes, that followed. But then this. Teaching hospitals cannot compete in a marketplace. Absent teaching hospitals, there would be no medical schools. Not literally, but significantly in that the flow of resources to the great scientific institutions would fall off, and very possibly a great age of science would be foreshortened.

On January 2, 1996, the *New York Times* published a special section under the headline: "Outlook '96, The Economy: Increas-

---

*In the first quarter of 1996 the cost to employers of providing medical and other fringe benefits fell for the first time since the Bureau of Labor Statistics began its Employment Cost Index in 1982.

ing the Demand for Health Care Services": "The providers of
health care can hardly wait as the latest crop of 50-year-olds crosses
the threshold to the aches and pains of middle age. Having grown
up expecting and generally finding care that was both affordable
and accessible, those graying boomers will now need it a lot more,
and that should translate into bonanzas for drug makers, and many
physicians and hospitals, not to mention the makers of artificial
knees for worn-out joggers who refuse to slow down. 'Inexorably,
demand goes higher,' said John F. Hinelong, a health care securities
analyst with Donaldson, Lufkin & Jennrette."

The Finance Committee now proceeded to draft a health care
bill. Concerning this troubled, complicated subject there is one
simple, central fact to keep in mind. *No health care bill was ever
reported to the floor of the House of Representatives.* The President's
party had a solid majority there. The House leaders and the Committee chairmen had simply assumed that the President's bill would
be drafted—three committees had jurisdiction—reported, and
passed. But the polity was changing and the House of Representatives reflected this, much as the framers had hoped.

Michael Barone would later write that America was returning to
a Tocquevillian time. The era of Big—Big Business, Big Labor, Big
Government, Big Plans—was giving way to a postindustrial decen-
tralized, dispersed society which would once again choose to be
lightly governed. What we now saw was wondrous, whatever you
think of the outcome. The people were changing their minds, and
the House was accordingly changing *its* mind. There was a sense in
which no one knew this; and yet, they did know. They *acted* as if
the change had taken place. In the House, the Committee on
Education and Labor, which had been leading the way for universal
health care for the better part of half a century, found it could not
even agree on a bill. In Ways and Means, which has to raise the
money and is rarely ardent in such matters, Rostenkowski cobbled
together a Democratic majority and sent a bill to the Rules Committee. But there was no majority *there*. Again, in a constitutional
mode, the Senate was behind the times in thinking we should move
forward.

On July 2 the Finance Committee reported out a health care bill which would have been substantial in an earlier period. Coverage, if not universal, would be getting close. Our hearings had established that costs were indeed coming under control through managed care. The Finance Committee bill would seem to have been the first ever to address the new, familiarly "unanticipated" crisis of medical schools and teaching hospitals in the age of commodification. A tax of 1.5 percent would be levied on private health insurance for a Graduate Medical Education Academic Health Centers Trust Fund, bringing in some $6.4 billion per year at the outset. Another 0.25 percent levy was dedicated to a Biomedical and Behavioral Research Trust Fund.

All excellent, but none of it was ever going to become law. This reality had still not dawned. The front-page story in the *New York Times*, by Robin Toner, reporting that we had finished our work, nicely captures the illusions of the moment.

Last Panel Sends Its Health Plan to Party Leaders

The Senate Finance Committee today approved legislation that fell short of President Clinton's goal of universal health insurance but promises to expand coverage significantly without requiring employers to pay for it. Its action finally concluded the difficult, six-month journey of health care legislation through a maze of major Congressional committees. The vote clears the way for leaders to try to meld the various committee bills into packages that can attain majorities in the full House and Senate.

By a vote of 12 to 8, with little ceremony, a weary Finance Committee in a largely deserted Capitol approved a bill that seeks to cover 95 percent of Americans by the year 2002 and creates a commission to recommend further action if that goal goes unmet. Nine of the panel's eleven Democrats and three Republicans voted for the measure, which several of the Democrats viewed as largely a means of getting the health care struggle beyond the difficult and divided committee, where it has been stalled for months.

President Clinton, in a relatively restrained statement, said the vote by the Finance Committee "moves health care reform another step closer to final passage." But Mr. Clinton added, "I remain firmly committed to guaranteed health coverage for every American that can never be taken away." Sounding the theme that the White House plans to escalate in the weeks to come, Mr. Clinton declared, "We must achieve universal coverage if we are to reform our health care system and assure hard-working, middle-class Americans that they will have health care when they need it."

With committee work largely behind them, Democratic leaders hope to push for passage of a bill by the full House and Senate in August, which would be followed by a conference committee from both houses to negotiate the differences and final passage of health care legislation by early October.

A dispatch that will live in the annals of innocence. For health care reform was by now over and finished and failed. The House, which would have had to go first as this was a revenue bill, had been unable to bring any measure to the floor. As noted, the Committee on Education and Labor, with jurisdiction over Medicare, never found a majority for *any*thing. In other circumstances—earlier circumstances—the Finance Committee bill might have passed the Senate at least. Three Republicans voted for the measure, Chafee of Rhode Island, Danforth of Missouri, and Durenberger of Minnesota. But the three did not include the Republican leader, Bob Dole. Earlier he had indicated he could work with the President—had passed a note at a Committee hearing: "Time for Moynihan-Dole?" I had passed this on. But there was in the White House no thought of settling for anything save less than the President had called for. Rockefeller of West Virginia, an unmovable supporter of universal care, had voted No on the Finance Committee bill (along with Baucus of Montana). And so it all came to nothing.

This was July. A year or so later President Clinton would tell Haynes Johnson and David S. Broder that by June the White House knew that health care was over. In their fine narrative, *The System: The American Way of Politics at the Breaking Point,* they record: "In our experience as reporters, there have been few moments when a President has sat in the Oval Office and said, flat out and without a trace of rationalization or self-pity, 'I made a blunder.' But the next sentence was even more striking: 'I set the Congress up for failure,' Clinton said. He set himself up for failure, too, he said, but Congress 'had to stand with it' sooner—in 1994—'and I didn't, and I feel badly about that. We had an opportunity, and our leaders thought we might make it. But I think that our system probably cannot absorb this much reform with this much involved that quickly.'"

I don't much hold with the latter, nor should we teach it. Had the White House been willing to accept near universal health care, with a prescient provision for medical schools and teaching hospitals, had Rockefeller of West Virginia agreed, as presumedly he would have done, then by a solid 13–7 bipartisan vote the Senate Finance Committee would have shown that a very great deal could have been done, and done reasonably well. The failure was political, not systemic. The administration would settle for nothing less than, as the *Times* would put it, "a medical monstrosity."

An election season had already commenced. The Moynihan Committee, as the Federal Elections Commission puts it, was in place. Chester Straub, John Westergaard, Steven Mann, Nina Rosenwald, a core group unchanged in eighteen years. Liz as ever. For a change we had some money, and what looked like an easy race. The New York Republicans were after the incumbent, Democrat Mario M. Cuomo; for Senate they nominated Bernadette Castro, a personable Republican fundraiser but with no previous government experience.

Withal, trouble came, as trouble will. Reverend Alfred Sharpton announced that he expected the Democratic Convention to nominate him as well as me, such that we would both be on the ballot in the September primary election. I had to allow that if this were done I would not accept the party nomination, and run as an independent. The usual. I allowed that if the Reverend wanted to circulate petitions and get on the ballot in that way, I would not challenge his signatures. Not so usual, but there you are. That is how it turned out.

Sharpton had appeared in New York politics in a conventional role, a preacher protesting. He was now, however, moving toward an ethnic nationalism that is to be encountered among peoples far and near over much of history. In a lecture at Kean College in New Jersey on February 13 of that year he had told a student audience: "White folks was in the caves while we was building empires . . . We built pyramids before Donald Trump even knew what architecture was . . . We taught philosophy and astrology [*sic*] and mathematics before Socrates and them Greek homos ever got around to it . . . Do some cracker come and tell you, 'Well my mother and father blood go back to the Mayflower,' you better hold your pocket. That ain't nothing to be proud of, that means their forefathers was crooks."[7]

At the Democratic convention, as recorded by Nicholas Goldberg of *Newsday,* Sharpton denounced me in a "fiery speech . . . as a closet conservative who is overzealous on welfare reform, unconcerned about health-care reform, and insensitive to the plight of blacks, Latinos, gays and women." On it went, until the September primary election when he carried 25.3 percent of the vote. A Marxist candidate, Lenora Fulani, gathered 21 percent of the vote against Cuomo, but this was small comfort. Thus the returns in Brooklyn. In Bensonhurst, Moynihan 95.0 percent; in Bay Ridge, Moynihan 87.7 percent; in Bedford-Stuyvesant, Moynihan 16.9 percent.

The Senate recessed at last, and I campaigned across the state. To be in the Chenango Valley of an October morning is reward enough; I was known and welcomed. That I was seen to have been wary of the administration health care bill did no seeming harm. A group of "militants" demanding a single-payer Canadian-style national health scheme harassed me a bit. A rally was organized near our home in Delaware County, complete with wheelchairs and placards: "Health Care Coverage as Good as Congress Has!" Banners: "Ithaca Democratic Socialists of America." In 1991 I had been Senator Kerrey's sole cosponsor of a single-payer, Canadian-style bill, so why had these folk invaded Delaware County? But no matter, few New Yorkers seemed put out that the health plan had faltered.

I did, however, stumble upon an issue. At an editorial board meeting in Syracuse I was reciting my achievements as Chairman to an assertively uninterested audience when I happened to add "and we decriminalized babysitting." Of a sudden, the editors were listening. I got the point and carried the message across the state. People knew exactly what I was talking about. Here was something they could relate to, that mattered to them *personally*. The issue had arisen in the first days of the new administration. The President's first choice for Attorney General turned out not to have paid Social Security taxes on household help and had to withdraw. The same with the President's second choice. Whereupon the problem arose to harass all manner of nominees. Domestic workers had first been covered by Social Security in 1950. Payroll taxes were owed after wages of $50 per quarter. The amount was left there, so that in time even occasional babysitters were covered. But three-quarters of the taxes due were never paid. People didn't know they owed them; now they did. Now they had reason to wonder if they had not somehow violated a federal law they had never heard of. Compliance required quarterly filings, forms, receipts. As if the Smith family was a corporation that employed Mary Ellen from next door for $5 each Saturday night, amounting to $60 for the quarter. A fine rite of passage was of a sudden troubled and problematic. The penalty for noncompliance extended to prison—the welfare state grown grotesque.

Without much notice, none of any kind from the administration preoccupied with health care, I had put together a bill that set the threshold for withholding and paying Social Security taxes on domestic workers at an annual amount of $1,000, thereafter indexed for inflation. Payments henceforth would be included with the annual income tax filing, the familiar W-2 form. Domestic workers under age 18 were exempt. The bill passed the Senate by unanimous consent on May 25; a conference report passed October 6.

For all that "nannygate" had near to preoccupied the administration in its early days, it quite disappeared from their view. Millions of citizens of voting age owed such taxes. The bill was retroactive to January 1, 1994. Those who hadn't paid taxes for a domestic worker or babysitter hired since then would now have broken no law; those who had paid were as likely as not due a refund. Henceforth the whole horror would be gone. Government is *not* out to put you in prison. But there was no Oval Office signing ceremony, not even a presidential statement. The Social Security Domestic Employment Reform Act of 1994 was signed aboard Air Force One in a batch of some 27 bills, some naming post offices, others courthouses, one recognizing "the achievements of radio amateurs" and establishing "support for such amateurs as national policy." Even so, this was about all I talked about in the last weeks of the campaign, something every audience immediately understood and seemingly appreciated.

The polls closed at 9:00 P.M. on November 8. At 9:03, the AP wire out of Albany reported the results: "Sen. Daniel Patrick Moynihan . . . won a fourth term Tuesday, overwhelming Republican challenger Bernadette Castro in a race that was never in doubt. A preliminary exit poll found Moynihan was a clear choice among almost all demographic groups: men, women, whites, blacks, young, old, rich, and poor as well as self-described independents. But even as the 67-year-old Moynihan was scoring his third lopsided victory in a row, his powerful role as chairman of the Senate Finance Committee was imperiled by Republicans bidding to gain control of the Senate."

We went over to Grand Central for a last rally, thanked all, returned to the hotel, and watched the rest go down. In New York, the Governor, Lt. Governor, our candidate for Attorney General, all lost. H. Carl McCall was elected Comptroller; but he and I were now the only statewide Democrats left standing. The next morning the press was generous. The *New York Times:* "That rare creature, the well-liked politician, survives in New York." But by mid-day, full returns were in and the election turned out to have been closer than the polls had predicted. I carried only 16, mostly urban, counties outside of New York City. The vote dropped off to a margin of 658,233. Sufficient to be sure, but the seeming consensus of 1988 had dwindled at home, while in the rest of the nation it had quite vanished.*

1994–95: Welfare Reform

Welfare in America began as reform. On January 25, 1909, President Theodore Roosevelt convened The White House Conference on the Care of Children. Matthew Crenson of Johns Hopkins records it was the first conference of its kind in American history. Some 200 persons attended: Jacob Riis, Jane Addams, Booker T. Washington, Theodore Dreiser. Reform meant an end to orphanages, the beginning of direct aid to "parents of worthy character," allowing children to remain in their homes, or, in time, foster homes. The conference asked the question: Is this the way of the future? Crenson comments: "With this question, [reformers] crossed a fault line of American social policy. The proposition implicitly advanced was the payment of cash subsidies to the destitute parents of children who might otherwise become candidates for the orphanage. The proposal anticipated contemporary welfare policy." Within two years of the White House conference, "mothers' pensions" had been established in Chicago, for example. By 1920 they had been created in 40 of the 48 states. In 1935 the federal government folded the arrangement into the Social Security Act as Aid to Dependent Children (in 1962 renamed Aid to Families with Dependent Children). Orphanages were not to fade away. Sixty years later the Speaker of the House of Representatives would be calling for their return.

Well before Gingrich, it had been clear that something had gone wrong. The Family Support Act of 1988 had redefined the status of recipients of Aid to Families with Dependent Children, Title

---

*"Republican challenger Bernadette Castro" evidently knew something was afoot. In the week before the election she lent her campaign $352,810 (used exclusively to pay for negative advertising) without reporting it to the Federal Election Commission. This surely helped her to break the 40 percent mark, ending with 41.5 percent. Our campaign could have matched this and might have done so had we known, and this in turn might have affected the outcome. In 1996 the Castro campaign agreed to pay a $22,000 civil penalty to the FEC.

IV-A of the Social Security Act. President Reagan had signed the legislation in a Rose Garden ceremony:

> I am pleased to sign into law today a major reform of our nation's welfare system, the Family Support Act. This bill, H.R. 1720, represents the culmination of more than 2 years of effort and responds to the call in my 1986 State of the Union Message for real welfare reform—reform that will lead to lasting emancipation from welfare dependency.
>
> It is fitting that the word "family" figures prominently in the title of this legislation. For too long the federal Government, with the best of intentions, has usurped responsibilities that appropriately lie with parents . . . In so doing, it has reinforced dependency and separated welfare recipients from the mainstream of American society. The Family Support Act says to welfare parents, "We expect of you what we expect of ourselves and our own loved ones: that you will do your share in taking responsibility for your life and for the lives of the children you bring into this world."
>
> Well, the Family Support Act focuses on the two primary areas in which individuals must assume this responsibility. First, the legislation improves our system for securing the support from absent parents. Second, it creates a new emphasis on the importance of work for individuals in the welfare system.
>
> Under this bill, one parent in a two-parent welfare family will be required to work in the public or private sector for at least 16 hours a week as a condition of receiving benefits. This important work requirement applies to families that come onto the welfare rolls as a result of the unemployment of the principal wage earner. It recognizes the need for a family's breadwinner to maintain the habits, skills, and pride achieved through work. This work requirement also allows us to expand coverage for two-parent families to all States without dangerously increasing welfare dependency. A key part of this bill is to make at least one of the parents in a welfare family participate in meaningful work while still getting a needed cash support.
>
> Single parent families also share in the message of hope underlying this bill. They, too, will know that there is an alternative to a life on welfare. To ensure that they get a better start in life, young parents who have not completed high school will be required to stay in or

return to school to complete the basic education so necessary to a productive life. Other parents will be offered a broad range of education, employment, and training activities designed to lead to work.

To provide new employment opportunities to welfare recipients, States will be entitled to receive $6.8 billion over the next 7 years. They also will receive the funding necessary to provide child care and Medicaid benefits. This financial assistance represents a significant and generous national commitment to enhancing the self-sufficiency of welfare recipients. To ensure that meaningful numbers of recipients actually do benefit from welfare reform, each State must be required to involve increasing percentages of welfare families to participate in employment and training activities over time.

The Family Support Act also contains significant reforms in our nation's child support enforcement system. These reforms are designed to ensure that parents who do not live with their children nevertheless meet their responsibilities to them. To improve the adequacy of child support awards, judges and other officials will be required to apply support guidelines developed by their States for setting award amounts. And to help ensure that the child support awarded actually is paid, child support payments will be automatically withheld from the responsible parent's paycheck.

Governor William J. Clinton of Arkansas, then chairman of the National Governors' Association, was on hand. The legislation had passed out of the Senate 96–1, owing much to the governors' bipartisan support. Which was much in order, as the legislation was drafted in response to experimentation that had commenced in states from Massachusetts across to California in the 1980s, all in a proper federal mode. What could reasonably be called social learning was beginning to suggest ways *out* of dependency. In the 1980s, welfare dependency came to be seen as a new social problem that required thinking anew. How is this to be demonstrated? Not easily. But I was there; I saw it happen.

If you would mark a beginning, Lewis Thomas's 1980 article would do. Enough, he wrote, of this "worrying ourselves half to death" over our health: "We do not have time for this sort of thing anymore, nor can we afford such a distraction from our other, considerably more urgent problems. Indeed, we should be worrying that our preoccupation with personal health may be a symptom of copping out, an excuse for running upstairs to recline on a couch, sniffing the air for contaminants, spraying the room with deodorants, while just outside, the whole of society is coming undone."[8] I knew Thomas; he was watching New York City, where the ratio of "nonmarital" births had passed 40 percent, heading for the halfway mark in 1993. Fifty-four percent in Manhattan.

The Family Support Act argued that welfare was to be seen as a temporary circumstance. Now the idea of specific time limits appeared. In *Poor Support* (1988) David Ellwood, an economist at Harvard, argued that this could be achieved by intensive, what surgeons would call heroic, interventions. More spending; more scrutiny; more, yes, interfering. Clinton opened his presidential campaign with an address at Georgetown University in October 1991. In it he proposed to "end welfare as we have come to know it." This became a central theme of the campaign. In 1993 Ellwood came to Washington as Assistant Secretary for Planning and Evaluation in the Department of Health and Human Services.*

But a year went by and there was no bill. Health care was the administration's first priority, to the point of preoccupation. On January 6, 1994, I told an editorial board meeting at the *New York Post* that welfare reform had become "boob bait for the bubbas." Which I ought never to have done; but I did. The following Sunday when I appeared on *Meet the Press* to discuss welfare reform and health care, David Broder asked me what I had meant by that. I answered: "I don't want in any way to suggest that health is not a priority or that what the President makes a priority is not a priority for me. But . . . we don't have a health care crisis in this country. We do have a welfare crisis."

No matter, it was not until June 21, 1994, that the Work and Responsibility Act was sent to the Congress. It was much, perhaps

---

*In a paper published in May 1996 Ellwood would write of the original Clinton welfare reform plan: "We had satisfied organized labor; most liberal advocacy groups were not adamantly opposed." This was the most to be hoped for: "not adamantly opposed" to the efforts of a liberal administration working with a Democratic Congress. The 1994 elections left these groups in shock, disbelief, and paralysis.

most, of what Ellwood would have wanted, but it had taken a year and a half, and the election season was already begun. It was not meant to be taken seriously, and wasn't.

By contrast, the Contract with America stated that in the first 100 days of a Republican Congress there would be a vote on ten bills, the third of which was "Welfare reform: The government should encourage people to work, *not* to have children out of wedlock." The latter clause was a clue to what had happened in the welfare debate. As the 1980s went by, the reform energies that had led to the Family Support Act gave way on the right to a far more radical view. Welfare ceased to be seen as a possible solution to problems; it was now defined as the source. There was not that much to show for the 1988 statute. The number of AFDC cases continued to rise, passing the 5 million mark before peaking in March 1994. The number thereafter did decline considerably, but was this the business cycle? the JOBS program (Job Opportunities and Basic Services)? Who was to say? No one knew.

The new Congressional majority would not have cared for causes in any case. A new vocabulary had quite supplanted the old. Welfare was child abuse; to end child abuse, end welfare. "As we know it," as someone had said. The reasoning, occasionally quite explicit, was that ending welfare would make the lives of illegitimate babies so unendurable that mothers would forbear to bear more. Cruelty to children—"tough love"—became an instrument of social policy. No Social Darwinist can ever have dreamed of a measure such as that now set forth by Washington "think tanks" with an insouciance that verged on the insensate. Essays appeared: "Welfare Reform and the Death of Marriage." Stop subsidizing illegitimacy or see the fall of civilization. In fairness, the conservatives were serious. Liberals never had been, and were now merely silent.

In the course of this nondebate, Douglas J. Besharov and Karen N. Gardner addressed the subject in *The Public Interest*. Their paper, "Paternalism and Welfare Reform," began: "After years of collective denial, most politicians (and welfare policy makers) have finally acknowledged the link between unwed parenthood and long-term welfare dependency, as well as a host of other social problems. But it is one thing to recognize the nature of the problem and quite another to develop a realistic response to it. For, truth be told, there has been a fair amount of wishful thinking about what it takes to help these most disadvantaged parents become self-sufficient."

The authors described three large, expensive, carefully measured experiments. The programs cost about $10,000 per year per adult in addition to "welfare" cost as such. As per usual, seemingly as ever, there was little or nothing to show. They closed on a note perhaps not that far distant from the abolitionists, but surely more moderate: "Aristotle is credited with the aphorism, 'Virtue is habit.' To him, the moral virtues (including wisdom, justice, temperance, and courage), what people now tend to call 'character,' were not inbred. Aristotle believed that they develop in much the same way people learn to play a musical instrument, through endless practice. In other words, character is built by the constant repetition of divers good acts. These new behavior-related welfare rules are an attempt, long overdue in the minds of many, to build habits of responsible behavior among long-term recipients; that is, to legislate virtue." Which none, as yet, knew how to do.

What we did know, or had to assume, was that "progressive" social policy was producing a progressive social calamity. Society was coming undone. Or much of it. At about this time Nicholas Eberstadt published a thought experiment, "Prosperous Paupers." Not a pretty term; not intended to be. "Imagine with me that we find a time machine, which transports us back to the year 1935. We are in the midst of the Great Depression, near its depths. Imagine further that we somehow manage to buttonhole one of the men or women then in Washington busily formulating President Franklin Roosevelt's New Deal." Eberstadt mentions Frances Perkins, who, come to think, once remarked to me that she had envisioned the typical AFDC recipient as a West Virginia miner's widow. Imagine, Eberstadt continued, a per capita GDP that had grown near four-fold. Imagine that "future generations would never again face anything like the unemployment crisis of the 1930s." Imagine the virtual end of agricultural field labor. Imagine the end of legalized racial segregation. Imagine an expenditure of nearly a quarter trillion dollars a year to assist the needy. Would the New Dealer in turn have imagined that by the last decade of the century nearly a quarter of the population would be on "relief"? That some 53 percent of African American households would be receiving some form of means-tested assistance, twice the 26 percent rate estimated in 1935 by the National Resources Planning Board? No, it had to be the system we had created, which was to say welfare. He concludes:

Judged purely by its performance specifications, AFDC can therefore be accurately described as a policy instrument for financing illegitimacy in the contemporary United States. By extension, depending upon their particulars, other government social support programs can be seen, in greater or lesser degree, as vehicles for financing the out-of-wedlock lifestyle. To observe that such programs underwrite out-of-wedlock or single-parent lifestyles is not to judge whether they create the syndromes they support, but simply to recognize what they do.

The second observation can be offered as a sort of "thought experiment." Imagine that all of the incentives—or if you will, disincentives—embedded in today's U.S. social welfare programs were suddenly transported back in time—not to our New Deal reformer's time but back to Salem, Massachusetts, around 1660 or 1670. Now let us wonder: How many additional out-of-wedlock births might have occurred in Salem, Massachusetts, in the midst of the Puritan era, in the face of all the perverse incentives of the modern welfare state? Like all thought experiments, this one cannot be answered conclusively. But my guess would be very few. The reasoning behind my guess is that most people in Salem, Massachusetts, in those years thought that engaging in what we now sometimes term "disorganized lifestyles" would lead them to Hell. And there were a lot of people in Salem, Massachusetts, around 1660 and 1670 who believed in Hell.

To sum up: Today's antipoverty efforts confront problems that were not faced by the New Dealers—and may not even have been imagined by them. (These problems, on the other hand, were imagined by the Puritans—although it is doubtful that many Puritans would have predicted such problems would ever be so rampant in their City on a Hill.) The problems to which I refer devolve from predictably injurious patterns of individual and parental behavior. These injurious patterns do not explain all of the social problems that we confront in our nation today. But they may account for a great fraction of the domestic problems we confront.

A revolution in personal behavior and personal attitudes has taken place in the United States since the New Deal. That revolution has coincided with a great surge in policy experimentation, as we have attempted to apply the techniques of problem-solving governance to an increasingly ambitious agenda of social concerns. For better or worse, we have been living through interesting years.

We have learned, to our sorrow, that the state is a limited and highly imperfect father for the family. Given the comprehensive proposals currently pending for the restructuring of our health care system, I fear that we may learn that the state is also a limited and highly imperfect mother for the family. No matter how expertly devised the policy, no matter how dedicated the civil servants, no matter how generously funded the initiatives, antipoverty and social policy programs will be judged a failure in any confrontation against the perverse patterns of behavior that characterize so much of what troubles us about modern U.S. life.

The reassertion of individual and familial responsibilities, I believe, is central to the revitalization of our society. It is also central, I believe, to dealing with the dysfunctions that sadden and dismay us most about our national condition. But how such a resurgence is to be accomplished generally and effectively—much less how our governmental institutions are to abet in such a resurgence—is far from clear to me.

By now, anyone serious about social policy knew this; withal it had taken an Eberstadt to put it so painfully. But we also knew that a pathology that had taken two—or was it three?—generations to evolve would not be undone by one bill emerging from the House of Representatives. Dealing with the dysfunctions "that sadden and dismay us" would require a generation of something like social mobilization. But bad as things were, they could be made indescribably worse.

Undeterred, or disbelieving, the new House promptly passed H.R. 4, The Personal Responsibility Act of 1995, repealing Title IV-A of the Social Security Act, Aid to Families with Dependent Children,[9] replacing it with a block grant to states, accompanied by a five-year time limit, a "family cap" forbidding additional payment for additional children, and such like statutory stricture. Nothing so radical had been seriously proposed in the House of Representatives since the Social Security Act itself. A measure that would have been unthinkable a year earlier now passed 234–199.

The Clinton administration determined to go along. In May the Senate Finance Committee, having received the House bill, voted out a somewhat modified version. A bit more in the way of social services, but repealing Aid to Families with Dependent Children. The Secretary of Health and Human Services declared herself "pleased that the legislation eliminated some of the extreme and punitive provisions of the bill passed by the House of Representatives." In the *New York Times* Robert Pear had this: "An Administration official, speaking on the condition of anonymity, said, 'AFDC is the bone that the Clinton White House can throw to the hounds at the door, the people who want to make radical changes in the welfare state.' The official said the White House had not made a major effort to preserve the entitlement of poor people to welfare benefits because such an effort would be 'more trouble than it's worth' in political terms."

A tactic took shape. Democrats would *demand* that the Republicans add *a little* extra money for various services, notably child care, a particular enthusiasm of the Children's Defense Fund, with which the First Lady and Secretary Shalala had been closely associated. We were back at family preservation, preoccupied with this or that marginal, even questionable, program, while putting millions of children at grievous risk. Three-quarters of AFDC children had received benefits for more than five years; to cut them off at that point, in cities such as Detroit, where in 1993 67 percent of children were on AFDC at one time or another, would ask for social devastation.

The White House would not talk with me about this; they talked *about* me, instead. Nothing out of the ordinary; after "boob bait" I did have it coming, and it came in the form of a front-page story in the Sunday *New York Times* of June 18:

Moynihan Battles View He Gave Up on Welfare Fight

If ever there was a legislative moment made for Senator Daniel Patrick Moynihan, it ought to be now, as Congress attempts a vast overhaul of 60 years of antipoverty policy. By virtue of his position as ranking Democrat on the Senate Finance Committee, Mr. Moynihan will officially lead his party on the floor of the Senate as it pushes for a Democratic vision of welfare for a new century. He will bring more than three decades of serious scholarship on American poverty and dependency to what is expected to be a fiercely political and partisan fight.

But Mr. Moynihan, in the view of some involved in the welfare struggle, is less an eager warrior than a lion in winter these days, angry and depressed at the conservative turn that "welfare reform" has taken, frustrated with the Clinton Administration and warning bleakly of the consequences of measures with broad support in both parties, like time limits on welfare benefits. "This is just a huge leap in the dark," said the 68-year-old New York Democrat, first sent to the Senate in 1976.

Critics argue that he has allowed the debate to pass him by, missing opportunities to take the edge off the most radical Republican proposals. For his part, Mr. Moynihan . . . argued that the defining characteristics of modern poverty—the family breakdown and chronic dependency—were extraordinarily complex and that the 1988 welfare overhaul that he sponsored reflected "about as much as anybody knows" about the remedies. He has proposed a bill that would expand that law—which pushes states to develop a variety of jobs programs for welfare recipients—"on the not-very-inspiring grounds that that's all we know."

Mr. Moynihan erupted when a reporter suggested that his stance was being perceived as defeatist, a throwing-up-the-hands rationalizing for abandoning efforts at another major overhaul. "That is not a defeatist message," he said, his voice rising in anger, but instead the message of people who have studied the issue "for 35 years, who saw it coming and have been marking it along while everyone else was in denial."

"People who say that nothing can be worse than the present system, just you wait and see," he added. "We are dealing with a profound social change. And those of us who first spotted it are entitled to be heard a generation later when we are saying we still don't understand it."

Still, to many on Capitol Hill Mr. Moynihan is out of step with an era when 9 in 10 Americans say they want fundamental changes in the welfare system. Pollsters tell Democrats that, above all else, they cannot appear to be attached to the status quo. Moreover, many politicians in both parties have come to believe that the status quo in social welfare policy *should* be profoundly changed, given the persistent problems of illegitimacy and dependency.

Mr. Moynihan speaks with passion about a poverty that is inextricably tied to "a volcanic change in family structure, for which there is no comparable experience in human history." "No one is near a hypothesis, let alone a general theory," to explain it, he said. "It is not going away, and to take away the life-support system for children growing up in it is an act of unprecedented social vindictiveness."

It was not the language of welfare reform in the 1990's.

As, indeed, it was not. A Quinnipiac College poll toward the end of the year found 57 percent of whites and 35 percent of African Americans in favor of a reduction in welfare benefits which Governor George E. Pataki had proposed, while 60 percent and 41 percent, respectively, agreed it would be a "good thing" if welfare recipients left New York as a result of benefit cuts.

Thus, the summer of my discontent. Nothing I did connected, save with the Catholic Bishops and the editorial board of the *Washington Post,* institutions in no noticeable need of my advice. On September 7, H.R. 4, The Personal Responsibility Act, as amended, was taken up by the full Senate. On behalf of himself and other Democrats, the minority leader Tom Daschle offered as a substitute the Family Self-Sufficiency Act, a "modified amendment . . . which abolishes the existing AFDC program and replaces it with a Temporary Employment Assistance Program (TEA) which provides conditional assistance of limited duration." This failed on a party line vote, with all Democrats save Baucus of Montana in favor. I voted for it, as the next morning I would offer as a substitute the Family Assistance Act of 1995, building, as I chose to think, on what we had done in 1988. Neither amendment would pass, but I could hope for a respectable showing if I kept this side of mutiny. Daschle had failed 45–54; the next day I lost 41–56. Senators Bingaman, Harkin, Kohl, and Nunn joined Baucus in voting against. A week later the House bill passed 87–12, with three-quarters of Democratic Senators, 35 in all, joining 52 Republicans to repeal for the first time ever a title of the Social Security Act, the provision for dependent children. Eleven Democrats voted No: Akaka of Hawaii, Bradley of New Jersey, Kennedy of Massachusetts, Kerrey of Nebraska, Lautenberg of New Jersey, Leahy of Vermont, Moseley-Braun of Illinois, Moynihan of New York, Sarbanes of Maryland, Simon of Illinois, and Wellstone of Minnesota.

The advocacy groups were silent. Going back at least to the 1960s, Washington had developed an extraordinary range of lobbyists for social programs corresponding to the interest lobbies—railroads—that emerged in the nineteenth century. The distinction wasn't all that great. Social programs had become an increasing source of something very like wealth—witness the nursing home lobby that had got hold of a third of Medicaid expenditure. But many advocates were disinterested in any financial sense. This allowed a measure of self-righteousness not always suppressed as the groups went about expressing outrage that the amount of program increases was being reduced. Now, however, when something of great consequence was seemingly about to happen, the advocates fell silent.

This came to me as I spoke on the morning of September 14. Debate was to commence at 10:00 A.M. The Republican managers had some business with the House and asked if I would simply hold the floor until 10:30 A.M. I found myself alone. I commenced thinking out loud:

▼

On this, the likely final day of the debate on the welfare reform measure before us, it is worth noting that in the lead story of the *New York Times* this morning we read that "the White House, exceedingly eager to support a law that promises to change the welfare system, was sending increasingly friendly signals about the bill."

That is a bill that would repeal Title IV-A of the Social Security Act of 1935 that provides aid to dependent children. It will be the first time in the history of the nation that we have repealed a section of the Social Security Act. That the White House should be eager to support such a law is beyond my understanding and, certainly in 34 years' service in Washington, beyond my experience. If this administration wishes to go down in history as one that abandoned, eagerly abandoned, the national commitment to dependent children, so be it. I would not want to be associated with such an enterprise, and I shall not be.

The administration has abandoned us, those of us who oppose this legislation. Why do we not see the endless parade of petitioners, as when health care reform was before us in the last Congress—the lobbyists, the pretend citizen groups, the real citizen groups? None are here. I can recall the extraordinary energy that went into any change in the welfare system 30 years ago, 25 years ago. Fifteen years ago, if there was a proposal to take $40 out of some demonstration project here on the Senate floor, there would be 40 representatives of various advocacy groups outside.

There are very few advocacy groups outside today. You can stand where I stand and look straight out at the Supreme Court—not a person in between that view. Not one of those flaunted, vaunted advocacy groups forever protecting the interests of the children and the helpless and the homeless and the what-you-will. Are they increasingly subsidized and therefore increasingly co-opted? Are they silent because the White House is silent? They should be ashamed. History will shame them.

One group was in Washington yesterday, and I can speak with some spirit on that. This was a group of Catholic bishops and members from Catholic Charities. They were here. They were in Washington. Nobody else. None of the great marchers, the great chanters, the nonnegotiable demanders.

What is to be said of a White House that was almost on the edge of excess in its claims of empathy and concern in the last Congress but is now prepared to see things like this happen in the present Congress? I had no idea how profoundly what used to be known as liberalism was shaken by the last election. No president, Republican or Democrat, in history, or 60 years' history, would dream of agreeing to the repeal of Title IV-A of Social Security. I cannot understand how this could be happening. It has never happened before.

Scholars have been working at these issues for years now, and the more capable they are the more tentative and incremental their findings. I cited yesterday a research evaluation of a program, now in its fifth year, of very intensive counseling and training with respect to the issue of teen births—with no results. It is a very common encounter, when things as profound in human character and behavior are dealt with. The capacity of external influences to change it is so very small.

And that we should think otherwise? That men and women have stood in this chamber and talked about a genuine crisis—and there is that. And I have said, if nothing else comes out of this awful process, at least we will have addressed the central subject. But if it is that serious, how can we suppose it will be changed by marginal measures? It will not.

Are there no serious persons in the administration who can say, "Stop, stop right now! No, we won't have this"?

▲

On September 21, these remarks were reprinted by the *Washington Post*, to accompany an article by Paul Offner, a person of wide experience in welfare administration and planning, also formerly of the staff of the Finance Committee.

A Truly Awful Welfare Bill

Democrats who voted for this one should stop kidding themselves—it's a disaster.

Senate Democrats are humiliating themselves. Having failed to push welfare reform when they controlled the Senate, and not wanting now to take a stand that will be unpopular with the voters, many of them voted this week for the Dole bill, which they regard as an abomination.

Last Thursday the Senate adopted a compromise amendment crafted by Majority Leader Bob Dole and Democratic Leader Tom Daschle that threw a few bones to Democrats. States must continue spending at least 80 percent of the money that they're currently devoting to welfare; $1 billion is provided to help states whose caseloads rise in recessionary times; and $3 billion is added to fund day care for welfare mothers who go to work or enroll in job training.

Are these guys serious? The Dole bill cuts off benefits for most welfare families after five years. When it is fully phased in, 3 million children will be removed from the rolls. Moreover, if the objective is putting welfare mothers to work, it's going to be a flop. By freezing federal funds for the welfare block grant at their current level, Dole guarantees that states won't have the money to put people in jobs.

According to the Congressional Budget Office, by the year 2000, states will receive more than $2 billion less in federal funds than they would receive under current law. Meanwhile, the CBO projects an increase in welfare caseloads, mostly as a result of demographics (the number of women of prime child-bearing age is projected to grow over the next 15 years).

On the David Brinkley show last Sunday, Sen. Dole got it right: There's not that much difference between the House and Senate welfare bills. The effort by Clinton and Daschle to pretend otherwise is silly. Having been outgunned and outmaneuvered by the Republicans, they're now trying to find defensible reasons for supporting a truly awful bill—one that cuts off benefits to millions of poor children, while making it measurably more difficult to put welfare mothers to work, which, after all, is everyone's objective.

For the record, three weeks later Jennifer Dixon of the Associated Press reported: "Liberal advocacy groups lined up Thursday to denounce Republican welfare legislation as reckless and immoral."

On October 24 the House/Senate conference on H.R. 4 convened in the great Ways and Means Committee room in the Longworth Building. The meeting was confined to opening statements.

I cited the *Washington Post:* "The fundamental flaw in this legislation is that it abandons the principle that the federal government will maintain at least some basic system of support for the nation's poor, especially poor children." Also Michael Wines of the *New York Times,* who had written that Democrats "have now acceded to what had been unthinkable: the end of the very entitlement that guarantees federal aid to the poor." I cited the administration position on the bill as set forth in a letter from Alice M. Rivlin, Director of the Office of Management and Budget: "The Administration is pleased that Congress finally may be within striking distance of passing comprehensive welfare reform. In spite of the positive changes made by the Family Support Act of 1988, the welfare system still fails to serve the taxpayers who pay for it and the people who are trapped in it. The American people have waited a long time for this historic moment. [*Sic.*] We owe it to the people who sent us here not to let this opportunity slip away by doing the wrong thing or failing to act at all."

Whereupon I called and raised: "Just how many millions of infants we will put to the sword is not yet clear. There is dickering to do. In April, the Department of Health and Human Services reported that when fully implemented the time limits in the House bill would cut off benefits for 4,800,000 children. At that time, the Department simply assumed that the administration would oppose repeal. But the administration has since decided to support repeal. HHS has done a report of the Senate bill on the impact on children, but the White House will not release it. Those involved will take this disgrace to their graves. The children alone are innocent."

We knew there was a report. For one thing, the Office of Management and Budget requires one; for another, we had been told. This was Tuesday. By Friday Elizabeth Shogren of the *Los Angeles Times* had it on the front page:

Welfare Report Clashes with Clinton, Senate

A sweeping welfare reform plan approved by the Senate and embraced by President Clinton would push an estimated 1.1 million children into poverty and make conditions worse for those already under the poverty line, according to a Clinton Administration analysis not released to the public.

The White House received the study, conducted by the Department of Health and Human Services, before Clinton signaled that he would not veto any final welfare measure that looks like the Senate package. Since then, the findings have been carefully guarded by the White House for fear that it would reflect badly on the President, according to sources in the Administration involved in welfare reform.

A copy of the analysis—stamped with the word "draft" and dated Sept. 14—was made available to *The Times*. It predicts that the Senate measure, which is not as tough as a competing House welfare reform bill, would create new hardships on many children.

The Senate measure, which passed, 87 to 12, with broad bipartisan approval, would end the 60-year federal guarantee of cash assistance to poor mothers with children and give states lump-sum block grants to create their own programs. Federal spending would be frozen for five years, and recipients would be required to work after two years and would be limited to five years of assistance in a lifetime.

"The severity of the impact of [the Senate welfare bill] on poor families exacerbates the deteriorating economic situation for these families," according to the analysis.

Next, Judith Havemann and Ann Devroy of the *Washington Post* reported that not only was there a report, but that "[Secretary] Shalala had carried it into a meeting with Clinton in an unsuccessful attempt to persuade him to reject the Senate version of welfare reform as well as the House version. She used the figures to say that the Senate bill was going to be tough on kids, too, according to their preliminary analysis, and White House officials should look seriously before they embraced it, an official said. Clinton went ahead and expressed tentative support for the measure on Sept. 17."

Department staff was now talking to the press; possibly even White House staff. I now switched, as Havemann and Devroy record:

Moynihan has been single-minded in using the missing study this week to try to embarrass Clinton into reconsidering his abandonment of the federal guarantee of welfare benefits for all eligible Americans.

Ending the entitlement, or guarantee, is central to both the House and Senate versions of the bill.

He said yesterday he had now "liberated" the president from his prior embrace of the legislation. "It is clear the study was kept from the president. The president could never have endorsed the Senate bill if he understood what was in the package," Moynihan said. When the senator was informed Clinton had been given the study, he said perhaps Clinton had not read it. "The president is handed a lot of paper," he said.

"The basic issue is that we are dismantling the Social Security Act . . . Now that this information is available, the president is liberated. He is free to withdraw this support because he never would have given it in face of these facts," he said.

The numbers were nothing special, but they were *numbers*. The bill would increase the child poverty rate from 14.6 percent to 16.1 percent; an additional 1.1 million children would fall below the poverty line. Welfare is not about poverty; it is about dependency; poverty data are not especially reliable. No matter, we now had numbers; Havemann would later suggest that this transformed the argument and it surely did. Or rather, Shogren and she and Devroy did.

To this service by the American press, as I would see it, add a sparkling turn by Jason DeParle in the *New York Times Magazine,* "Welfare, End of." A computer hacker in the year 2015 accesses *The Interactive Encyclopedia* entry for "welfare," subtopic, "end of." He learns that the President and Congress got together in 1995 and ended the bad old ways. Not long thereafter a tide of homeless children swarmed over the cities. Of which, the twenty-first-century encyclopedia entry notes: "A handful of critics accurately predicted that ending welfare would bring rising numbers of 'street families,' just as the closing of mental hospitals had produced 'street people' in the 1970s and 80s. In his memoirs former President Clinton described his handling of the issue as 'one of my greatest regrets.'"

Presidents spend no little of their time planning their memoirs, so I cannot doubt DeParle got through. At the very least, he got through to his readers. An editorial note in the January 7, 1996, issue of the *New York Times Magazine* explains: "Jason DeParle's cautionary tale about welfare's demise drew the most mail, with readers overwhelmingly agreeing with his bleak predictions. One New Yorker summed the article up as 'a vision that would reduce even Swift to tears of laughter—and despair.'"

On December 12 I gave a long statement on the floor which was printed in the next edition of the *New York Review of Books* with considerable seeming impact. It was as if the argument was being heard for the first time.

▼

Congress Builds a Coffin

We are now in the final days of the first session of the 104th Congress. In a short while we will have worked out some accommodations on the budget. We must do this, for we will now be engaged in the establishment of some measure of peace and lawful conduct in the Balkans. It would be unforgivable to put our military in harm's way abroad without first getting our affairs in some minimal order here at home.

I am fearful, however, that as we close out this session we will also close down the provision for aid to dependent children that dates back 60 years to the Social Security Act of 1935. If this should happen, and it very likely will, the first and foremost reason will be the monstrous political deception embodied in the term "welfare reform."

In my lifetime there has been no such Orwellian inversion of truth in the course of a domestic debate. "Welfare reform" in fact means welfare repeal. The repeal, that is, of Title IV-A of the Social Security Act. Everyone is to blame for this duplicity, everyone is an accomplice.

For practical purposes, we can begin with the celebrated Contract with America, which pledged that within 100 days, a "Republican House" would vote on ten bills, including "3. *Welfare reform.* The government should encourage people to work, *not* to have children out of wedlock."

This in itself was unexceptional, especially the second clause. By 1994 the nation had become alarmed by an unprecedented rise in illegitimacy, to ratios altogether ahistorical—from practically nil to almost one-third in the course of a half-century. Since illegitimate children commonly end up supported by Aid to Families with Dependent Children (AFDC), a causal connection was inferred. *Not proven.* We know desperately little about this great transformation, save that it is happening in all the industrial nations of the North Atlantic.

Undeterred, the new House majority promptly passed a bill which repealed AFDC. Such an act would have been unthinkable a year earlier, just as repealing Old Age pensions or Unemployment Compensation, other titles of the Social Security Act, would be today. At a minimum, it would have seemed cruel to children. But the new Republicans succeeded in entirely reversing the terms of the debate. Instead of aiding children, AFDC was said to harm them. Last month, a Republican member of the House remarked on the importance of child care: "Because our welfare reform package is going to remove people from welfare and get them to work. We understand that child care is a critical step to ending the cruelty of welfare dependency." What once was seen as charity, or even social insurance, is redefined as cruelty.

This happens. Social problems are continuously redefined. Malcolm Gladwell of the *Washington Post* has noted that "in the nineteenth century, the assumption had almost always been that a man without a job was either lazy or immoral. But following the depression of the 1890s, the Progressives 'discovered' unemployment." Which is to say, a personal failing became a societal failing instead. This redefinition has wrought what would once have seemed miracles in the stabilization of our economy. Mass unemployment is now history. On the other hand, nothing such can be said for the attempt to dissociate welfare dependency from personal attributes, including moral conduct.

As we would say in the old Navy, I am something of a plank owner in this regard. It is just 30 years since I and associates on the

policy planning staff of the Department of Labor picked up the
onset of family instability in the nation, in this case among African
Americans. Interestingly, this followed our having failed to establish
that macroeconomic problems were the source of the trouble. In
the event, I was promptly accused of "blaming the victim." For the
30 years that followed there was an awful tyranny of guilt monger-
ing and accusation that all but strangled liberal debate. One consequence was that when a political force appeared that wished to
change the terms of debate altogether, "established" opinion was
effortlessly silenced and displaced.

Again, Gladwell: "But if anything is obvious from the current
budget fight and Capitol Hill's commitment to scaling back welfare
and Medicaid while lavishing extra billions on the Pentagon, it is
that this once formidable confidence has now almost entirely
slipped away. This is what has given Washington's current re-exami-
nation of the size and shape of government its strange ambivalence.
In most revolutions the defenders of the status quo have to be
dragged from power, kicking and screaming. In this revolution, the
defenders of the old activism toward the poor surrendered willingly,
with the shrugs and indifference of those who no longer believed
in what they stood for either."

This was painfully evident in the Senate. On August 3, 1995, the
Republican majority introduced a "welfare reform" bill which abolished AFDC. That same day, the Democratic minority introduced
a competing "welfare reform" bill—which also abolished AFDC.
On the minority side an enormous fuss is now being made over
adding a little extra child care, some odd bits of child nutrition aid,
perhaps a little foster care; literally arranging flowers on the coffin
of the provision for children in the Social Security Act. Coming
from devious persons this would have been a conscious strategy—
distracting attention from what was really going on. But these were
not, are not, devious persons. Sixty years of program liberalism—a
bill for you, a bill for me—had made this legislative behavior seem
normal. The enormity of the event was altogether missed.

I hope this is not mere innocence on my part. The *Washington
Post* editorial page has been unblinking on this subject. An editorial

of September 14 described the bill on the Senate floor as "reckless," adding with a measure of disdain: "Some new money for child care may . . . be sprinkled onto this confection." Those seeking to define welfare repeal as welfare reform by "improving" the Republican measure should have known better; but I truly think they did not. In recent years, "child care" has been something of a mantra among liberal "advocates" for the poor. For all its merits, it has awesome defects, which are the defects of American social policy. The most important is it creates two classes of working mothers: one which gets free government-provided child care, another which does not.

The Clinton administration arrived in Washington sparkling with such enthusiasms. At this time, I was chairman of the Committee on Finance, charged with producing $500 billion in deficit reduction, half through tax increases, half through program cuts. I thought deficit reduction a matter of the first priority, as did my fabled counterpart in the House, Dan Rostenkowski, chairman of Ways and Means. In the end, we got the votes. Barely. Fifty, plus the Vice-President's in the Senate. But all the while we were taking on this large—and, as we can now say, hugely successful—effort, we were constantly besieged by administration officials wanting us to *add* money for this social program or that social program. Immunization was a favorite. *My* favorite in this miscellany was something called "family preservation," yet another categorical aid program (there were a dozen in place already) which amounted to a dollop of social services and a press release for some subcommittee chairman. The program was to cost $930 million over five years, starting at $60 million in Fiscal Year 1994. For three decades I had been watching families come apart in our society; now I was being told by seemingly everyone on the new team that one more program would do the trick.

The new Family Preservation program was included in the President's first budget, but welfare reform was not. In fact, the administration presented no welfare plan until June of 1994, a year and a half after the President took office. At the risk of indiscretion, let me include in the record at this point a letter I wrote on July 28, 1993, to Dr. Laura D'Andrea Tyson, then the distinguished chair-

man of the Council of Economic Advisers, regarding the Family
Preservation program:

Dear Dr. Tyson:

You will recall that last Thursday when you so kindly joined us at a
meeting of the Democratic Policy Committee you and I discussed
the President's family preservation proposal. You indicated how
much he supports the measure. I assured you I, too, support it, but
went on to ask what evidence was there that it would have any effect.
You assured me there were such data. Just for fun, I asked for two
citations.

The next day we received a fax from Sharon Glied of your staff with
a number of citations and a paper, "Evaluating the Results," that
appears to have been written by Frank Farrow of the Center for the
Study of Social Policy here in Washington and Harold Richman at
the Chapin Hall Center at the University of Chicago. The paper is
quite direct: "Solid proof that family preservation services can effect
a state's overall placement rates is still lacking."

Just yesterday, the same Chapin Hall Center released an "Evaluation of the Illinois Family First Placement Prevention Program: Final
Report." This was a large-scale study of the Illinois Family First
initiative authorized by the Illinois Family Preservation Act of 1987.
It was "designed to test effects of this program on out-of-home
placement of children and other outcomes, such as subsequent child
maltreatment." Data on case and service characteristics were provided
by Family First caseworkers on approximately 4,500 cases; approximately 1,600 families participated in the randomized experiment.
The findings are clear enough.

Overall, the Family First placement prevention program results in
a slight increase in placement rates (when data from all experimental
sites are combined). This effect disappears once case and site variations are taken into account. In other words, there are either negative effects or no effects.

This is nothing new. Here is Peter Rossi's conclusion in his 1992
paper, "Assessing Family Preservation Programs." Evaluations conducted to date "do not form a sufficient basis upon which to firmly
decide whether family preservation programs are either effective or
not."

May I say to you that there is nothing the least surprising in either of these findings? From the mid-60s on this has been the repeated, I almost want to say consistent, pattern of evaluation studies. Either few effects or *negative* effects. Thus, the negative income tax experiments of the 1970s appeared to produce an *increase* in family break-up.

This pattern of "counterintuitive" findings first appeared in the '60s. Greeley and Rossi, some of my work, Coleman's. To this day I can't decide whether we are dealing here with an artifact of methodology or a much larger and more intractable fact of social programs. In any event, by 1978 we had Rossi's Iron Law. To wit: "If there is any empirical law that is emerging from the past decade of widespread evaluation research activities, it is that the expected value for any measured effect of a social program is zero."[10]

I write you at such length for what I believe to be an important purpose. In the last six months I have been repeatedly impressed by the number of members of the Clinton administration who have assured me with great vigor that something or other is known in an area of social policy which, to the best of my understanding, is not known at all. This seems to me perilous. It is quite possible to live with uncertainty, with the possibility, even the likelihood that one is wrong. But beware of certainty where none exists. Ideological certainty easily degenerates into an insistence upon ignorance.

The great strength of political conservatives at this time (and for a generation) is that they are open to the thought that matters are complex. Liberals have got into a reflexive pattern of denying this. I had hoped twelve years in the wilderness might have changed this; it may be it has only reinforced it. If this is so, current revival of liberalism will be brief and inconsequential.

Respectfully,
Daniel Patrick Moynihan

Note that concluding paragraph: If we don't get as good at asking questions as conservatives have become, "the current revival of liberalism will be brief and inconsequential." This was summer 1993. In the course of the recent debate on "welfare reform," specifically on September 14, I took occasion to note that almost the only serious critique of the Republican proposal, and its Democratic variant, was coming from conservative social analysts and social scientists. Let me cite three such criticisms which in sum, or so I would argue, make a devastating case against what Congress and the administration seem bent on doing.

First, George Will, who in the high tradition of conservative thought asks us to consider the unanticipated consequences of what we are about to do to children in the course of disciplining their parents. He wrote in September: "As the welfare reform debate begins to boil, the place to begin is with an elemental fact: No child in America asked to be here. No child is going to be spiritually improved by being collateral damage in a bombardment of severities targeted at adults who may or may not deserve more severe treatment from the welfare system."

Let me attach a number to this statement. In 1968, as part of the social science undertakings associated with the Economic Opportunity Act of 1964, the federal government helped establish the Panel Study of Income Dynamics at the Survey Research Center of the University of Michigan. The thought was to follow cohorts of real, named individuals over the years to see how income rose and fell over time. Earlier this year, using this data, Greg J. Duncan and Wei-Jun J. Yeung calculated that of children born between 1973 and 1975, some 24 percent received AFDC at some point before turning eighteen. Among African Americans this proportion was 66 percent, while for whites it was 19 percent. All told, some 39 percent of this cohort received AFDC, Food Stamps, or Supplementary Security Income.[11] And so we know what we are talking about. A quarter of our children.

A year ago November, James Q. Wilson gave the Wriston lecture at the Manhattan Institute, entitled "From Welfare Reform and Character Development." He began by insisting on how little we know:

Let me confess at the outset that I do not know what ought to be done and assert that I do not think anyone else knows either. But I think that we can find out, at least to the degree that feeble human reason is capable of understanding some of the most profound features of the human condition. What we may find out, of course, is that we have created a society that can no longer sustain a strong family life no matter what steps we take. I am not convinced of that, for the very people who express the deepest pessimism are themselves leading, in most cases, decent lives amid strong human attachments and competent and caring families.

What we worry about is the underclass. There has always been an underclass and always will be one. But of late its ranks have grown, and its members have acquired greater power to destroy their own children and inflict harm beyond their own ranks. The means for doing so—guns, drugs, and automobiles—were supplied to them by our inventive and prosperous economy. We must either control more rigorously those means or alter more powerfully the lives of those who possess them. I wish to discuss the latter, because the public is rightly dubious about how great a gain in public safety can be achieved by the legal methods at our disposal and is properly indignant about the harm to innocent children that will result from neglecting the processes by which the underclass reproduces itself.

The great debate is whether, how, and at what cost we can change lives—if not the lives of this generation then those of the next.

He then set forth three precepts. Note that the first is precisely where George Will began.

First precept: Our overriding goal ought to be to save the children. Other goals—reducing the cost of welfare, discouraging illegitimacy, and preventing long-term welfare dependency—are all worthy. But they should be secondary to the goal of improving the life prospects of the next generation.

Second precept: Nobody knows how to achieve this goal on a large scale. The debate that has begun about welfare reform is largely based on untested assumptions, ideological posturing, and perverse priorities. We are told that worker training and job placement will reduce the welfare rolls, but we know that worker training and job placement have so far had at best very modest effects on welfare rolls. And few advocates of worker training tell us what happens to children whose mothers are induced or compelled to work, other than to assure us

that somebody will supply day care. We are told by others that a
mandatory work requirement, whether or not it leads to more mothers working, will end the cycle of dependency. We don't know that
it will. Moreover, it is *fathers* whose behavior we most want to
change, and nobody has explained how cutting off welfare to mothers will make biological fathers act like real fathers.

We are told that ending AFDC will reduce illegitimacy, but that is,
at best, an informed guess. Some people produced many illegitimate
children long before welfare existed, and others in similar circumstances now produce none, even though welfare has become quite
generous. I have pointed out that group homes and boarding schools
once provided decent lives for the children of stable, working-class
parents who faced unexpected adversity, but I do not know whether
such institutions will work for the children of underclass parents
enmeshed in a cycle of dependency and despair.

Third precept: The federal government cannot have a meaningful
family policy for the nation, and it ought not to try. Not only does
it not know and cannot learn from "experts" what to do; whatever
it thinks it ought to do, it will try to do in the worst possible way:
uniformly, systematically, politically, and ignorantly. Today official
Washington rarely bothers even to give lip service to the tattered
principle of states' rights. Even when it allows the states some freedom, it does so only at its own pleasure, reserving the right to set
terms, issue waivers, and attach conditions. Welfare politics in Washington is driven by national advocacy groups that often derive their
energy from the ideological message on which they rely to attract
money and supporters. And Washington will find ways either to deny
public money to churches (even though they are more deeply engaged in human redemption than any state department of social
welfare) or to enshroud those churches that do get public money
with constraints that vitiate the essential mission of a church.

Finally, to address Wilson's point that any welfare program significantly funded from Washington will be run "uniformly, systematically, politically, and ignorantly": I don't disagree. The Family
Support Act of 1988 had two basic premises. The first was that
welfare could not be a way of life, that it had to be an interlude in
which mothers learn self-sufficiency and fathers learn child support,

and also that this goal was to be pursued in as many different ways as state and local governments could contrive. I would like to think that I am not the only person still in Washington who recalls that in debate we would continually refer to the experiments being carried out by a liberal Democratic governor in Massachusetts, Michael Dukakis, and a conservative Republican governor of California, George Deukmejian. Our expectations, very much under control I should say, were based on the careful research of such programs by the Manpower Demonstration Research Corporation based in New York.

On December 3 Douglas J. Besharov of the American Enterprise Institute, the third of the conservative analysts I will cite, wrote in support of the welfare measure now in conference, stating that the experience of the JOBS program under the Family Support Act showed just how innovative and responsible states can be. He said: "Since 1992, the federal government has allowed states almost total freedom to reshape their welfare systems through the waiver process. According to the Center for Law and Social Policy (CLASP), as of last week, 42 states had requested waivers and well over half had already been granted."

As some will know, earlier this year I introduced the Family Support Act of 1995, seeking to update the earlier legislation, given seven years' experience. In the current issue of the *National Journal*, in which I am referred to as the "champion" of "left-of-center advocacy groups," this measure, which got 41 votes on the Senate floor, is simply dismissed: "Moynihan's bill is principally a vehicle for defending the status quo." Dreadful charge, but not unwarranted. The status quo is meant to be one of experiment and change. And it is. I so state: the idea of changing welfare has even taken hold in New York City!

Now to what I think of as a constitutional question, the source of my greatest concern.

I have several times now related an event which took place in the course of a "retreat" which the Finance Committee held last March 18 at the Wye Plantation on Maryland's Eastern Shore. Our chairman, Senator Packwood, asked me to lead a discussion of welfare legislation, the House bill, H.R. 4, having by then come over to the Senate, where it was referred to our committee. I went through the House bill and called particular attention to the provision denying AFDC benefits to families headed by unwed females under eighteen years of age. I said that these were precisely the families we had been most concerned about in the Family Support Act.

The welfare population is roughly bi-modal. About half the families are headed by mature women who for one reason or another find themselves alone with children and without income. AFDC is income insurance, just as unemployment compensation is income insurance. Or, if you like, social insurance, which is why we call it Social Security. These persons are typically in and out of the system within two years. The other AFDC families, rather more than half, *begin* as AFDC families. Young women with children typically born out of wedlock. These are the families the Family Support Act was concerned with. There are millions of families in just this circumstance.

A few days later, a colleague on the Finance Committee came up to say that he had checked on this matter at home. In his state there were *four* such families; two had just moved in from out of state. I can imagine the state welfare commissioner asking if the Senator wanted to know their names!

Here is the point as I see it. Welfare dependency is huge, but it is also concentrated. That portion of the caseload that is on welfare for two years or less is more or less evenly distributed across the land. But three quarters of children who are on AFDC at any point in time will be on for more than five years. They are concentrated in cities. In Atlanta, 59 percent of all children received AFDC benefits in the course of the year 1993; in Cleveland, 66 percent; in Miami, 55 percent; in Oakland, 51 percent; in Newark, 66 percent; in Philadelphia, 57 percent.

By contrast there are many states which do not have large cities and do not have such concentrations. The Department of Health and Human Services has estimated the number of children who would be denied benefits under the 60-month time limit contained in both the House and Senate welfare bills, now in conference. For California, 849,300; for neighboring Nevada, 8,134. For New York, 300,527; for neighboring Vermont, 6,563.

If welfare were a smallish problem—if this were 1955, or even 1965—an argument could be made for turning the matter back to state government. But it is now so large a problem that the state government where it is most concentrated simply will not be able to handle it. On December 3 Lawrence Mead had an excellent article in the *Washington Post* in which he described the recent innovations in welfare policy, all provided under the Family Support Act, in Wisconsin. His article is entitled: "Growing a Smaller Welfare State: Wisconsin's Reforms Show That to Cut the Rolls, You Need More Bureaucrats." It begins: "The politicians debating welfare reform would have us believe that their efforts will greatly streamline the current system, help balance the nation's books and reverse the growing tide of unwed pregnancy among the poor. What they aren't telling us is that, at the state and local level, the federal cuts in the offing are apt to increase—not shrink—the size of the welfare bureaucracy."

Mead's point is one we understood perfectly at the time we enacted the Family Support Act. The cheapest thing to do with chronic welfare-dependent families is simply to leave them as they are. Changing them in ways that Wilson speaks of is labor intensive, costly, and problematic. A nice quality of the Wisconsin experiments is that job search begins the day an adult applies for welfare. But this takes supervision. Mead notes that high-performing areas "feature relentless follow-up of clients to see that they stay on track." The term "client" is important; it is a term of professional social work. This sort of thing is not for amateurs.

Most importantly, Mead concludes: "Even with Wisconsin's successes so far, important questions remain unanswered: What happens to the people who were formerly on the welfare rolls? Are they better or worse off than before? Can they sustain themselves long term? Anecdotes don't suggest great hardship, but nobody knows for sure. And what evidence is there that this approach can flourish in inner cities where the social problems are far more serious? In

Milwaukee, which has half the state's welfare caseload, the success has been far more modest than in the rest of the state. These questions need answers before a case can be made that Wisconsin is the model on which other states should base their reforms. But this much is clear: Wisconsin's fusion of generosity and stringency does represent what the voters say they're looking for." In Milwaukee, 53 percent of children are on AFDC in the course of a year.

I have been taken to task for suggesting that the time limits in the House and Senate bills will produce a surge in the number of homeless children such that the current problem of "the homeless" will seem inconsequential. So be it; that is my view. I believe our present social welfare system is all but overwhelmed. Witness the death of Elisa Izquierdo of Brooklyn. If 39 percent of all children in New York City were on AFDC at some point in 1993, I would estimate for Brooklyn the proportion would have been at least half, probably more. Hundreds of thousands—I said hundreds of thousands—of these children live in households that are held together primarily by the fact of welfare assistance. Take that away and the children are blown to the winds. A December 6 administration analysis concludes that the welfare conference agreement will force 1.5 million children into poverty.*

Republicans must look to their own consciences. I would appeal to that of my own party. A few weeks ago our distinguished Majority Leader, Senator Bob Dole, stated that he hoped to bring "welfare reform" to the floor within a week. "It is very likely next week there will also be a conference report on welfare reform. I think we have about concluded the conference. The original bill passed in the Senate by a vote of 87 to 12. We believe we have

*The six-year-old Elisa Izquierdo was beaten to death, allegedly by her drug-ridden mother. In time City and State agencies issued fierce investigations. "After Death of 6-year-old Girl, Report Shows System's Collapse." The press accounts described a "litany of inattention and ineptitude by child welfare workers." Welfare agencies "so mismanaged and out of control" that such children were sitting ducks for violence and death." None of the reports, none of the appropriate responses by the Governor and Mayor, addressed the thought that the system was overwhelmed. Its professionalism hales from a wholly different time when the City could afford to think of all those involved as "clients"—certainly not criminals—with an almost obsessive concern for confidentiality. A time warp; nothing more. But wait the day these children are living in the streets.

retained most of the Senate provisions in the conference, and I ask my colleagues on both sides—this bill had strong bipartisan support—to take a close look. Eighty-eight percent of the American people want welfare reform. We will have it on the floor, we hope, next week. We hope the President of the United States will sign it. In my view, it is a good resolution of differences between the House and the Senate. We still have one or two minor—well not minor—issues in disagreement we hope to resolve tomorrow, and then we hope to bring it up by midweek next week."

What is one to say? The Senate bill did indeed have "strong bipartisan support." If we do get a conference committee report, it will pass and will, I am confident, be vetoed. What I fear is that the repeal of the Social Security Act provision will return as part of a general budget reconciliation, and that bill *will* be signed into law. Should it do so, the Democratic Party will be to blame, and blamed it will be. It will never again be able to speak with any credibility to the central social issue of our age.

We will have fashioned our own coffin. There will be no flowers.

December 14, 1995

▲

The welfare bill came to the Senate for final passage on December 22. This time every Democrat, again save Baucus of Montana, voted against it and the measure was vetoed. Mark Hatfield of Oregon crossed the aisle and also voted Nay, thus, for my part, defining the issue as one of principle. Or so I consoled myself at the end of a year for which there was little else to show.

Consolation was fleeting. Early in 1996 the National Governors' Association reached a bipartisan accord to abolish AFDC and turn the federal money over to the states as a block grant with a five-year limit. LaDonna Pavetti at The Urban Institute calculated that the first year such a limit might take effect—say 2001—some 3,552,000 children would be cut off. For onto three decades liberal opinion had dealt with the crisis of family break-up with a more or less succession of responses: first, it wasn't happening; next, it wasn't all that bad, might even be good for you; finally, it couldn't be all that bad because the symptom, welfare dependency, was widely distributed in the population, and duration relatively brief.

Welfare officials and assorted interest groups had successfully extended the rules of confidentiality that began out of concern for individual child welfare into a near impenetrable system of state secrecy about what was going on at large. One consequence was that in the end even liberals did not know just how bad the situation was. Pavetti now demonstrated that the mean duration of time on welfare of persons ever on welfare was 12.98 years. A five-year limit would devastate this population—unless it were made up of able-bodied malingerers, which on the statistical evidence it simply was not. In enormous proportion, these were essentially failed persons.

Pavetti went further to show that of the first cohort of 3.5 million children to be dropped from the AFDC system, 49.3 percent—1,751,000—would be black, and 19.2 percent—891,500—Hispanic. At a hearing of the Senate Finance Committee, Senator Carol Moseley-Braun raised the issue of disparate impact. The two of us wrote the President:

> March 4, 1996
>
> Dear Mr. President:
>
> As you may know, the Finance Committee has been holding hearings on the National Governors' Association welfare and Medicaid proposals. Secretary Shalala appeared before the Finance Committee last Wednesday and stated with regard to welfare: "As the President said in January, we should take advantage of bipartisan consensus on time limits."
>
> May we ask you to reconsider? If a five-year time limit is enacted this year, it would take effect in 2001. At that point, income support would end for some 3,552,000 children. By 2005, this number would have increased to 4,896,000. More than two-thirds of these children will be black or Hispanic (49.3 percent black, 19.2 percent Hispanic). The impact on urban areas ought surely to concern us as well. In Illinois, for example, 244,000 children will have been dropped by the year 2005. In New York City, we estimate 254,000. To drop 2,414,000 black and Hispanic dependent children from our federal life support system would surely be the most brutal act of social policy since Reconstruction.

We cannot avoid the judgment that this disparate impact on minorities—which Secretary Shalala did not dispute—would likely give rise to a civil rights cause of action.

May we speak to you on this matter?

There was no reply. Shortly thereafter, the administration sent to Congress The Budget for Fiscal Year 1997. Section 7 was entitled, "Making Work Pay."

In 1994, the President sent Congress a dramatic welfare reform plan to: time-limit welfare benefits; establish tough work requirements and provide child care for welfare recipients; impose tough child support enforcement measures on non-custodial parents; increase State flexibility to run public assistance programs; and protect children. That proposal triggered many others—in Congress and from the nation's governors.

The President is determined to keep working with Congress to enact a bipartisan welfare reform bill. In this budget, the President proposes a revised plan to replace the current welfare system with one that requires work and provides child care so people can leave welfare for work. *This new plan saves about $40 billion over seven years* while promoting sweeping work-based reform and protecting children.

Welfare Reform
To succeed, welfare reform must focus on moving those who can work to independence through: tough work requirements; child care; incentives to reward States for placing people in jobs; a continued financial commitment by States to reform; a flexible program structure that can respond quickly to fluctuations in welfare caseloads and adapt to local needs; a strong national nutritional safety net; and protection for children even if their parents lose assistance.

Moving People from Welfare to Work
Welfare reform is mainly about work. The President's plan would repeal Aid to Families with Dependent Children (AFDC) and create a new, time-limited, conditional entitlement to cash assistance. As soon as they join the rolls, beneficiaries would have to develop and sign a personal responsibility contract with their welfare office. Within two years, able-bodied parents would have to work or lose their

benefits—and after five years, they no longer would get cash benefits. [Emphasis added.]

We are here at the junction of two large events. The strategy of starving the federal government of revenue was commencing to bite. It was now on to fifteen years since President Reagan had stated: "There were always those who told us that taxes couldn't be cut until spending was reduced. Well, you know we can lecture our children about extravagance until we run out of voice and breath. Or we can cut their extravagance by simply reducing their allowance."

From 1981 to 1996 the budget of the Justice Department—law enforcement—grew by 600 percent. Judiciary and Treasury—law enforcement—did almost as well. But for the rest, as President Clinton proclaimed in his 1996 State of the Union Address, "the era of big government" was over. Departments such as Transportation, Energy, Agriculture, Labor, Housing and Urban Development lost personnel. As did Defense. The President's seven-year balanced budget called for a reduction of upwards of one-third in domestic discretionary spending—that is, other than for entitlements.

When David Ellwood first wrote of time limits on welfare, he intended a large increase in federal outlays to make it possible. Prior to his confirmation hearing as Assistant Secretary of Health and Human Services for Policy Planning in 1993, he called on the Committee Chairman as protocol decreed. He recollects that I told him that in two years' time he would return to Harvard and write a fine book on how he had failed. "For there is no money." In the event he departed in seventeen months.

The second development was not as concise, but unmistakable even so. The week before the President's budget was sent to Congress, *National Journal* ran a long section on "Budget," beginning with welfare:

Looking for a Voice

The Republicans' grip on Congress and a majority of the national governorships means tough sledding for defenders of the poor. A

Democratic President committed to welfare reform makes things tougher still.

The way welfare advocates tell it, the poor are getting mugged. In the current Congress, virtually every poverty program stands to have its pocket picked. Republican proposals to cut spending for the social safety net are described as the "most dramatic ever." A Clinton Administration official exclaims: "We're talking about huge changes in the incomes to the poorest in America."

But something is wrong; something is missing. The response of progressive groups to the Republican-led assault has been scattered and ineffectual. Pickets and demonstrations have been rare. Where are the howls of protest? Hardly a soundbite has nipped at the heels of the national news.

Last September, in the midst of the Senate debate over welfare reform, Daniel Patrick Moynihan, D-NY, wondered what was taking place. "Why do we not see the endless parade of petitioners, as when health care reform was before us in the last Congress—the lobbyists, the pretend citizen groups, the real citizen groups? None are here . . ."

Shaken by Moynihan's charge, advocates for the poor replied that they were overwhelmed, fighting a "100-front" war against the 100-day legislative siege laid by the Republican Contract with America. "Most social welfare organizations felt there were so many proposed cuts that it was bewildering to keep up with them," said Ronald F. Pollack, the executive director of Families U.S.A. Foundation, a nationwide health care consumer organization.

Pollack had been counsel to the National Welfare Rights Organization, which in the early 1970s organized the opposition to President Nixon's Family Assistance Plan. *National Journal* noted, "He recalls that the organization at one time mobilized 20,000 people to march on the capital." And the issue? the outrage? President Nixon had proposed a guaranteed income that was not large enough; there was a slight penalty for adults who refused jobs. The Family Support Act of 1988 included a similar provision. *Congressional Quarterly* recalled, "The so-called workfare provision was anathema to many liberals . . . some of whom referred to it as 'slavefare.'"[12] But this was all now. As ever, Meg Greenfield put it most pointedly and yet gently: "Listening to many white liberals,

you get the idea that they have finally found racial politics disappointing: too complicated, too ambiguous, too likely to go unre-
warded either by the blacks they rather condescendingly thought
they were championing or other white liberals who have recently
gone AWOL on the cause." Indeed, the political surprise of the
1996 political season was the success of an assertively right-wing
Pat Buchanan rousing the resentments of blue-collar workers thinking about *their* jobs. The *New Yorker* reported that William Julius
Wilson was "furious" at the Republican Congress for proposing to
impose a five-year time limit without an accompanying employment
program for those whose benefits had ended, and for their male
counterparts, but this was rare.[13] Besides, Democrats agreed.

I will leave the matter with a comment by John J. DiIulio, Jr., in
the Winter 1996 issue of the *Public Interest:* "It took liberals 30
years to figure out that Daniel Patrick Moynihan was probably right
about black families, urban poverty, and welfare policies in the mid
1960s; unfortunately, it may take conservatives as long to fathom
that he was right about these issues in the mid 1990s too."

What I have been right about, if indeed anything, is that the
United States is evolving into a new kind of society; Daniel Bell has
described it as postindustrial. Seymour Martin Lipset, James S.
Coleman, James Q. Wilson, and many others have limned, en-
larged, illuminated this still-elusive theme. We have been at this for
some while, getting on to 40 years of friendship and collaboration.
There is a record, or so I believe, of having anticipated some matters
of consequence. Accompanied at times by angry rejection. I have
spent most of these 40 years in government and politics and have
seen a good many new matters resolved with striking success: such
that many of the other arrivals on Capitol Hill are scarcely aware
that they were once thought intractable. This then is a source of
solace, but only so much.

In a final chapter, "The Coming of Age of American Social
Policy," I contend that the main issues that have bedeviled us in
the past first appeared in European settings. These cluster around
two interrelated themes: expanding citizenship in a posttraditional
society, much in the mode described by T. H. Marshall; and attain-

ing stability and social equity in the new industrial economies. No sequence is suggested here; voting rights precede unemployment insurance in some settings, follow them in others. Still, the basic models and model responses were European. The 1909 White House Conference on Dependent Children had exulted that soon now the United States would catch up with the social welfare systems in England, France, and Germany. That was the ideal and that was the goal.

No longer. We are dealing now with issues of social policy that first arose in the United States. And so to these reflections. In the Godkin Lectures at Harvard in 1986 I commented: "The central conservative truth is that it is culture, not politics, that determines the success of a society. The central liberal truth is that politics can change a culture and save it from itself." Some of what follows may advance this thesis and the possibilities it suggests.

Pindars Corners, New York
July 1996

~ 1 ~

Three Decades of *The Public Interest*

The Public Interest first appeared in the fall of 1965, a moment of high optimism concerning the American condition. It was surely the case that the first editors, Irving Kristol and Daniel Bell, shared this optimism, but from a distinct perspective. For them, the great triumph of the time was not the Great Society but rather the end of ideology, the falsification of the Marxist doctrine of inexorable, all-defining, all-consuming class conflict. That issue had preoccupied the European and American left. (The proposal for a new journal was agreed to at a meeting in Sidney Hook's apartment in New York City.)

In 1985, in the twentieth-anniversary issue, Glazer, in an article "Interests and Passions," would write of them: "They did not think that in advanced industrial societies, such as the United States or Western Europe, interests caused any necessary and fatal division among social classes: All could agree on courses of action that satisfied more or less the interests of workers and employers, property owners and tenants, farmers and consumers, renters and investors. Thus, whatever fine distinctions the editors and founders may have made over the 'end of ideology' thesis, they believed that there was no sound basis for Marxist ideology, or other ideologies that posited the incapacity of capitalist society to provide stability, growth, and a decent life to the various classes that made it up."

To be beyond all that was a liberating experience indeed, and a personal triumph for the likes of Kristol and Bell. Economic determinism persisted withal. Glazer put it in the twentieth-anniversary issue: "*The Public Interest* was launched under the sign of the interests." But, he continued, "it now operates in an environment in which the passions are dominant." What had intervened? Riot, nihilism, war, assassination, social dysfunction of every sort. Economics had not proved sufficient.

In the same twentieth-anniversary issue, James Q. Wilson wrote of "The Rediscovery of Character: Private Virtue and Public Policy." He began:

> The most important change in how one defines the public interest that I have witnessed—and experienced—over the last twenty years has been a deepening concern for the development of character in the citizenry. An obvious indication of this shift has been the rise of such social issues as abortion and school prayer. A less obvious but I think more important change has been the growing awareness that a variety of public problems can only be understood—and perhaps addressed—if they are seen as arising out of a defect in character formation.
>
> *The Public Interest* began publication at about the time that economics was becoming the preferred mode of policy analysis. Its very first issue contained an article by Daniel Patrick Moynihan hailing the triumph of macroeconomics: "Men are learning how to make an industrial economy work" as evidenced by the impressive ability of economists not only to predict economic events accurately but to control them by, for example, delivering on the promise of full employment. Six months later I published an essay suggesting that poverty be dealt with by direct income transfers in the form of a negative income tax or family allowances. In the next issue, James Tobin made a full-scale proposal for a negative income tax and Virginia Held welcomed program planning and budgeting to Washington as a means for rationalizing the allocative decisions of government, a topic enlarged upon the following year by a leading practitioner of applied economics, William Gorham. Meanwhile, Thomas C. Schelling had published a brilliant economic analysis of organized crime and Christopher Jencks a call for a voucher system that would allow parents to choose among public and private purveyors of education. In a later issue, Gordon Tullock explained the rise in crime

as a consequence of individuals responding rationally to an increase in the net benefit of criminality.

In this same issue Daniel Bell noted the "rise of the ethnic as a feature of American life," not least as an important means of getting "a piece of the (affirmative) action" which the federal government now provided: "Most sociologists had assumed that ethnicity was an atavistic feature of modern life, and that with the deeper identification of individuals with their occupations, professional, or class positions, these alignments would be the major axes of group attachments in the country. Subsequently the idea arose that ethnicity is a 'primordial' sentiment, an inherent, indigenous feeling of belonging. But the puzzle, therefore, for many sociologists, was how to explain the resurgence of ethnicity, especially among second- and third-generation descendants, as against an adherence to class."

It was Glazer who first pointed this out in *The Social Origins of American Communism* (1961). As I once put it, what Karl Marx wrote in the British Museum, Nathan Glazer disproved in the New York Public Library. Communism in America had been an ethnic phenomenon. *Beyond the Melting Pot* (1963), on which I collaborated, should be read as a test of the Marxist premise of class cohesion. If this was to emerge anywhere in a multiethnic city it would be New York; it hadn't. Nor was there any empirical evidence that the influence of ethnicity differed anywhere else—in fact, there was much to the contrary.

For a period in the 1970s I served as American Ambassador to India and saw the fissiparous powers of ethnicity in South Asia. Why not North Asia? In 1975 I returned by way of China (where I was the guest of our mission chief George Bush); I wrote a "Letter from Peking" for the *New Yorker*[1] in which I allowed that the People's Republic would surely be around for a bit. So had the Soviet Union, and it "may have considerable time left before ethnicity breaks it up. Red China works too, and is likely to last even longer." Ten years later, the breakup seemed closer at hand, but American government could not grasp this. It had spent the first part of the 1980s obsessed with communists in Central America, in time putting the Constitution itself in jeopardy in the Iran-Contra affair. Hence, my topic for the twentieth-anniversary issue: "The Paranoid Style in American Politics Revisited." Richard Hofstadter had been a member of *The Public Interest* circle before his death in 1970. His great essay had been given as the Herbert Spencer Lecture at Oxford, just hours after the assassination of John F. Kennedy. It was an eerie evocation of things to come, some of it on the left, as in the motion picture *JFK,* but more importantly the movements on the right, which have brought us to right-wing violence for the first time in several generations. I wrote of this. Assassinations linger, societies sicken, as I had sensed at the time.

I do not know how much explanatory power this thesis has, and there was but little response to the paper. Yet, government *was* missing things. In a sequence of specific events in October and December 1988, the leaders of the Soviet Union sued in effect for peace. Specifically, on October 11, 1988, Eduard Shevardnadze, USSR Minister of Foreign Affairs, journeyed to Paris to speak to the United Nations Educational, Scientific, and Cultural Organization (UNESCO), the first Soviet Foreign Minister to do so. His address, he stated, was "inspired by Mikhail Gorbachev's words that the goals for which the UNESCO was set up are of special importance." UNESCO was not working and well he knew why: the Soviets had sabotaged it: "As we delve into the roots of the trouble, we don't try to shift the blame on others. We submitted to the influence of confrontation, and adopted its spirit as we sought to repulse ideas alien to us. The exaggerated ideological approach undermined tolerance intrinsic to UNESCO. We [now] refuse to act as judges, and we start our criticisms with ourselves. We call on everybody to learn the lessons of the past as UNESCO revival is starting. The organization shall be one universal whole to respond to the emergent wholeness of the world. UNESCO shall embark on the course determined in its Charter and become a genuine center of cooperation. Thus we see the goal of its revival."

He set forth an astounding—for a Soviet Foreign Minister—set of principles for the future: "*Free choice,* which implies that one must not claim the right to final judgment, nor impose ideas, doctrines or models of development; *political and cultural pluralism,* which implies that no commitment to one's beliefs can any more justify their messianic promotion; *reliance on dialogue,* not on confrontation, and on the balance of interests, not on the balance of forces; *exclusion of the self-acting component of ideological differences from international affairs,* and measures to guarantee national security in the context of universal security; *peace through wisdom,* not through force; *force of politics,* not politics of force; *supremacy of international law in international affairs."*

Two months later, on December 7, 1988, Gorbachev himself journeyed to New York to address the United Nations General Assembly. His address was the plainest possible abandonment of Marxism-Leninism. "We in no way aspire to be the bearer of ultimate truth." To the contrary, law must govern: "the political, juridical and moral importance of the ancient Roman maxim: *Pacta sunt servanda!*—Agreements must be honoured!"

Then this: "Our idea is a world community of states with political systems and foreign policies based on law. This could be achieved with the help of an accord within the framework of the U.N. on a uniform understanding of the principles and norms of international law; their codification with new conditions taken into consideration; and the elaboration of legislation for new areas of cooperation. In the nuclear era, the effectiveness of international law must be based on norms reflecting a balance of interests of states, rather than on coercion. As the awareness of our common fate grows, every state would be genuinely interested in confining itself within the limits of international law."

No one in Washington could follow him. The Soviets could see they were beaten; we could not. (While Ambassador to the United Nations in the mid-1970s, I had argued that they *could* be beaten. The doctrine of *detente* held otherwise; my tenure was brief.)

All of which has been described elsewhere. What is not resolved, and needs work, is why we failed to sense our success. In his Iliadic memoir, *Events Leading to My Death,* Howard K. Smith recounts America's "Age of Responsibility" as the great republic rose to the challenge of totalitarianism. Nothing like that will likely ever happen quite like that again. But Smith closes with the caution that danger never disappears; it merely presents itself in unfamiliar forms. A tentative guess is that while caught up in the Cold War abroad we quite missed that fact that at home, and in the North Atlantic as you could say, the acute disorders of industrialism which had been thought unsolvable were largely resolved. Or, if you like, moderated to the point of acceptability. This came about through intellectual disciplines, far more than through politics. (Which is only symmetrical; Marxism was an intellectual discipline.) In the first issue of *The Public Interest,* in an article "The Professionalization of Reform," I more or less bet that this was going to happen. Thirty years later I returned to this theme unapologetic but, well, thirty years older.

▼

The Professionalization of Reform (1965)

Our best hope for the future lies in the extension to social organization of the methods that we already employ in our most progressive fields of effort. In science and in industry we do not wait for catastrophe to force new ways upon us . . . We rely, and with access, upon quantitative analysis to point the way; and we advance because we are constantly improving and applying such analysis.

The passage above, as succinct a case for social planning as could be made, is not a product of either the thought or the institutions of the liberal left. It is, rather, a statement by the late mathematical economist Wesley C. Mitchell. And it has recently been approvingly reprinted at the beginning of a report on "The Concept of Poverty" published by the Chamber of Commerce of the United States.

The report itself, the work of businessmen and scholars, is perhaps the most competent commentary on the government's antipoverty program yet to appear. It is replete with citations of articles in *Social Research* and *Land Economics,* and of data from the *Statistical Abstract of the United States;* the perspective ranges from friendly references to the works of Friedrich Engels, to more detached assessments of contemporary tracts. ("Michael Harrington, author of a widely read book on poverty, *The Other America,* has written, 'Any gain for America's minorities will immediately be translated into an advance for all the unskilled workers. One cannot raise the bottom of society without benefiting everyone above.' This is almost precisely wrong.") But the report is less significant for what it says than for what it is: an example of the evolving technique and style of reform in the profoundly new society developing in the United States. Lacking a better term, it might be described as the professionalization of reform.

Writing for the British journal the *New Society* just prior to the assassination of President Kennedy, Nathan Glazer described the process: "Without benefit of anything like the Beveridge report to spark and focus public discussion and concern, the United States is passing through a stage of enormous expansion in the size and scope of what we may loosely call the social services—the public programs designed to help people adapt to an increasingly complex and unmanageable society. While Congress has been painfully and hesitantly trying to deal with two great measures—tax reform and a civil rights bill—and its deliberations on both have been closely covered by the mass media, it has also been working with much less publicity on a number of bills which will contribute at least as much to changing the shape of American society."

The vast Mental Retardation Facilities and Community Mental Health Centers Construction Act had just become law. The no less enormous vocational education bill was moving steadily through Congress. The Kennedy administration had earlier obtained such measures as the Area Redevelopment Act, the Manpower Development and Training Act, and the Public Welfare Amendments of 1962. "Waiting in the wings" were a domestic peace corps and an ambitious youth conservation corps, while the community action programs developed by the President's Committee on Juvenile Delinquency and Youth Crime, established in 1961, were scheduled for new and expanded funding.

It is a special mind that can as much as keep the titles of those programs straight. But the most interesting thing about all this sudden expansion of social services was that it had behind it, as

Glazer noted, "nothing like the powerful political pressure and long-sustained intellectual support that produced the great welfare measures of the New Deal—Social Security, Unemployment Insurance, Public Welfare, Public Housing." The "massive political support and intellectual leadership that produced the reforms of the thirties" simply did not exist; yet the reforms were moving forward.

Glazer accounted for this in terms of the emergence of a large body of professional persons and professional organizations that had taken on themselves the concern for the 20 to 30 percent of the population that was outside the mainstream of American prosperity. Intellectuals knew little about the subject, and were not much interested. Organized labor, while both concerned and knowledgeable, had had but limited success in involving its membership in such efforts. As a result, "The fate of the poor is in the hands of the administrators and the professional organizations of doctors, teachers, social workers, therapists, counselors and so forth. It is these who, in a situation where the legislation and programs become ever more complex, spend the time to find out—or rather have brought home to them—through their work the effects of certain kinds of measures and programs, and who propose ever more complex programs which Congress deliberates upon in the absence of any major public interest. When Congress argues these programs, the chief pressures upon it are not the people, but the organized professional interests that work with that segment of the problem, and those who will benefit from or be hurt by the legislation."

The antipoverty program that was being developed even as Glazer wrote is far the best instance of the professionalization of reform yet to appear. In its genesis, its development, and now in its operation, it is a prototype of the social technique of action that will almost certainly become more common in the future. It is a technique that will not appeal to everyone, and in which many will perceive the not altogether imaginary danger of a too-powerful government. But it is also a technique that offers a profound promise of social sanity and stability in time to come.

There are two aspects of the poverty program which distinguish it from earlier movements of its kind: The initiative came largely from within. And the case for action was based on essentially esoteric information about the past and probable future course of events.

The most distinctive break with the past is with regard to initiative. War on poverty was not declared at the behest of the poor. Just the opposite. The poor were not only invisible, as Michael Harrington described them, they were also for the most part silent. John F. Kennedy ventured into Appalachia searching for Protestant votes, not for poverty. There he encountered the incredible pauperization of the mountain people, most particularly the soft coal miners, an industrial work force whose numbers had been reduced by nearly two-thirds in the course of a decade—but with hardly a sound of protest. The miners were desperately poor, shockingly unemployed, but neither radical nor in any significant way restive. In 1964, in the face of the historic Democratic sweep, Harlan County, Kentucky, returned a freshman Republican Congressman.

True, the civil rights movement was well established and highly effective during this period, but it was primarily concerned with just that: the demand for the recognition of the civil rights of the Negro American. While the movement would clearly in time turn to the problem of poverty and of the economic position of the Negro, it had only begun to do so, as in the March on Washington in August 1963, and its economic demands were still general and essentially traditional, as for example an increased minimum wage.

Apart from the always faithful labor movement, the only major lobbies working for any of the programs that came together to form the war on poverty were the conservationists supporting the youth conservation camps, and the National Committee on the Employment of Youth, an organization representing a variety of groups in the social welfare field. The essential fact is that the main pressure for a massive government assault on poverty developed within the Kennedy-Johnson administration, among officials whose responsibilities were to think about just such matters. These men now exist, they are well paid, have competent staffs, and have access to the

President. (Many of these officials, of course, were originally brought to Washington by the New Deal: they are by no means all *nuovi huomini*.) Most importantly, they have at their command an increasing fund of information about social conditions in the United States.

Almost all this information is public, but the art of interpreting it is, in a sense, private. Anyone is free to analyze income statistics, or employment data, or demographic trends to his heart's content. But very few persons in the beginning years of the present decade were able to perceive in those statistics the gradual settling of a poverty class in America. A number of officials in the federal government (mostly academicians on leave) were. Leaving aside the question of whether or not they were right—a question which must always be open—it is clear that the judgment they reached was quite at variance, almost poles apart, from the general public understanding of the time.

Whereas the public, both high and low in the intellectual hierarchy, saw income distribution steadily compressing, saw the Negro American more and more winning his rightful place in society, saw prosperity spreading through the land, the men in the government saw something quite different: an income distribution gap that had not budged since the end of the war, and had in fact worsened sharply for Negroes, a rising measure of social disorganization among poor families and poor communities, a widening gap between the prospects of the poor and those of the middle class.[2]

In President Johnson these officials found a chief executive who knew a good deal about poverty, and seemingly everything about politics. In a matter of weeks from the time he assumed office, the array of programs and bills Glazer had described as "waiting in the wings" were mustered into a coherent legislative program, reinforced by some entirely new ideas, and moved out under the banner of a war on poverty. It was an issue that united rather than divided, and the ranks of its supporters if anything swelled as it moved through the legislative process.

There is nothing, as such, startling about these developments.

They have been foreseen, with either hope or fear, by many persons
for many years. However, in recent times a number of events have
occurred which very much hasten the process, and make it of
greater moment. These have to do (1) with the almost sudden
emergence of the fact that the industrial nations of the world seem
finally about to learn how to manage their economies, (2) with the
professionalization of the middle class, and (3) with the exponential
growth of knowledge.

The Economic Revolution

Recent years, with the steady advance of technology, have given
birth to a good number of neo-apocalyptic views of the future of
the American economy, most of them associated with the concept
of automation. No one should doubt there is something called
automation going on, and that it does change things. However,
there is no evidence whatever that it is in fact transforming American society, or any other society. It is simply the newest phase in a
process that has been under way for at least two centuries, and will
presumably go on and on, past any immediate concern of this age
or the next.

At the same time, there is a good deal of evidence, if that is the
term for what are little more than everyday impressions, that in the
area of economic policy there has occurred a genuine discontinuity,
a true break with the past: Men are learning how to make an
industrial economy work.

What is involved is something more permanent than simply a run
of good luck, or specially refined intuitions on the part of persons
responsible for the economic affairs of one nation, or a group of
nations. Rather it is the fact that for two decades now, since the
end of World War II, the industrial democracies of the world have
been able to operate their economies on a high and steadily expanding level of production and employment. Nothing like it has ever
happened before in history. It is perhaps the central fact of world
politics today. The briefest recollection of what happened to those
economies in the two decades that followed the First World War

will suggest why. Moreover, it is a development that has all the markings of a scientific event, of a profound advance in knowledge, as well as of an improvement in statecraft.

In the beginning was the theory. With but little data either to support or confound them, economic theories multiplied and conflicted. But gradually more and better data accumulated: progress begins on social problems when it becomes possible to measure them. As the data accumulated and technology made it possible to calculate more rapidly, the theories gradually became able to explain more, and these in turn led to the improvement in the data. John Maynard Keynes at King's College, Cambridge, and Wesley C. Mitchell at the National Bureau of Economic Research in New York are supremely good symbols of the two processes that ended up in a deeply symbiotic relationship.

And then one day it all more or less hangs together and the world is different, although of course not quite aware of the change. Governments promise full employment and then produce it. (In 1964 unemployment, adjusted to conform more or less to United States definitions, was 2.9 percent in Italy, 2.5 percent in France and Britain, and 0.4 percent in Germany. Consider the contrast with post–World War I.) Governments undertake to expand their economy at a steady rate—and do so. (In 1961 the members of the Organization for Economic Cooperation and Development, which grew out of the Marshall Plan, undertook to increase their output by 50 percent during the decade of the 1960s. The United States, at all events, is right on schedule.)

The ability to predict events, as against controlling them, has developed even more impressively—the Council of Economic Advisers' forecast of GNP for 1964 was off by only $400 million in a total of $623 billion; the unemployment forecast was on the nose.

There is a temptation, of course, to go too far in presuming what can be done with the economy. The international exchange system is primitive, and at the moment menacing. The stock market can be wildly irrational. There are, as Hyman Lewis points out, competing theories of investment which could bring us to unsettling dilemmas. We in the United States have not achieved full employment. We have accepted the use of federal taxing and spending powers as a means of social adjustment, but so far only in pleasant formulations. Our willingness to raise taxes, for example, is yet to be tested. In general, the political component of political economy remains very much uncertain. Thus the British, again to cite Lewis, have the best economists but one of the less successful economies. But the fact remains that economics is approaching the status of an applied science.

In the long run this econometric revolution, assuming it works itself out, is bound to have profound effects on the domestic politics of all the nations involved. The central political issue of most industrial nations over the past century and a half has been how to make an economy work. Almost every conceivable nostrum, from the nationalization of the means of production, distribution, and exchange to the free coinage of silver, has been proposed, and most have been tried. Usually without success. In the United States, for one administration after another, economic failure has led to political failure. But if henceforth the business cycle has a longer sweep, and fewer abrupt downturns, the rise and fall of political fortunes may follow the same pattern. Once in power, a party may be much more likely to remain so. Or in any event, the issues that elect or defeat governments could be significantly different from those of the past.

The more immediate impact of this econometric revolution in the United States is that the federal government will be endowed, more often than not, with a substantial, and within limits predictable, rise in revenues available for social purposes. Significantly, the war on poverty began in the same year of the great tax cut. The President was not forced to choose between the measures; he was able to proceed with both. In that sense, the war on poverty began not because it was necessary (which it was) but because it was possible.

The singular nature of the new situation in which the federal government finds itself is that the immediate supply of resources available for social purposes might actually outrun the immediate demand of established programs. Federal expenditures under existing programs rise at a fairly predictable rate. But, under conditions of economic growth, revenues rise faster. This has given birth to the phenomenon of the "fiscal drag"—the idea that unless the federal government disposes of this annual increment, either by cutting taxes or adding programs, the money taken out of circulation by taxes will slow down economic growth and could, of course, at a certain point stop it altogether.

Thus, assuming the continued progress of the economy in something like the pattern of recent years, there is likely to be $4–5 billion in additional, unobligated revenue coming in each year. But this increment will only continue to come on condition that it is disposed of. Therefore one of the important tasks to which an administration must address itself is that of devising new and responsible programs for expending public funds in the public interest.

This is precisely the type of decision-making that is suited to the techniques of modern organizations, and which ends up in the hands of persons who make a profession of it. They are less and less political decisions, more and more administrative ones. They are decisions that can be reached by consensus rather than conflict.

The Professionalization of the Middle Class

"Everywhere in American life," Kenneth S. Lynn reports, "the professions are triumphant." The period since the G.I. Bill has witnessed an extraordinary expansion of higher education. In the United States, a quarter of the teenage population now goes on to some kind of college, and among specific class and ethnic groups the proportion is as high as three quarters. The trend is unmistakable and probably irresistible: in the course of the coming decades some form of higher education will become near to universal. But most importantly, for more and more persons the form of education will involve professional training. This is not the same thing as traditional higher education; it does not produce the same types of persons.

The difference has been most succinctly stated by Everett C.

Hughes: "Professionals *profess*. They profess to know better than others the nature of certain matters, and to know better than their clients what ails them or their affairs." And he continues: "Lawyers not only give advice to clients and plead their cases for them; they also develop a philosophy of law—of its nature and its functions, and of the proper way in which to administer justice. Physicians consider it their prerogative to define the nature of disease and of health, and to determine how medical services ought to be distributed and paid for. Social workers are not content to develop a technique of case work; they concern themselves with social legislation. Every profession considers itself the proper body to set the terms in which some aspect of society, life or nature is to be thought of, and to define the general lines, or even the details, of public policy concerning it."

As the number of professionals increases, so also does the number of professions, or neo-professions. More and more, middle-class persons are attracted by the independence of judgment, esoteric knowledge, and immunity to outside criticism that characterize professionals. As Everett Hughes puts it: "The YMCA secretary wants his occupation recognized not merely as that of offering young men from the country a pleasant road to Protestant righteousness in the city, but as a more universal one of dealing with groups of young people. All that is learned of adolescence, of behavior in small groups, of the nature and organization of community life is considered the intellectual base of his work."

There are now an extraordinary number of such persons in America. Those Americans classified as professional and technical workers have just passed the 9 million mark—more than the number of "managers, officials, and proprietors," more than the craftsmen and foremen. And of this group, an enormous number are involved in various aspects of social welfare and reform. Through sheer numbers they would tend to have their way; but as professionals in a professionalizing society, they are increasingly entitled to have their way. That is how the system works.

One of the more powerful demonstrations of the influence of professional thinking on programs of social reform is the provision of the Economic Opportunity Act that community action programs be carried out with the "maximum feasible participation" of the poor themselves. This is one of the most important and pioneering aspects of the entire antipoverty program. But typically this measure was inserted in the legislation not because of any demand of the poor but because the intellectual leaders of the social welfare profession had come to the conclusion that this was indispensable to effective social action. Typically also, the literature describes the process in terms of the use of the "indigenous nonprofessional"— persons identified by the fact that they are not professional. A somewhat ironical turn of events in this area is the role the community action programs are playing in recreating the ethnic political-social organizations of the big city slums—the dismantling of which was for so long the object of political and social reformers in the United States!

The prospect of large-scale opposition to the new professions is, for the moment at least, limited because the professionalization of the middle class has led to a no less extraordinary opening up of careers to talent. The time when any considerable number of persons of great ability and ambition have found their way out of poverty blocked by their inability to obtain an education has all but passed. (There are still many, many persons whose natural abilities are stunted by poverty, but that is another matter.) A nationwide survey of 1960 high school graduates, Project Talent, found that about 97 percent of those in the top 1 percent in aptitude and 93 percent of those in the top 5 percent entered college within a year. Among the next 5 percent (the 90th to 94th percentile), 86 percent did so. As a general proposition, ability is recognized and rewarded in America today as at no time in history. (Michael Young's forecast of the revolt of the lower quartile against the ultimate injustice of a society based on merit may not be discounted, but it is not, on the other hand, scheduled until 2031.)

It is possible that this process, just because it is successful in drawing up talent from lower economic and social groups, will deprive those groups of much of their natural leadership and make them all the more dependent on professionals. Kenneth Clark has noted that the degree of recruitment of civil rights leaders into "establishment" organizations verges on raiding—and has raised suspicions of hidden motives. On the other hand, there is rather a pronounced tendency for persons from such groups, when they do rise to the middle class, to settle into professions which involve work with the very groups they left behind. Thus, in a certain sense the poor are not so much losing their natural leaders as obtaining them through different routes.

The Exponential Growth of Knowledge

Among the complexities of life is the fact that the American business community, in a period when it was fiercely opposed to the idea of economic or social planning, nonetheless supported, even pressed for, the development of a national statistical system which has become the best in the world and which now makes certain types of planning and regulation—although quite different from the collective proposals of earlier eras—both feasible and in a measure inevitable. Much as mountains are climbed, so statistics are used if they are there. As an example, trade union wage settlements in recent years have been profoundly influenced by the wage-price guidelines set by the federal government. This could not possibly have occurred on an essentially voluntary basis were it not that the Bureau of Labor Statistics has developed the technique of measuring productivity—and has done so accompanied, step-by-step, by the business and labor advisory committees that work with the Bureau.

A measure of the near quantum change that has only recently occurred in the information available for social planning in the United States (the development work began long ago, but the pay-off has been rather recent) may be suggested by the fact that the nation went through the Great Depression of the 1930s without ever really knowing what the rate of unemployment was! This was then a measurement taken but once every ten years, by the census. Today, of course, employment and unemployment data are collected monthly and debated in terms of the decimal points.

Similarly, the census has been quietly transformed from a ten-times-a-century proceeding to a system of current accounts on a vast range of social data.

Most of the information that went into the development of the antipoverty program was essentially economic, but the social data available to the President's task force was of singular importance to shaping the program, and in turn the program will greatly stimulate the collection of more such. The nation is clearly on the verge of developing a system of social statistics comparable to the now highly developed system of economic statistics.

The use of all such statistics is developing also. A vast "industry of discovery," to use William Haber's description of events in the physical sciences, is developing in the social sciences as well. Computer technology has greatly enhanced the possible uses of such data. Just as the effort to stimulate the American economy is now well advanced, the simulation of social processes, particularly in decision-making, is also begun and may be expected to produce important, if not indeed revolutionary, insights. Such prospects tend to stir some alarm in thoughtful persons, but it may be noted the public has accepted with calm, even relish, the fact that the outcome of elections is now predicted with surpassing accuracy. If that most solemn of democratic rituals may be simulated without protest, there is not likely to be much outcry against the simulation of various strategies of housing integration, or techniques of conflict resolution, or patterns of child rearing.

Expenditure for social science research was somewhere between $500 and $600 million in 1964. This was only 10 percent of the $6 billion spent in the same year on the life and physical sciences (including psychology), and much less a proportion of the $19 billion spent on research and development altogether. Nonetheless it represents a sixfold growth in a decade. There is, moreover, some indication social scientists are not yet thinking in the money terms that are in fact available to them. Angus Campbell suggested recently that social scientists still think in budgets of thousands of dollars when they should be thinking of millions. "The prevailing format for social research is still the exploitation of opportunities which are close at hand, easily manageable, and inexpensive." But, he adds, "there are a good many social scientists who know very well how to study social change on a broad scale and are intensely interested in going about it." The Survey Research Center at the University of Michigan, which Campbell directs, has under way a year-long panel survey of the impact of the 1964 tax cut on the nation's taxpayers, a specific example of the use of social science techniques in the development of economic policy.

All in all, the prospect is for a still wider expansion of knowledge available to governments as to how people behave. This will be accompanied by further improvement of the now well-developed knowledge of what they think. Public opinion polls are already a daily instrument of government decision-making (a fact which has clearly affected the role of the legislature). In combination these two systems of information make it possible for a government to respond intelligently and in time to the changing needs and desires of the electorate. The day when mile-long petitions and mass rallies were required to persuade a government that a popular demand existed that things be done differently is clearly drawing to a close. Indeed, the very existence of such petitions and rallies may in time become a sign that what is being demanded is *not yet* a popular demand.

The Perils of Progress

The professionalization of reform will proceed, regardless of the perils it presents. Even in the face of economic catastrophe, which is certainly conceivable if not probable, the response will be vastly more systematic and informed than any of the past.

A certain price will be paid, and a considerable risk will be incurred. The price will be a decline in the moral exhilaration of public affairs at the domestic level. It has been well said that the civil rights movement of the present time has at last provided the youth of America with a moral equivalent of war. The more general effect of the civil rights movement has been a much heightened public concern for human dignity and welfare. This kind of passion could seep out of the life of the nation, and we would be the less for it.

The risk is a combination of enlightenment, resources, and skill which in the long run, to use Harold D. Laswell's phrase, becomes a "monocracy of power."

But the potential rewards are not less great. The creation of a society that can put an end to the "animal miseries" and stupid controversies that afflict most peoples would be an extraordinary achievement of the human spirit. The argument may be made, for example, that had the processes described in this article not progressed as far as they had by 1961, the response of the federal government to the civil rights revolution would have been thoroughly inadequate: that instead of joining with and helping to direct the movement, the national government would have trailed behind with grudging, uncomprehending, and increasingly inadequate concessions that could have resulted in the problem of the Negro American becoming insoluble in terms of existing American society.

The prospect that the more primitive social issues of American politics are at last to be resolved need only mean that we may now turn to issues more demanding of human ingenuity than that of how to put an end to poverty in the richest nation in the world. Many such issues might be in the area of foreign affairs, where the enormity of difficulty and the proximity of disaster is sufficient to keep the citizens and political parties of the nation fully occupied. And there is also the problem of perfecting, to the highest degree possible, the quality of our lives and of our civilization. We may not be accustomed to giving political priority to such questions. But no one can say they will be boring or trivial!

▲

What is to be made of these closing passages? The Vietnam war surely set the limits of professionalization. The public never demanded such a war, or saw the compelling need for it. It was the decision of a tiny handful of professionals in government, and ruined two presidencies. Professionals who, for one thing, never noticed the Sino-Soviet split of the same decade; so much for expertise. As for "the quality of our lives," the environmental movement of the next decade surely represented such a development; in part, I would hazard, in response to too much in the way of foreign affairs. As for the proposition that we might "now turn to issues more demanding of human ingenuity than how to put an end to poverty in the richest nation in the world," I equivocate. The crisis of dependency that developed three decades later was addressed early on as merely a problem of poverty. This may in part have been a result of a relative absence of data (see Chapter 6).

▼

The Professionalization of Reform (1995)

Thirty years ago, in the first article of the first issue of *The Public Interest,* I published some observations on "The Professionalization of Reform" which thirty years later can be read, selectively, without overmuch embarrassment. I had served as Assistant Secretary of Labor for Policy Planning and Research in the Kennedy years and had carried on under Johnson. The memory is almost lost now, but the Kennedy years were a time of almost feverish efforts to get around the disinclination of Congress to spend money. My first meeting in the Oval Office involved a pay raise for government employees. Even Congress would want to side with the National Association of Letter Carriers! Then a double dividend for Veterans Administration life insurance. Next a tax cut. Then revenue sharing, the chairman of the Council, Walter E. Heller, reasoning that if Congress would not spend the money, possibly the governors would. This mode took us through the decade with but a single recession at the very end.

The Nixon administration continued in just this vein. Revenue sharing was enacted. A guaranteed income was proposed and almost enacted. George P. Shultz became director of the new Office of Management and Budget. A University of Chicago economist, he set about elaborating a formal definition of a full employment budget, one in which outlays equal revenues at full employment. Absent full employment, a *deliberate deficit* would stimulate the economy in that direction. On into the seventies when *five* successive tax cuts were enacted.

The success was stunning: so much that it has gone almost unnoticed. The wild gyrations of a capitalist economy gave way to a sequence of more or less uniform business cycles in which the economy grew, faster, then slower, but with only one significant decline. Before 1929 the average business cycle contraction lasted nearly 21 months following an average expansion of slightly more than 25. Over the past 50 years, the average recovery has lasted 50 months, with contractions shortened to an average of 11. In all this past half century, the largest *decline* in output was 2.2 percent, in 1982. Compare that with a drop of 9.9 percent in 1930; followed by 7.7 percent in 1931; followed by 14.8 percent in 1932. As of mid-1995, for example, we are in our tenth postwar expansion which reached its 58th month in January. During the half century period, the size of our economy has quadrupled, and real income per person has more than doubled. Wealth accumulated but society decayed.

The Health Care Imbroglio

A pattern emerged. Great undertakings are proposed in political campaigns, often crafted by professional techniques such as polling and focus groups. If the campaign succeeds, the undertaking is taken as validated. Experts are set to work and the bill emerges. In this regard there has been no equal to the health care reform project of the Clinton administration during the 103rd Congress. Health insurance had been on the national agenda at least since 1934 when Roosevelt set up the Committee on Economic Security which drafted the Social Security Act of the following year. It had not been solely a Democratic concern; the Nixon administration, as usual, had proposed a considerable health measure. But it was rejected by

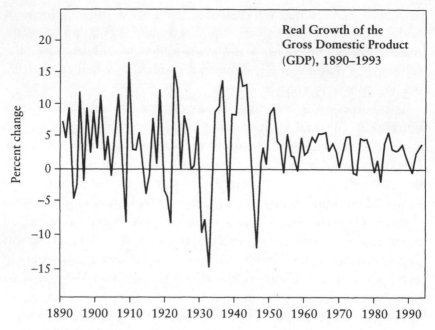

Between 1890 and 1945, real growth in the economy dropped by 5 percent on three occasions, by 10 percent on two occasions, and on two other occasions dropped almost 15 percent. Since 1945, and the Employment Act of 1946, there have been five mild declines, and only a single serious one, that of the recession of 1982, say 2–3 percent. I took this graph to the Senate floor daily (as well as to a Sunday morning appearance on *Meet the Press*) during the debate over a constitutional amendment requiring an annual balanced budget. The amendment failed by one vote. (Data provided by the Department of Commerce, Bureau of Economic Analysis; chart prepared by the Joint Economic Committee.)

a Democratic Congress out of a proprietary sense that this was by rights a Democratic issue. Now, seemingly, the Democratic moment had come.

But where, in the main, New Deal initiatives came as responses to popular demand, variously expressed, by 1993 health care insurance was a latent issue. Five in six Americans had health insurance. Most of the poor got it free from the government; it was subsidized for all of the elderly. Hence, it was an issue mainly for those who thought it *should* be an issue. Which is to say, professionals. The administration organized a task force of some 500 persons, sworn to secrecy, who set about reorganizing, and pretty much taking control of one-seventh of the American economy. After the better part of a year, they produced a 1,342-page bill. Martha Derthick commented: "In many years of studying American social policy, I have never read an official document that seemed so suffused with coercion and political naiveté as the draft report of the president's health security plan that emerged last fall, with its drastic prescriptions for controlling the conduct of state governments, employers, drug manufacturers, doctors, hospitals, and you and me."

I was then chairman of the Senate Finance Committee, which had principle jurisdiction over the measure in the Senate, and perforce I came to know the details of the proposal with a measure of thoroughness. In that process I became one of possibly a dozen persons outside the task force who knew that the legislation would cut the number of doctors in the United States by one-quarter, and the number of specialists by one-half.

For some time a debate had been going on within the various professions involved concerning these two questions, driven not least by the fact that much of medical education and training is subsidized with public monies. Economists such as Alain Enthoven have addressed such questions as "physician oversupply" and "geographic maldistribution." Writing in the *Journal of the American Medical Association* in 1994, Richard A. Cooper, M.D., of the Medical College of Wisconsin, observed that "a consensus has developed that better balance in the proportion of primary care physicians and specialists must be achieved" and that this consensus was being quantified. More of the former, fewer of the latter. He noted, however, that primary care is "population based"—indeed, had settled in at about 75 to 85 primary care physicians per 100,000 population. By contrast, "The driving force behind much of specialty medicine is science, and the specialty workforce is largely technology based." Good subject, not least in this heroic age of medical science. The problem was that the Clinton task force did not want to debate the issue; they desired, rather, to decree the outcome, and to enact it surreptitiously as a mode of cost control. The tale of the Clinton task force will one day be told, but as the result of a lawsuit some documents are already available in the National Archives.

On March 31, 1993, Working Group 12 addressed this issue to Tollgate 5: "Problem: An increasingly overabundant number of medical graduates are entering specialty fields instead of primary care fields (family practice, general pediatrics, general internal medicine)." The Working Group proposed the following solution:

- Provide [by federal law] that at least 50% of residency graduates enter primary care practice.

- *Limit federal funding for first-year residency positions to no more than 110% of the size of the graduating class of U.S. medical schools. This would further support the action to limit specialty residency positions.* [Emphasis in original.]

There followed on April 26, 1993, a dissent signed by some thirteen members of Working Group 12, having been written by a physician at the Veterans Administration.

FOR OFFICIAL USE ONLY
SUBJECT: Proposal to cap the total number of graduate physician (resident) entry (PGY-1) training positions in the USA to 110% of the annual number of graduates of US medical schools.
ISSUE: Although this proposal has been presented in Tollgate documents as the position of Group 12, it is not supported by the majority of the members of Group 12 (listed below).

REASONS NOT TO CAP THE TOTAL NUMBER OF
US RESIDENCY TRAINING POSITIONS FOR
PHYSICIAN GRADUATES
1. This proposal has been advanced by several Commissions within the last two years as a measure to control the costs of health care. While ostensibly advanced as a manpower policy, its rationale lies in economic policy. Its advocates believe that each physician in America represents a cost center. He not only receives a high personal salary, but is able to generate health care costs by ordering tests, admitting patients to hospital and performing technical procedures. This thesis may be summarized as: TO CONTROL COSTS, CONTROL THE NUMBER OF PHYSICIANS.
2. Capitalist economic theory does not support this argument. Manpower theory does not support this argument.

3. Economic theory would argue that to reduce costs one should increase the number of physicians. If each physician is a cost center then one should reduce incentives to increase procedures, admissions and tests, or control the costs of these items, rather than limit the number of physicians. Those desiring to limit physician numbers point out that while the number of graduates was doubled beginning in 1975 from 7500 to 15,000 per year, costs of care rose markedly. The physician increase was deliberate social policy to address shortages of physicians and access problems, which were partially but not wholly solved by this increase. The growth of health care costs in the same 15 year span can certainly be attributed more accurately to distorted reimbursement incentives for physicians and the entire health care sector and to runaway inflation in technical costs.

4. Capitalist manpower theory would argue that controlling demand by limiting supply is perverse. Managed competition seeks to control demand and uses physicians as the agents to manage access to services. By reversing the incentives, the same provider becomes the controller rather than the generator of costs.

5. On the demand side of the supply/demand equation there is little support for limiting the number of health care providers. Under the Clinton Health Plan the demand for primary care and generalist physicians vastly outstrips supply. Insuring universal access will add 35 million people to the health care network and no modeling has been done of the manpower requirement to assure access to care for this influx. Even under present access to care we do not have enough minority physicians, primary care physicians or physicians willing to work in remote rural and embattled inner city areas.

6. While there is agreement that the US needs a better balance in its physician production between generalists and specialists, there is not even strong evidence that there are too many specialists in practice for the actual needs of the population under current access to health care, let alone what might be needed under universal access. Manpower modeling under universal access was not undertaken by Group 12. While the last major physician manpower study, the GEM-NAC [Graduate Medical Education National Advisory Committee] Report (1974) projected physician excess in some specialties by 1990 under unchanged access, a recent examination of only 6 specialties by COGME [Council on Graduate Medical Education] (1990) found shortages for generalist physicians, psychiatrists, child psychiatrists, and surgeons. The AAMC [Association of American Medical Colleges] study (1989) concluded that current rates of production

of physicians would not lead to a surplus. All manpower studies done of MD/DO [Medical Doctor/Doctor of Osteopathy], and very poor tools for determining demand, even under present conditions. No modeling of universal access has been done. It is of interest that pediatrics societies contested the finding of COGME that there would not be a shortage of pediatricians, arguing for a model examining the need for pediatricians to care for the uninsured.

7. Some who argue for capping physician supply invoke the ratio of physicians to total population in other industrialized countries. At the present time the US ratio of MD/DO to population is exactly at the median for industrialized nations . . . On the face of it this does not seem a strong argument for limiting physicians. This raw ratio also does not address the US problems of physician mix or patient access.

8. Attempts within the profession to limit physician number are severely limited by the FTC [Federal Trade Commission]. The FTC has brought suit against the ACGME [Accreditation Council on Graduate Medical Education] and physician specialties who believe they have too many members. Despite the FTC, these specialties have reduced the number of physicians in certain disciplines by strict quality control of resident training programs. More could be done in this area by private sector mechanisms if the ACGME were granted some relaxation of FTC restrictions.

9. The proposal under consideration, to cap the number of entry resident training positions to 110% of US graduates, is not even a true manpower control policy. The number of graduates of US medical schools is not limited by this policy. In effect, the policy would merely limit the entry of foreign medical graduates into US practice, since they must take US residency training to achieve licensure. At worst, enactment of this proposal could lead to US medical graduates, whose average debt upon graduation is $57,000, [being] unable to enter residency training because of displacement by foreign physicians in competition for a limited number of slots.

10. The most insidious part of the proposal to cap entry slots to graduate medical education is that it carries in its wake the necessity to create a vast regulatory apparatus to implement it. The total number of GME [Graduate Medical Education] slots is not under central control, nor are they federally funded. Medicare pays an estimated 22% of the salaries for resident physicians as part of its fair share because they provide care for Medicare patients.

11. If it were to prove necessary in future to control physician supply, the control point would be the number of entry positions to medical schools in this country. In 1990 the AAMC manpower study concluded that the number of entry positions should not be increased but did not need to be decreased. Through private sector accreditation of medical schools LCME [Liaison Committee on Medical Education] the annual number of allopathic physician graduates has not increased in the last decade. While the number of osteopathic graduates is increasing because of a doubling of the number of schools of osteopathy since 1975, these graduates tend to go into primary care and practice in non-urban settings.

12. The physician manpower problems to be solved in this country are ones of specialty mix, current shortages of generalists and certain specialists, and potential greater shortages once universal coverage is achieved, geographic distribution of physicians to rural and inner city sites and achieving greater racial, ethnic and gender diversity in the physician workforce. NONE OF THESE PROBLEMS IS SOLVED, AND SOME ARE EXACERBATED, BY LIMITING ACCESS TO GRADUATE TRAINING FOR PHYSICIANS OR ATTEMPTING THROUGH OTHER MEANS TO LIMIT THE TOTAL SUPPLY OF PHYSICIANS IN THE US.

13. To end on a philosophic note, when the proposal to cap training slots was presented to the residents of the major US universities last weekend, they were incredulous that the US government would advance as sound social policy a proposal to limit access to one of the three learned professions with its millennial history of achieving social good. They further recognized that in America open access to careers in these professions has been a traditional path for immigrant social mobility.   4-26-93

A Sin of Omission

The administration bill, when it came, included a "Subtitle A—Workforce Priorities under Federal Payment," which provided for a National Council on Graduate Medical Education in the Department of Health and Human Services which would ensure that by 1998–99 "not less than 55 percent" of medical school residents complete a program in primary care. The explicit 110 percent residency cap was replaced by a cap to be determined by the Council. In the Congress, the House Education and Labor Committee draft bill was specific, setting the 110 percent ratio; others left it to the Council, but clearly this was to be its goal. The one exception was the bill reported by the Senate Committee on Finance, which would have nothing to do with either.[3]

These are, were, legitimate issues of debate. The problem, and I take this to be the fatal failing of the process, is that neither was debated. The dissenters on Working Group 12, for all the quirkiness—just what is "capitalist manpower theory"?—made legitimate points. These were never made public. The Clinton administration devoted most of its energies for a year and more to health care reform without once openly addressing this issue. Not even in the semiprivacy of the Cabinet Room.

The principal campaign document was *Health Security: The President's Report to the American People,* an ambitious, all-purpose, glossy affair issued in October 1993. Of 136 pages, there is one section, "Doctors in the United States: An Unhealthy Mix," eleven lines in all, devoted to primary physician supply: "Health care reform will increase the demand for primary care physicians, nurses and other health professions, correcting the long-standing incentives that discouraged medical students from becoming family doctors. But change won't happen quickly. To encourage American teaching hospitals to switch some residency positions from specialist to primary care, the federal government must make it more worthwhile to train them. Consequently, rather than pay for graduate medical education without regard to specialty, public and private investment will redistribute the balance between residency slots devoted to primary care and those devoted to specialty training."

There is no mention whatever of limiting the number of hospital residencies to 110 percent of U.S. medical school graduates. In retrospect, it is not hard to understand the administration's reluctance to be open about all this. Begin with the fact that this was an administration of fervid, professed liberals, the youth of the 1960s at last in power. To be liberal means to wish the third world well. Surely not to slam the golden door on the swarthy sons and daughters of India, Pakistan, and the Philippines. Like some nasty, hateful racist Chinese Exclusion Act. (Recall the point made by the Working Group 12 dissidents. The 110 percent ratio would not reduce the number of graduates if U.S. schools increased *their* enrollment.)

Then there was the problem of the poor. The municipal hospitals of a city such as New York depend heavily on the services of interns who have come from elsewhere. Some are Americans who went abroad for medical school. Some are young foreigners who have come here for the best internships in the world, fully intending to return home. (Much as Americans once interned in Paris.) But most are, in fact, immigrants, and fine doctors we are fortunate to have. Take them out of New York City, hospitals and health care in New York collapses. Such liberals could hardly be seen to propose that either. As for specialists, all right-thinking folk know them to be elitists; but then, they do help when complications set in. Best be discreet. And then there was the dirty little secret. The health care reformers soon discovered that they had no money. And so to provide universal health insurance, they had to provide less health care. By cutting the number of doctors. Now, not all would agree with that characterization; but something very like that did happen.

The *professions* said nothing. The final paragraph in the Working Group 12 dissent refers to a conference on health care reform sponsored by the Association of American Universities in Washington, April 17–18, 1993. Pretty much everyone was there. The *Executive Summary* gets the facts straight.

> The implications of health care reform for academic health centers fall into three broad categories: teaching, research and patient care. Following are the general trends presented at the conference:
>
> • Education: Inevitable limits on number of sub-specialty training programs and positions in US. Reduction of the overall number of positions to 105–110 per cent of US medical school graduates.

But if any of the university officials present was "incredulous" at the suggestion, they remained silent. More thanks then to Walter

Reich, M.D., Senior Scholar at the Woodrow Wilson International Center for Scholars. He was in touch with the Finance Committee regularly on the subject of "a deliberate dumbing down of medicine." A letter of August 29, 1994, had this: "There's also something profoundly anti-intellectual, even medieval, about the effort to abolish medical specialization. Knowledge, in the case of modern medicine, can result in large expenses. Get rid of that knowledge, some argue, and you can get rid of those expenses. In fact, this approach is so illogical and strange that characterizing it as medieval does a profound disservice to what was, in comparison to this age of anti-medical-scientism, an intellectually luminous epoch. Attempting to dismantle the edifice of specialization seems akin, somehow, to the deliberate torching of the great library in Alexandria. This is enlightened social policy?"

When all else fails, the press is supposed to step in. It did not. A search of the Nexis database located only three articles, out of thousands on the general subject, which focused on this issue. The *Los Angeles Times,* March 22, 1993, "U.S. Incentives for More Family Doctors Weighed" by Marlene Cimons. The *New York Times,* September 15, 1993, "Clinton Seeks to Regulate Medical Specialties" by Robert Pear. The *New York Times,* January 24, 1994, "New York Hospitals Fear Harm in Plan to Reduce Specialization" by Todd S. Purdum. Toward the end of the 103rd Congress there were occasional articles citing protests by me and Senator D'Amato that the administration bill would devastate the New York City hospital system which for most of this century has, in fact, provided universal health care for the city. But these were pretty much of the Congressman Opposes Base Closing genre. The best explanation is that there was no national debate and accordingly the press did not report one.[4]

The Price Paid

In the end, of course, nothing came of the whole effort. Neither body of Congress even voted on a health care bill. A whip count in the House showed that the Democratic votes weren't there. The

Senate was in much the same situation. Something so large and potentially controversial could only be dealt with in a bipartisan setting. It was decided *not* to attempt this at a Cabinet Room meeting of February 7, 1994, and from that day forward the legislation was doomed. That being the date the discussion *began* in the Finance Committee.

But there was more. Michael Polanyi would say: "People change their minds." On large matters. Suddenly. Without notice. I would suggest that something such happened to the professionalization of reform. Even in 1965 one could note a popular unease. After *all* we had done for Appalachia, in 1964 Harlan County, Kentucky, returned a freshman Republican Congressman. Professionalization would continue, "but," as I pointed out in 1965, "a certain price will be paid, and a considerable risk will be incurred." The "price will be a decline in the moral exhilaration of public affairs at the domestic level." The risk "a combination of enlightenment, resources, and skill which in the long run, to use Harold D. Laswell's phrase, becomes a 'monocracy of power.'" What I missed was the resentment that would grow.

A new breed of Republican did *not* miss it. For much of the postwar era Republicans competed with Democrats to fulfill pretty much the same domestic agenda. I served in two Republican cabinets, and I know this, even if most Democrats don't, or don't want to. But then this changed. Republicans became a party of ideas in their own right. The great strategic goal of the new thinking was to undo the opportunities for greater government created by the Democratic "Economic Revolution." The deficit came to be the first fact of national government. Whatever program professionals might think best could not be afforded. This had led to the fatal complexity and coerciveness of health care reform. Which, in turn, brought on what George Will called "the cymbal-crash elections of 1994." There followed a surge of programmatic initiatives unknown since the New Deal. Designed to undo the New Deal.

▲

— 2 —

Repealing Economics

In the Congressional elections of 1994, Republicans of radical purpose won a majority in the House of Representatives with a platform calling for a radical scaling back of the powers of the national government. In the preceding half century they had twice won single-term majorities, in 1946 and again in 1952, but as a part of a response to larger events, the end of World War II, the election of President Dwight D. Eisenhower. 1994 was different. The House Republicans won on their own, as a party of ideas, and of change.

The "supreme coort," as Mr. Dooley observed at the outset of the century, seemed content to follow "th' iliction returns." Soon after the 1994 election the Court, in *United States v. Lopez*, held a federal statute unconstitutional for the first time since the New Deal. Something such had happened before. In 1936, in *Carter v. Carter Coal Co.*, the Court struck down a wage and hour statute for the coal mining industry. Then came the 1936 elections. The next year, in *N.L.R.B. v. Jones & Laughlin Steel Corp.*, the Court addressed essentially the same question and found that the act's regulation of *intra*state matters was "substantially related" to *inter*state commerce and was, accordingly, within the reach of the Commerce Clause, Article I, Section 8. Now, in *Lopez*, the Court found that the Gun-Free School Zones Act of 1990 exceeded Congress's authority under the same said clause. Note the subject matter—the desperate notion that possibly the *federal* government could keep guns out of schools. Note also the loss of any memory of earlier constitutional tests which such legislation would have to meet. The bill had passed the Senate by a voice vote.

As the millennium approaches, the national government of the United States shows signs of a crisis of legitimacy. Who knows but this is somehow cyclical: the original crisis of the Articles of Confederation and the touch-and-go emergence of the present Constitution; the Age of Jackson ("John Marshall has made his decision, now let him enforce it"); the Civil War; the industrial strife of the late nineteenth century; the Espionage Act of 1917 and the Attorney General's raids at the end of the Wilson era; the New Deal; the 1960s. Now something not dissimilar.

The question of legitimacy, of ultimate authority, is as old as political philosophy. Hannah Arendt has noted that the Constitution itself is silent on the question of ultimate authority. Accordingly, we must look to the Declaration of Independence which "still bears clear signs of divine origin, such truths are, as Jefferson wrote in the original draft of the Declaration of Independence, 'sacred and undeniable.'" By the twentieth century, however, what Karl Frederich termed a "procedural and pragmatic" view had taken hold in American political philosophy, or at least the most influential branches. Stability was seen to derive from economic development. Karl Frederich had not the least doubt: "The ruler who improves the standard of living will be considered legitimate."[1]

There had been an historic increase in living standards following World War II. In 1947, as the postwar boom commenced, average hourly wages (in 1977 dollars) in the United States stood at $3.07. They rose *each* year until 1973, when they peaked at $5.38. Thereafter wages declined more or less steadily until 1989; when George Bush took office, they had dropped to $4.80, lower than the level when Lyndon B. Johnson left office twenty years before. By 1989 average weekly earnings were barely what they had been in 1959; net of Social Security taxes, they were lower. Real median family income reached $32,109 in 1973; it proceeded to decline, and only just got back to that level in 1989. This recovery was achieved mostly by families doubling up in the workforce. For the first time in history, it appeared that the coming generation of Americans would be less well off than their parents; this, after the great ascent of the 1950s and 1960s.

Much of this may be illusion. In a 1996 paper "The American Real Wage since 1963: Is It Unchanged or Has It More than Doubled?" Robert Gordon argues the latter. Working from a growing consensus, which he had helped get started, that the Consumer Price Index overstates increases in the cost of living by a *large* factor—one percentage point is one-third!—and noting that fringe benefits as a share of total compensation doubled (from 9 percent to 19 percent) between 1963 and 1995, he finds a solid two plus percent annual growth. Enough to double in 35 years. Small consolation, however, if you're feeling down, and many Americans were. Corporate "downsizing" became a theme, withal the economy had added 27 million jobs since 1979. The Reagan prosperity. The pronounced Clinton recovery seemed to make no impress.

Just at the moment when government had reason to be well enough satisfied, it turned out the citizenry was anything but. And why was the workforce getting worse off if not because government is too big and costs too much? Democrats cottoned on. In 1976 Jimmy Carter ran for President in this key: "Our government in Washington now is a horrible bureaucratic mess. It is disorganized; wasteful; has no purpose; and its policies—when they exist—are incomprehensible or devised by special interest groups with little or no regard for the welfare of the average American citizen." And: "We've developed in recent years a welfare government . . . We've seen evolve a bloated, confused, bureaucratic mess. The American people believe that we ought to control our government. On the other hand, we've seen government more and more controlling us." But Republicans had a prior claim on this issue, and it was soon theirs, with Democrats reduced to a wan "Me, too," the epithet which had haunted Republicans who had earlier tried to join in the prevailing Democratic ethos.

It happens there was certain left-right symmetry in this crisis strategy. Thus, in the mid-60s, the antipoverty programs of the Johnson administration, and the preceding juvenile delinquency programs of the Kennedy moment, precipitated municipal turbulence in New York City under newly elected Mayor John V. Lindsay. "Welfare rights" became a focus of organizing efforts, the object being to get as many persons as possible *on* welfare rather than *off.* Charles R. Morris, who was an Assistant Budget Director and later director of the city's welfare and Medicaid programs, describes the onset of a certain kind of radical frenzy, much associated with the Columbia University School of Social Work, in his 1980 *The Cost of Good Intentions: New York City and the Liberal Experiment:*

> A turning point came with the publication of an article by [Richard] Cloward and [Francis Fox] Piven in the *Nation* on May 2, 1966, which set out for the first time a coherent strategy for the movement. They argued that the existing system survived only by intimidating and underpaying clients. (A massive campaign to enroll eligible clients and to get full benefits for those already on the rolls would cause the system's financial collapse and ensure its replacement by an equitable, federally administered program of guaranteed income maintenance.) The tactics should include a mass educational campaign and public disruption of local welfare offices. The disruption, it was argued, was necessary to enhance the clients' sense of power in dealing with the system and to increase the pressure on state and local governments to pass the burden to the federal government. The article generated immense excitement among radical anti-poverty workers.

Morris continues with the dispassion of an investment banker, which he later became. "The radicals failed in their quest for national reform. Although they nearly succeeded in bankrupting local governments, as they had intended." He is here referring to the National Welfare Rights Organization, which took off in this setting. "To liberal reformers the sharpest disappointment was the sudden upsurge in dependency." Welfare rolls in New York City doubled; it had been thought, somehow, that they would decline. A complex fate ensued. President Richard M. Nixon proposed a guaranteed income. The National Welfare Rights Organization helped defeat it on grounds that it was insufficient, effectively allying themselves with those who thought the idea absurd. Welfare benefits, in AFDC terms, commenced a long, still unbroken decline. The immiserization of a once potentially prosperous population commenced. A decade later, New York City *was* bankrupt.[2]

As if some law of physics was in effect, an equal and opposite response occurred in the nation at large. State legislatures commenced to petition the Congress to "call a Convention for proposing Amendments" to the Constitution (Article V). The petitions, otherwise a phantasmagoria of style and format, had a uniform purpose, a constitutional amendment to require the federal government to have a balanced budget. An *annual* balanced budget. As New York City grew hopelessly entangled with welfare applications and appeals and protests, Mitchell Ginsberg, the decent, idealistic welfare commissioner, dispensed with time-consuming application forms and home investigations in favor of a simple declaration of eligibility and need. No further questions asked. Morris writes: "The move drew plaudits from HEW [Department of Health, Education and Welfare in Washington] and the *New York Times,* but the sobriquet 'Come-and-Get-It Ginsberg' from the *Daily News.*" That is to say, the tabloid with far the largest circulation among the working-class readers in the city. It is beyond the reach of any social science that I know of to connect the general war on poverty fracas of the 1960s with the movement for a balanced budget amendment of the 1970s, but the sequence seems too direct to dismiss. In the end, some 30 states sent petitions, four short of the needed 34. This, too, is suggestive. No state was willing to cast the deciding vote in aid of terminating the federal highway program, or whatever. Even so, the issue was abroad.

The 104th Congress convened January 3, 1995. The House of Representatives promptly passed H.J. 1, a bill that would send a balanced budget amendment to the several states for ratification. Section 1 of the amendment read: "Total outlays for any fiscal year shall not exceed total receipts for that fiscal year, unless three-fifths of the whole number of each House of Congress shall provide by law for a specific excess of outlays over receipts by a rollcall vote."

In the Senate, debate began on January 31, 1995. For someone of the Kennedy era, it defied understanding. Did the Senate not know what it would mean to clamp an agricultural plant-cultivate-harvest-market cycle onto the largest industrial economy on earth? Something we had never dreamed of when ours was essentially an agricultural economy? Some did not, some did not care. The deficits of the 1980s—Republican deficits—were taken, even so, as evidence that Democrats were reckless and ruinous.

Indeed, a crisis of legitimacy *was* at hand. In the 1994 senatorial elections in Tennessee, a majority of voters with household incomes under $15,000 had voted Republican. *No more Tennessee Valley Authority?* Who can say what connection was made. The matter required considerable debate. Not filibuster, merely debate. Senator Robert C. Byrd of West Virginia organized the opposition, which I joined in three long speeches on Monday, Wednesday, and Friday of the week of February 5th.

The first showed that the current deficit is a recent event that marked a sharp departure from the fiscal challenges of earlier administrations, which were directed primarily to the persistent "full employment surplus," with its accompanying downward pressure on consumer demand. The second related the singular events of the 1980s which led to huge deficits and a correspondingly huge debt, contending that there is no reason whatever to think we would repeat this behavior, or misbehavior, especially now that the events are better understood. The final paper explored the folly and danger of writing into the Constitution restraints concerning fiscal policy which would have been inappropriate to a small eighteenth-century republic and would be absurd and potentially destabilizing to a world power of the twenty-first.

▼

The Era of Surplus, 1960–1980
Full Employment Budgets and the Problems of "Fiscal Drag"

Representative democracy in the United States is fully capable of balancing the nation's accounts without an amendment to the Constitution. Deficits are not endemic to democracy.

As recently as the Nixon administration, the President's economic planners faced a problem of *surplus* in the national accounts, and thought it wise to *create* deficits in order to move the economy toward full employment. In those not-notably-distant years, full employment with price stability was the central goal of fiscal policy; this had been indicated by the Employment Act of 1946, which established the Council of Economic Advisers, and became steadily more feasible as economic projections became steadily more reliable.

The Nixon administration inherited a difficult economic situation. Contrary to advice from the Council, President Lyndon B. Johnson had been unwilling to raise taxes to pay for the increased outlays occasioned by the Vietnam war. The result was inflation. This was stamped out, but then unemployment rose. It became necessary to stimulate the economy once again by *deliberately incurring a deficit*. George P. Shultz, then director of the newly established Office of Management and Budget, explained the policy in *The Budget of the United States Government, Fiscal 1973:* "The full-employment budget concept is central to the budget policy of this Administration. Except in emergency conditions, *expenditures should not exceed the level at which the budget would be balanced under conditions of full employment*. The 1973 budget conforms to this guideline. By doing so, it provides necessary stimulus for expansion, but is not inflationary [emphasis in original]."

George P. Shultz is one of the most admired public men of his generation. His service as Secretary of State in the Reagan administration won the esteem and gratitude of much of the world, along with that of the American people. It is useful to recall that he is by profession an economist, having once been dean of the School of Business at the University of Chicago. He had originally joined the Nixon administration as Secretary of Labor. He was speaking in terms then readily understood by fellow economists, but not always clear to laymen, such as myself. The key phrase in his policy statement is italicized: *"Expenditures should not exceed the level at which the budget would be balanced under conditions of full employment."* Which is to say that in the absence of full employment, as was the case in FY 1973, the federal government should deliberately contrive to *incur* a deficit equal to the difference between the revenues that would actually come in at levels of underemployment and those that would come in at full employment.

Far from being inevitable and unavoidable, there were points in the business cycle where a deficit had to be *created*. Otherwise surpluses would choke off recovery. The contrary thought, that budget deficits will be continuous and uncontrollable, is surely the oldest of prejudices against democracy. Which is to say the assertion that a majority will continuously vote itself benefits which the economy cannot sustain.

In an earlier age this supposed tendency was seen as a threat to property. Benefits would be obtained by confiscatory taxation—or plain confiscation. Hence, John Locke's prescription for a stable society: the security of "Life, liberty, and estate." In the Declaration of Independence, Thomas Jefferson devised a more felicitous formula: "Life, liberty, and the pursuit of happiness." Yet, there was never any doubt that the security of property was essential to such happiness. In *The Federalist* No. 10, James Madison addressed this issue with not the least apology. Ours would be a representative government, concerned to moderate, if not indeed to control, appetites.

> From this view of the subject, it may be concluded, that a pure Democracy, by which I mean, a Society, consisting of a small number of citizens, who assemble and administer Government in person, can admit of no cure for the mischiefs of faction. A common passion or interest will, in almost every case, be felt by a majority of the whole; a communication and concert results from the form of Government itself; and there is nothing to check the inducements to sacrifice the weaker party, or an obnoxious individual. Hence it is, that such Democracies have ever been spectacles of turbulence and contention; have ever been found incompatible with personal security, or the rights of property; and have in general been as short in their lives, as they have been violent in their deaths. Theoretic politicians, who have patronized this species of Government, have erroneously supposed, that by reducing mankind to a perfect equality of their political rights, they would, at the same time, be perfectly equalized and assimilated in their possessions, their opinions, and their passions.

In modern times a more common fear has been that the "excesses" of democracy would "debauch the currency" through the monetization of debt, which is to say inflation. Indeed, there have been such episodes, albeit relatively rare. Twentieth-century democracies have experienced fairly steady price increases. Yet nothing ruinous for most. Far the greater fact has been the economic growth of the twentieth century. Far from inhibiting such growth, democracy is now widely seen as an essential precondition. If democracy caters to wants more than to needs, it has proven itself reasonably capable of satisfying both, not least because we have developed a profession of economics which, if not in any sense perfected or even especially scientific, even so has a lot to show for itself. In the United States, for example, real per capita income has increased fourfold over the course of the twentieth century from about $4,300 to $20,500 per person!

The historian Alan Brinkley has recorded the development of the idea of federal spending as a route to prosperity, dating back to the 1890s, particularly for public works to counteract the business cycle. In the 1920s William Trufant and Waddill Catchings argued for public spending as an antidote to underconsumption, an idea that would come to dominate both theoretic, to use Madison's term, and applied economics. The theoretical approach to underconsumption is much associated with the publication in 1935 of John Maynard Keynes's *The General Theory of Employment, Interest and Money.* That master of the calling, John Kenneth Galbraith, records that by the autumn of 1936 *The General Theory* "reached Harvard with tidal force." There has been no other event like it in the history of the social sciences. The Great Depression, then two-thirds over, had seemingly falsified the central tenet of classical economics, which is that markets clear through the price mechanism—that whatever is offered for sale, including labor, is purchased. There were business cycles, to be sure, but, most important, there was said to be an inherent tendency for the system to return to an equilibrium in which all resources were fully employed. But for six years there had been no such return; none was in sight.

In *The General Theory,* Keynes demonstrated that there could be unspent savings, and that when this happened prices would not adjust downward to insure that the same volume of goods would be purchased with the reduced (after-saving) purchasing power. Galbraith summarizes: "Instead, output and employment fell until reduced profits, increased losses and the need to spend from past savings ensured that all income from current production or its equivalent was thus established, one with a lot of people out of work—the under-employment equilibrium." After an unprecedented period of depression, mounting crisis, and something like intellectual desperation, this had indeed the quality of revelation.

However, by the time any considerable portion of the economics profession had converted to Keynesianism, the Second World War had commenced. And so to a considerable irony, Keynesian economics was to be given its first trial not in the conditions of depression for which it had seemed designed but in the very opposite circumstances of a wartime economy, when the central problem was an excess of consumer demand and a shortage of consumer goods production.

Yet, in the crucible of war, the new doctrine produced, well, astonishing results. In a series of newspaper articles, Keynes set forth how to maintain price stability during wartime, and in the United States a new Office of Price Administration did just that. Until, that is, the war ended and wartime controls collapsed. Here are the inflation rates for that period: 1941, 9.7%; 1942, 9.3%; 1943, 3.2%; 1944, 2.1%; 1945, 2.3%.

With the war ended, Congress enacted the Employment Act of 1946. The authors of the legislation, and perhaps especially the committee staff, were convinced that this new economics could now be used as originally intended, which is to say to ward off a recurrence of the Great Depression of the 1930s. (It was widely assumed that the Depression would indeed resume at war's end. Hence, for example, the Interstate Highway Act of 1944, a public works program in the classic New Deal mode.) With the Employment Act, Congress declared it to be "the continuing policy and responsibility of the federal Government . . . to promote maximum employment, production and purchasing power," and at the same time established the annual Economic Report of the President, which steadily became a more detailed and instrumental document. In 1960, with the election of John F. Kennedy, the new economics was well established. Kennedy assembled a brilliant Council of Economic Advisers, Walter W. Heller, Kermit Gordon, and James Tobin. Although but little noted at the time, the present Senator from New York became Assistant Secretary of Labor for Policy Planning and Research. What I now report, I *saw*. I dare to think that what I saw is of great importance in the matter now before the Senate.

The unemployment rate had remained remarkably low throughout the postwar period. Then, in 1958 recession struck. The rate rose to 6.8 percent, two-and-one-half times the 2.9 percent rate of 1953. A recovery followed. But then stalled. By 1961, when the new President took office, it was back up to 6.7 percent. What had happened? In their first Annual Report to the President, in January 1962, the new Council of Economic Advisers offered a striking explanation. *The federal budget was running a surplus.* This was termed (somewhat awkwardly) "the full employment surplus."

Chart 6 in the Report, entitled, "Effect of Level of Economic Activity on Federal Surplus or Deficit," showed how this worked. Higher government expenditures during the 1957–58 recession helped to reduce the unemployment rate from 6.8 percent in 1958 to 5.5 percent in 1959. But the "Fiscal 1960 Program," the next to last of the Eisenhower administration, and which was, according to the Council, "the most restrictive program of recent years," had a large "full employment surplus" amounting to almost 2 percent of potential Gross National Product. This surplus came about as follows: As the recovery from the 1958 recession got under way, economic activity grew and so did the revenues of the federal government. *But Congress would not, or in any event, did not spend the additional revenue.* As a result, the recovery stalled. This untoward event was ascribed to "fiscal drag." (Nice term!) Accordingly, the President's economic advisers devised a "Fiscal 1962 Program" *with a built-in deficit*, which moved the economy closer to full employment. *To say again, the federal government had to find ways to prevent a recovery from stalling because of an accumulation of a budget surplus.*

The President's economists then proceeded to explain their actions and plans to reduce the "full employment surplus . . . a measure of the restrictive or expansionary impact of a budget program on over-all demand."

The Budget in 1958–60

The analysis of the budget program in terms of the full employment surplus points to a probable major cause of the incomplete and short-lived nature of the 1958–60 expansion. The most restrictive fiscal program of recent years was the program of 1960. Its full employment surplus exceeded any from 1956 to date . . . The full employment surplus declined sharply as a result of higher expenditures during the 1957–58 recession until it reached an estimated $3 billion in the second half of 1958. Thereafter, it rose gradually through most of 1959 but then increased sharply to about $12.5 billion in 1960. Thus, whereas the federal budget contributed to stability during the contraction phase of the cycle and during the first year of the expansion, it was altered abruptly in the direction of restraint late in 1959 at a time when high employment had not yet been achieved.

Federal Fiscal Activity in 1961–62

Immediately upon taking office, the new Administration moved vigorously to use the fiscal powers of the Federal Government to help bring about economic recovery. Federal procurement was accelerated by Presidential directive early in February, and tax refunds were also expedited . . . Changes in transfer programs added about $2 billion to the combined total of transfer payments for fiscal years 1961 and 1962. The Veterans Administration advanced the payment of $150 million of veterans' life insurance dividends into the first quarter of calendar year 1961, and then made an extra dividend payment of $218 million at midyear. The Congress promptly adopted a number of measures requested by the President. A Temporary Extended Unemployment Compensation Act was adopted, providing for extension of exhausted benefits and giving the Administration time to develop a comprehensive program for permanent improvement in unemployment compensation.

In time, the Council came forward with a proposal for a tax cut. Those were heady times. I recall visiting the White House mess in the company of that most eminent of public men, Arthur J. Goldberg, then Secretary of Labor, later an Associate Justice of the Supreme Court, and Permanent Representative to the United Nations. Heller was there and recounted in the most precise terms just how much GNP had been lost by congressional delay in the tax cut; just how much would be gained once it was enacted. His projections were perhaps too confident, but his principles were sound, as well as the practice that went with them. (That double dividend on G.I. Bill life insurance brought our family savings to just the point where we were able to buy the farm near Pindars Corners in Delaware County, which has been our home ever since!)

In the Economic Report of the President transmitted to Congress in January 1969, the Council of Economic Advisers, now headed by Arthur M. Okun, could report: "The full employment surplus was a particularly enlightening measure of fiscal policy in the early 1960's when the economy was far below its potential. Actual federal budgets were then in deficit. But after taking account of the large shortfall in tax revenues associated with the gap between potential and actual output, there was a large full employment surplus. It meant that the economy could realize its potential only if private investment far exceeded private saving. By that standard, discretionary fiscal policy was highly restrictive. The vigorous and unbroken expansion of the last 8 years is in dramatic contrast to the 30-month average duration of previous expansions. No longer is the performance of the American economy generally interpreted in terms of stages of the business cycle. No longer do we consider periodic recessions once every 3 or 4 years an inevitable fact of life."

The Johnson administration left office with too much of a deficit, which had to be reversed. And was. But the 1960s had produced an economics capable of understanding such matters to a degree never previously achieved. An understanding which we are asked to reject altogether by an amendment to the Constitution which economists of every political persuasion reject as potentially ruinous.

This consensus was stated February 3, in a statement issued by hundreds of such economists: "When the private economy is in recession, a constitutional requirement that would force cuts in public spending or tax increases could worsen the economic downturn, causing greater loss of jobs, production, and income." That insight is the great legacy of the economics that emerged from the Great Depression of the 1930s. It was hard won knowledge. It is not to be lost in the "turbulence and contention" that accompanied and now follow a single Congressional election.[3]

▲

▼

The Deficit Strategy, 1981–1985
"Starve the Beast"

On January 26, at the request of Chairman Bob Packwood, the Congressional Budget Office, in the person of Director Robert D. Reischauer, presented the Finance Committee with data comparing economic forecast and budget projection with those made by CBO before the enactment of the Economic Recovery Tax Act of 1981, ERTA as it is generally known. Here is Dr. Reischauer's testimony:

"Unlike the current *Economic and Budget Outlook,* CBO's budget reports issued before enactment of the 1981 tax cuts routinely projected that a continuation of current tax and spending laws would lead to large budget surpluses. CBO also warned that such levels of taxes and spending would act as a drag on the economy. The primary reason for those projections was that high inflation was expected to drive up revenues dramatically. Because key features of the federal individual income tax were not automatically adjusted for inflation, periods of high inflation—such as the late 1970s and early 1980s—pushed individuals into higher tax rate brackets and caused revenues to increase rapidly. In response, policymakers cut taxes every few years on an ad hoc basis."

Note the continuity of the "problems" faced by our analysts at the outset of the 1980s with those faced at the outset of the 1960s. The federal government was running an unacceptable surplus; a sure remedy was to cut taxes. Dr. Reischauer continued: "Illustrating this dilemma, in its February 1980 report *Five-Year Budget Projections: Fiscal Years 1981–1985,* CBO projected that revenues collected under current tax law would climb from about 21 percent of GNP in 1981 to 24 percent by 1985. Simple arithmetic pointed to enormous surpluses in the out-years. For example, current-law revenues exceeded outlays by a projected $98 billion for 1984 and $178 billion for 1985. Similarly, in its July 1981 report *Baseline Budget Projections: Fiscal Years 1982–1986,* CBO projected budget surpluses of between $148 billion and $209 billion for 1986, depending on the economic assumptions used. In the same report, CBO estimated that the 1981 tax cuts and other policies that were called for in the May 1981 budget resolution would generate a balanced budget or a small deficit (roughly $50 billion) by 1984—again, depending on the economic assumptions employed. That budget background led to the 1981 tax cuts. Given the best information available at that time, the Congress and the Administration reasonably thought that significant budget surpluses loomed under current law. Analysts differed, however, on whether the 1981 tax cuts would put the government on a balanced-budget footing or would lead to small budget deficits."

The Economic Recovery Tax Act of 1981 passed the Senate by an overwhelming 67–8 vote. I voted for it with the same measure of confidence that had led me to support earlier tax cuts. This was a familiar situation, well-enough understood. So I and others thought. We were ruinously wrong. At a hearing of the Finance Committee on January 31, Dale Jorgenson, Professor of Economics at Harvard University, called the 1981 tax cut "a fiscal disaster" because the federal government stopped raising the revenue it needed. In an instant, deficits, not surpluses, became our problem.

For certain, two things happened (beyond the bidding war that accompanied the enactment of ERTA, with Democratic members of Congress seeking to outdo the new Republican administration). The first was the action of the Federal Reserve designed to bring down the double-digit inflation of the late 1970s. In a not unfamiliar sequence, "the Fed" brought down the economy with it. A deep, deep recession commenced. In 1982 the unemployment rate reached 9.7 percent, the *highest* rate recorded since the Employment Act of 1946. Revenues fell off precipitously, largely the result of recession, but more steeply owing to the 1981 rate cut.

Now to a second, and to my view, more important event. Beginning in the 1970s a body of opinion developed, principally within the Republican Party, which held that government at the federal level had become so large as to be unacceptably intrusive, even oppressive. There is a continuity here. All those years trying to spend down surpluses had indeed brought about a great increase in the size of government. Of a sudden, deficits, if sizeable enough, gained a new utility. They could be used to *reduce the size of government*.

From the early 1980s, I found myself often making the point that in the Reagan White House and Office of Management and Budget, a huge gamble was being made. A crisis was being created by bringing about deficits intended to force the Congress to cut back certain programs.

I encountered great difficulty getting this idea across. No one believed what I was saying. The intentional nature of the Reagan deficits was not understood or admitted at the time, nor has it been very widely acknowledged since. Yet it did happen, and it has been well documented. The person principally involved, Mr. David Stockman, who was President Reagan's Director of the Office of Management and Budget, wrote a memoir of his time in Washington entitled *The Triumph of Politics*. He described in detail what happened and how it went wrong: how the Reagan Revolution—as based on the immutability of the Laffer Curve—had failed. According to Stockman, President Reagan's top economic advisers knew from the very beginning that supply-side economics would not and could not work. That superb journalist and historian, Haynes Johnson, wrote of this in his wonderful book *Sleepwalking through History: America through the Reagan Years,* published in 1991.

Johnson writes that the Reagan team saw "the implicit failure of supply-side theory as an opportunity, not a problem . . . [The] secret solution was to let the federal budget deficits rise, thus leaving Congress no alternative but to cut domestic programs." David Stockman writes in his book, "If I had to pinpoint the moment when I ceased to believe that the Reagan Revolution was possible, September 11, 1981 . . . would be it." It was then that Stockman realized that no huge spending cuts would ever come. He pleaded with the President and his colleagues in the Cabinet to do something. But nothing was done.

The President had claimed he "would use his pen" to veto "big spending" appropriations bills. But of the reality, Stockman wrote: "The President's pen remained in his pocket. He did not veto a single appropriations bill . . . Come to think of it, he did use his pen—to sign them . . . The 1983 deficit had . . . already come in at $208 billion. The case for a major tax increase was overwhelming, unassailable, inescapable, and self-evident. Not to raise taxes when all other avenues were closed was a willful act of ignorance and grotesque irresponsibility. In the entire twentieth-century fiscal history of the nation, there has been nothing to rival it."

And so, President Reagan became the biggest spender of them all! "By the mid-1980s the Reagan transportation budget in constant dollars topped Jimmy Carter's best year by 15 percent, Johnson's by about 40 percent, and Kennedy's by 50 percent. Big Government? That was something for the speechwriters to fight as long as they didn't mention any names . . . Spending continued largely unabated in all cases." I recall George Will speaking to a group of businessmen at breakfast in 1985 and saying, "I have a door prize of a toaster for anyone who can name one program that President Reagan promised to cut during his 1984 presidential campaign." Everyone in the room started looking around at his or her neighbor, clearly wondering, "Why can't I remember one?"

Whereupon Mr. Will came to their rescue, "Don't feel bad about your memory. There was none."

They created a crisis. We indulged ourselves, in the early 1980s, in a fantasy of young men who perhaps had too much power and too little experience in the real world. They thought they could play with fire, create a crisis. Well, the fire spread, and the numbers—the damages—are well known to all of us. On January 20, 1981, the federal debt stood at $940.5 billion, which was no great cause for concern. On December 31, 1983, I published an article in the *New Republic* entitled "Reagan's Bankrupt Budget," in which I noted, "The projected eight-year growth is $1.64 trillion, bringing us to a total debt, by 1989, of $2.58 trillion." As it turned out, the total debt in 1989 was $2.86 trillion. Not bad shooting. Four years later it was a little over $4 trillion.

I have spoken of two events of the 1980s. First, the tax cuts of 1981 followed by the severe recession of 1982. Next, the development within the incumbent administration of a grand strategy of using deficits to bring about a reduction in the size of government, followed by a disinclination to cut specific programs. Mr. Stockman's memoirs provide graphic examples of this latter development, including the celebrated counsel he gave the President on how much to cut them. Let me in passing mention a possible third event which led in part to the great increase in debt during the 1980s. This was recently alluded to by Lawrence J. Korb in an article in the *Washington Post*.

Dr. Korb, now at the Brookings Institution, contends that "the Reagan buildup" of the military was part of a deliberate strategy of engaging the Soviet Union in an arms race that would leave them bankrupt. The buildup, Dr. Korb continues, "was based not on military need but upon a strategy of bankrupting the Soviet Union. If the Reagan administration had budgeted only for military purposes, the 1985 budget would have been some $80 billion less. The 1995 defense budget is still at about 85 percent of its average Cold War level, and actually higher (even in inflation adjusted dollars) than it was in 1955 (under Eisenhower) and in 1975 (under

Nixon), when the Soviet Empire and Soviet Union were alive and well."

It is difficult to have been in Washington in those times and not to have been aware of such thinking in the environs of the White House. For the first four years of the Reagan administration, I was Vice Chairman of the Senate Select Committee on Intelligence, and one heard such thoughts. By this time, I was convinced that the Soviet Union would soon break up along ethnic lines and largely in consequence of ethnic conflict, and so was perhaps more attentive than some. Certainly, Raymond L. Garthoff, in his study *The Great Transition: American-Soviet Relations and the End of the Cold War* (Brookings, 1994) holds to the view that something of the sort Korb describes did take place.

He writes: "A final element in President Reagan's personal view was that not only was the Soviet system ideologically bankrupt and therefore vulnerable, but that it was also stretched to the utmost by Soviet military efforts and therefore unable to compete in an intensified arms race. As he put it in a talk with some editors, 'They cannot vastly increase their military productivity because they've already got their people on a starvation diet . . . If we show them [we have] the will and determination to go forward with a military buildup . . . they then have to weigh, do they want to meet us realistically on a program of disarmament or do they want to face a legitimate arms race in which we're racing. But up until now, we've been making unilateral concessions, allowing ours to deteriorate, and they've been building the greatest military machine the world has ever seen. But now they're going to be faced with [the fact] that we could go forward with an arms race and they can't keep up.' The Soviet system was indeed under growing strain, as would become increasingly evident throughout the 1980s. But most of the premises underlying Reagan's viewpoint were highly questionable: that the United States had not also been active in the arms competition and had been making unilateral concessions, that the Soviet Union was unable to match adequately a further American buildup, and that the Soviet Union would respond to such a buildup by accepting disarmament proposals that the United States would regard as 'realistic' (that is, would favor the United States more than the SALT II Treaty that had been produced under the strategic arms limitations talks conducted by the three preceding administrations but not ratified). But whatever their merit, they represented the thinking of the new president and his administration."

Just how much this thinking deepened the deficits of the 1980s is difficult to assess. It is now more a matter for historians. But it can hardly have helped. And so we come to a compound irony. The great struggles over the nature of the American economic system that raged from the Progressive Era to the New Deal ended in a quiet acceptance of the private enterprise economy so long as government could pursue policies that produced relatively full employment. Hardly a revolutionary notion, but surely an honorable undertaking. Even so, at first, this disposed American government toward deficit financing. Nothing huge; nothing unmanageable; but real. Which is to say, deficit spending as public policy.

How that would have troubled FDR! On election night of 1936, he was at Hyde Park surrounded by friends and overwhelmed by the electoral returns. The New Deal was triumphant. And so, as Alan Brinkley notes in *The End of Reform: New Deal Liberalism in Recession and War,* a few days later, boarding a train to return to Washington, he told well-wishers, "Now I'm going back . . . to do what they call balance the Budget and fulfill the first promise of the campaign."

Roosevelt never left off that rhetoric, but never left off spending either. Then came World War II, with genuine deficits. The Cold War followed and once again the United States has emerged intact and triumphant. But once again we find an administration, avowedly conservative in this case, assertively opposed to deficit spending, but more or less clandestinely pursuing just the opposite course.

And yet, may we not agree that both these tendencies are now abated, if not altogether spent? A post-Keynesian economics is no longer as confident of fiscal policy as was an earlier generation. A post–Cold War foreign policy has no need to concern itself with bankrupting the Soviet Union: the region is quite bankrupt enough, and indeed, receives American aid. Can we not then look upon our present debt much as the Truman and Eisenhower administrations looked upon the debt incurred during World War II? Pay it off and get on with the affairs of the nation. World War II and the Cold War were fought, in a legitimate sense, to defend the Constitution of the United States against all enemies, foreign and domestic. It would be awful if in this moment of victory we should choose to mutilate the basic law of the land for which so much was sacrificed.

▲

At this point in the now-televised Senate, I produced a bar chart prepared by the Council of Economic Advisers (see chart). Spending on government programs (omitting interest on the debt) was once again lower than revenues, just as it had been in the 1960s. To be sure, in the 1960s debt service was of no great consequence, nor would be for years to come. But program spending was not out of control. It *had* been during the Reagan-Bush years. So much for popular perception. It was the Clinton administration and the 103rd Congress that changed direction.

▼

The Prospect of Stability, 1993–1995

The great issue of the nineteenth century—the economic swings accompanied by vast unemployment—the issue which gave rise to the radical totalitarian movements that were to prove the agony of the twentieth century, that issue has been resolved. We have "fine-tuned," as the phrase went. The contradictory policies of 1969 were, in retrospect, a little too large, while the expansionary policy of 1972 came a little too late. But the theories seemed sound and the timing likely to improve. Both theory and practice centered on the problem of "underconsumption" and the avoidance of what

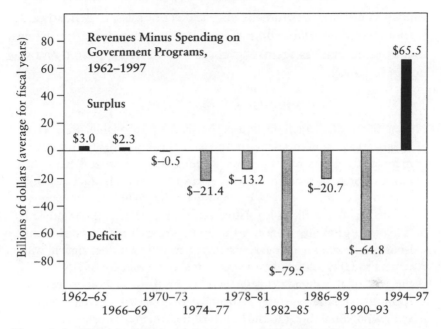

Through the 1960s the federal government ran a "primary" surplus, that is, revenues exceeded program outlays by $2–3 billion. This surplus disappeared in the 1970s owing largely to international economic turns. Large deficits began only with the 1980s. There was no external cause for these deficits; they were policy decisions. By the mid-1990s a considerable "primary" surplus had returned, albeit hidden by debt service.

was seen as the problem of persistent cyclical surpluses in the federal budget. Then came the Reagan Revolution. Earlier doctrines were succeeded by "supply side" economics. Huge deficits appeared which were *not* cyclical, and which were of no possible use. To the contrary, just yesterday at the Finance Committee, Matthew P. Pink, president of the Investment Company Institute, testified: "Government statistics show that personal saving as a percent of disposable personal income has tumbled over the last decade—from a high of 8.0 percent in 1984, to a low of 4.0 percent in 1993. If government deficits are factored in, the situation appears even more bleak: since the 1960s, "net national saving" has dropped from more than 8 percent to less than 2 percent today."

In 1984 the Council of Economic Advisers, then headed by

Martin Feldstein, the eminent Harvard economist, now head of the National Bureau of Economic Research, reported the grim news that a "structural" as against "cyclical" deficit had appeared and was not going away.

Reducing the Budget Deficit

Despite the dramatic reduction in the share of national income taken by government domestic spending and the fundamental improvement in the character of our tax system, the Nation still faces the serious potential problem of a long string of huge budget deficits. Vigorous economic growth can eliminate the cyclical component of the deficit. But without legislative action, the structural component is likely to grow just as fast as the cyclical one shrinks. The Administration's economic projections imply that the budget deficit will remain roughly $200 billion a year—or about 5 percent of GNP—for the rest of the decade unless there is legislative action to reduce spending or raise revenue. Deficits of that size would represent a serious potential threat to the health of the American economy in the second half of this decade and in the more distant future.

Deficit Projection

The cyclical component of the budget deficit is the part of the deficit that occurs because the unemployment rate exceeds the inflation threshold level of unemployment, i.e., the minimum level of unemployment that can be sustained without raising the rate of inflation. This excess unemployment raises the deficit by depressing tax revenues and by increasing outlays on unemployment benefits and other cyclically sensitive programs.

The remaining part of the budget deficit, known as the structural component, is the amount of the deficit that would remain even if the unemployment rate were at the inflation threshold level. The Administration estimates that the inflation threshold level of unemployment is now 6.5 percent and will decline in the coming years as the relative number of inexperienced workers declines and as the Administration's employment policies are enacted and take effect.

The 1983 deficit of $195 billion was divided about evenly between the cyclical and structural components. Because of the lower level of unemployment projected for 1984, a much larger share of the current year's deficit is structural. The projected deficit of $187 billion includes a cyclical component of $49 billion and a structural component of $138 billion. By 1989, the entire projected budget deficit is structural.

And so the idea of *making it go* away by amending the Constitution gained greater strength. This idea was already part of the public discourse. The "new economics" was hard to understand. It seemed to contradict common sense. Would it not be agreed that Herbert Hoover had the most practical and governmental experience in national and international economics of any American President before or since? And yet, he did not grasp any of this. Mind, the "new economics" had not yet evolved, but the point is that much of President Hoover's instinctive response to the Depression of the 1930s only worsened that depression.

President Roosevelt had more of an excuse, in that he knew nothing of economics, or as near as makes no matter. But his instincts were almost exactly those of his predecessor, even denouncing in 1932 the few countercyclical measures that Hoover had instituted.

In the 1970s a grassroots movement got under way to call a Constitutional Convention to adopt a balanced budget amendment. At a meeting of the Budget Committee, I asked the newest chairman of the Council of Economic Advisers, the estimable Charles L. Schultze, if he would "run" the 1975 recession on their computer. He agreed and reported back a while later. They had carried out the simulation. The computer "blew up." In specific terms, Dr. Schultze reported that federal spending dropped something like $100 billion, and *GNP dropped 12 percent*. Back, that is, to the wild swings of the last century. Save, that there might be no upswing.

I reported this in an article in the *Wall Street Journal* of March 1981 and asked if we really wanted to write algebra into the Constitution. Obviously, a majority, but not yet two-thirds, of the members of the United States Senate are disposed to do just that.

And so I have now asked Dr. David Podoff, sometime Chief Economist of the Senate Committee on Finance and now Minority Chief
Economist, if *he* would construct an example of what might occur
if we attempted to balance the budget. Dr. Podoff was trained at
MIT by a distinguished faculty, including three Nobel laureates,
Professors Paul Samuelson, Robert Solow, and Francisco
Modigliani. Not surprisingly, Podoff's analysis brings Schultze's
up-to-date, and quite confirms the judgment of the profession. It
is as follows:

Assume that for 1995 our $7 *trillion* economy is roughly at full
employment (which it is), and that under the requirements of the
Constitution the budget is balanced. The economy is then buffeted
by external or what economists call "exogenous" shocks. These
shocks, which could be due to financial dislocation in international
currency markets which disrupt trade (a second run on the Mexican
peso?), oil price shocks, or worldwide natural disasters, are assumed
to result in an increase in the unemployment rate from 5.5 to 8.5
percent. (At the height of the 1981–82 recession the unemployment rate reached 9.7 percent, so this is not an implausible level
for unemployment.)

Most economic models suggest that a 3 percentage point increase
in the unemployment rate is associated with a 7.5 percent reduction
in GDP. In turn, "sensitivity analysis" published by the Congressional Budget Office in its *Economic and Budget Outlook* indicates
that a reduction in the Gross Domestic Product of about $500
billion leads to an increase in the deficit of $150 billion, as tax
collections fall and outlays for unemployment compensation and
other income maintenance programs increase.

But now the budget must be balanced. Outlays are reduced
and/or taxes are increased by a total of $150 billion. This reduction
in the deficit leads to further decreases in output, which again
increase the deficit, which causes another round of budget cuts, and
on and on. *When this so-called multiplier process is finally completed,*
the downward spiral in economic activity will leave the economy in a
new low level equilibrium, with output 18 percent below its potential
and an unemployment rate of 12 percent.

Note the symmetry between Schultze's simulation of 1975 and Podoff's of 1995. Schultze projected a 12 percent drop of GDP in an economy operating at less than full potential, off about 5 percentage points. We were not then at full employment. By contrast, in 1995 we are close to full employment, which is a sufficient shorthand for potential Gross Domestic Product. Podoff suggests a drop of 18 percentage points. We may be onto an important economic insight here, but let us hope this remains in the realm of theoretic economics!

Laura D'Andrea Tyson, the current Chair of the Council of Economic Advisers, in the *Washington Post*, February 7, reinforced the perverse nature of balancing the budget in a recession. As she put it: "A balanced budget amendment would throw the automatic stabilizers into reverse. Congress would be required to raise tax rates or cut spending programs in the face of a recession to counteract temporary increases in the deficit. Rather than moderating the normal ups and downs of the business cycle, fiscal policy would be required to aggravate them."

Monetary policy could moderate the swing in economic activity described in the simulations above. But as Dr. Tyson further notes in her op-ed piece: "In a balanced-budget world—with fiscal policy enjoined to destabilize rather than stabilize the economy—all responsibility for counteracting the economic effects of the business cycle would be placed at the doorstep of the Federal Reserve."

The Federal Reserve Board, an appointed institution with overlapping terms, ought never to have delegated such fateful power. Under the amendment, Congress, relying on "estimates of outlays and receipts," is required to bring the budget into balance, or else waive such action by a three-fifths vote. This is to say, a minority of 40 votes in the Senate could block such action.

On February 3 our sometime President Pro Tempore, Senator Robert C. Byrd, invited Senator Paul S. Sarbanes, former chairman of the Joint Economic Committee, and this Senator to join him in the Mansfield Room to hear a number of economists, led by Jeff Faux of the Economic Policy Institute, present their views on the inadvisability and peril of this amendment. (Dr. Faux, incidentally, correctly predicted the devaluation of the Mexican peso in the course of the debate over the North American Free Trade Agreement.)

Among those who spoke, for himself and his fellow Nobel Laureates at MIT, was Robert M. Solow, who stated in part: "Many economists have pointed out how perverse the Amendment can be when the economy falls into recession. Then the appearance of a cyclical deficit is a desirable, functional event, not an undesirable one. At such a moment, the higher taxes or reduced transfers or lower expenditures that would be needed to restore balance will worsen the recession and do relatively little to reduce the budget deficit. Of course some escape mechanisms will be built into the Amendment. But they will inevitably be slow, uncertain in their scope, and subject to manipulation by a minority. (This would be an obvious occasion for dissidents to challenge the accounting conventions in use.)"

In the early 1980s, deficits were not viewed as a tool to stabilize the economy; rather, they were an ill-conceived strategy designed to *reduce the size of government.* A debt in excess of $4 trillion is the legacy. We should not use the legacy of the 1980s as an excuse to abdicate control of fiscal policy by passing a constitutional amendment. Abdication would, in the words of a statement issued February 3 by several hundred economists of every political persuasion, lead to the following results: "When the private economy is in recession, a constitutional requirement that would force cuts in public spending or tax increases could worsen the economic downturn, causing greater loss of jobs, production, and income." And, as noted in the examples of Dr. Schultze and Dr. Podoff, that is surely what will happen in a recession if we have a balanced budget amendment.

Not only were the budget policies of the early 1980s an aberration, which should not be used as a justification for adopting a constitutional amendment, but in the last two years we have at length been making progress toward achieving balance. In the *Economic and Budget Outlook: Fiscal Years 1994–1998* report of January 1993, CBO projected that, by the year 2000, the deficit would reach $455 billion and exceed 5 percent of GDP. In the *Economic and Budget Outlook: Fiscal Years 1996–2000,* issued last month, CBO now projects a deficit of $284 billion, or about 3 percent of GDP. The proposals recently submitted by the President in his FY 1996 budget message would reduce the deficit below 3 percent of GDP.

What accounts for this remarkable turnaround in the budget? Two interrelated factors. First, the administration proposed, and Congress adopted, a $500 deficit reduction package just last August. Second, the economy performed better than expected, in part, because Congress did adopt a creditable deficit reduction plan. In part also because, as Secretary of the Treasury Robert Rubin remarked to the Finance Committee this Wednesday, the deficit reduction program squeezed the "deficit premium," as he put it, out of real long-term interest rates. If financial markets do not believe a deficit is under control, they will levy a deficit premium on capital lending. In 1993 we clearly persuaded the markets that we were finally serious.

The legacy of debt for the twelve-year period 1980–92 will not go away quickly and can be seen in three aspects of fiscal and budget policy. Net interest on the increase in the publicly held debt is about $180 billion or roughly the size of the annual deficit. Even without a balanced budget amendment, fiscal policy remains paralyzed; as long as we are running deficits of $200 billion, for whatever reason, it is difficult to deliberately increase the deficit as an anti-inflationary measure. The public will just not accept that.

Yet the legacy of annual deficits of almost $300 billion must be reduced gradually, so as not to depress the economy. Consequently, we will continue to add to the debt. By the end of the century the gross federal debt will approach $7 trillion.

But it can be done! Note once more. Spending on government programs is less than taxes for the first time since the 1960s. If we keep at it, do more, the debt could start declining in five years surely. The decline accelerates as smaller debt leads to lesser borrowing for interest which leads to smaller debt. But can we not do this on our own, of our own free will? I say to Senators that it won't happen otherwise. The Courts, to which all disputes under this misbegotten amendment will be referred, are not capable of making even remotely sensible decisions on fiscal policy.

Some 40 years ago Guthrie Birkhead, sometime Dean of the Maxwell School of Citizenship and Government at Syracuse University, remarked that Americans are gadget-minded about government. The proposed balanced budget amendment is nothing if not a gadget. Allow me to offer a cautionary tale from New York history. On March 3, 1858, the *New York Times* reported from Albany that 86 state senators had presented a petition "so brief and so explicit" that it was given entire:

"The undersigned, citizens of the State, would respectfully represent: That owing to the great falling off of the Canal revenue, as well as the increasing drafts upon the State Treasury, and the large expenses of carrying on the several departments of the State Government, thereby swelling up the taxes; therefore, with the view of relieving the people from the large amount now unnecessarily expended to sustain the Executive and Legislative Departments, and to secure the *honest* and better administration thereof: your petitioners respectfully ask that your Honorable body pass an act for calling a Convention to so alter the Constitution as to abolish both the Executive and Legislative Departments, as they now exist, and to vest the powers and duties thereof on the President, Vice President, and Directors of the New York Central Railroad Company."

The *Times* special correspondent, an early advocacy journalist, explained that the proposal, while "intended as a joke," nonetheless conveyed "a bitter satire, a satire which is deserved and just," such were the depredations of the ruling Democrats. The time would come, he concluded, when "after long suffering" the people would rise and "retaliate."

Joke or not, the proposal passed the legislature, went on the ballot the next fall, and failed by only 6,360 votes. The amendment failed, but retaliation came even so. The New York Democrats scarcely held office for the rest of the century. Indeed, retaliation has pursued us into the twentieth century. The New York Democrats have controlled the New York State legislature for a total of four years in the whole of the twentieth century so far. Let Republicans beware: This amendment could pass!

▲

In the event, it failed by one vote, that of Senator Mark Hatfield, Republican of Oregon. A service to the nation beyond anything he had yet done, and he had done much. Republican Senators were otherwise unanimous; 14 Democrats joined to bring the final vote to 66 to 34. (A two-thirds vote of both Houses is necessary to propose an amendment to the Constitution; the House vote had been 300 to 132.)

In the meantime, the deficit reduction "package" of 1993 was taking hold. The Treasury Secretary testified that the deficit premium on interest rates had largely disappeared. Lower interest rates resulted in lower debt service; in time, it appeared we had cut some $600 billion all told. In August 1995, the Congressional Budget Office predicted a deficit of $161 billion for fiscal year 1995, half that of three years earlier. This would equal 2.3 percent of Gross Domestic Product, the smallest deficit relative to the size of the economy since 1979.

The deficit package had been principally my responsibility in the Senate. It had been as difficult as a thing could be; 50 votes plus the Vice President. In the final hours, Senator J. Robert Kerrey of Nebraska showed the stuff of which Medal of Honor recipients are made. He had wanted more reduction, but would save the presidency. All but one Republican Senator voted against us; two Democratic Senators who voted for the balanced budget amendment also voted against us. And yet, the center held.

In the fourth quarter of 1993 real domestic product grew at an annual rate of over 6 percent. (A 6 percent growth rate doubles the size of an economy in twelve years.) There was reason for relief: deficit down, growth up, Amendment dodged. Yet none came. The debt ceiling hove into view once again. It would have to be increased; interest payments do that. The government could stop yet again. Government stop? Indeed. In 1981, for the first time in history, the United States government stopped for lack of an approved budget. In 1814 the British burned the White House, the Treasury, and the Capitol, but there *was* a budget. As noted earlier, in the years after 1981 the government technically has closed down twelve times.

Postscript

In late 1963 an article by the political economist Oskar Morgenstern of Princeton University appeared in *Fortune* magazine with the title, "Qui Numerare Incipit Errare Incipit." This was the Roman maxim, "He who begins to count begins to err." The article was a condensation of a new edition of Morgenstern's book *On the Accuracy of Economic Observations*. The thesis in the original text was erudite and elegant. "In the *physical sciences* [his emphasis] it is customary to report data together with their carefully determined errors of observation." Not invariably, to be sure. "Thus it is not necessary every time to state the error in the measurement of the velocity of light because this value is indissolubly tied up with the theory of relativity." But the general rule obtains: when new measurements are made, the error must always be stated. By contrast, in the *social sciences* no such habits have developed.

He cited examples, notably: "Changes in consumers' total spending power are reported, and taken seriously, down to the last billion (i.e., about one-half percent!), price indexes for wholesale prices are shown to second decimals, when there have been so many computing steps that the rounding off errors alone may obliterate such a degree of precision." He was notably cautious concerning price indexes: "Partly because it is so surprisingly difficult to describe prices directly, and partly because there are so many prices, their representation through index numbers has assumed a great role. Index numbers are freely quoted and interpreted. In the manner already repeatedly referred to in this work, changes of indexes are taken to be significant, even when they occur in the last decimal digit; this, although they are neither exhaustive descriptions, nor can they be so accurately recorded as to warrant such descriptive detail." He thereupon turned to the supposed accuracy of unemployment figures, which were just then appearing on a monthly basis. In his *Fortune* article, he wrote of price indexes for both wholesale *and* retail prices, which is to say the Consumer Price Index.

Morgenstern's concern was for economics; it was "not nearly so much of a science as the free use of allegedly accurate figures would seem to indicate." The reliability of the data need not be an obstacle to the development of theory, if only the Council of Economic Advisers, the Federal Reserve Board, the various government departments would commence at once "to insist that economic statistics should not be released without an accompanying estimate of their error." The *Fortune* article caused something of a stir, notably as regards the unemployment rate, which in the early Kennedy years had become a monthly event of high drama. Business would declare the rate too high, labor insist it was too low, the President would take credit or assign blame as the opportunity presented itself.

I was then nominally in charge of the Bureau of Labor Statistics which, of course, was responsible for the unemployment data. Morgenstern's thesis overall could not be faulted. The notion that at that time we knew the national income or the rate of economic growth beyond approximation and direction was absurd, and none knew this better than those who compiled the data. (In particular, the notion of comparing one nation with another. Kuznets had observed that if the per capita incomes ascribed to most poor countries were just that, the inhabitants would have long since starved.) There was, however, a possibility that Morgenstern was mistaken in pointing to discrepancies between two employment series which, in fact and avowedly, measured different populations.

Meetings were held to consider whether I should write a letter to the editor of *Fortune*. In the event, I had the good sense not to take issue with the coauthor John von Neumann of *The Theory of Games and Economic Behavior*. This disappointed some, as very likely we did have him on a technicality. However, there was little argument that economic statistics were frequently obscure or skewed. In particular, among BLS veterans it was agreed that the Consumer Price Index considerably overstated the rise, inflation having become endemic, in the cost of living. At about this time, labor contracts were beginning to provide for cost of living adjustments, and the CPI was the agreed-on measure. Our statisticians were philosophical. After all, it was none of the government's business; and it *was* good for the workers.

A decade would pass and it would become very much the government's business, as set forth in a 1981 article in *The Public Interest*, "The Consumer Price Index: Measuring Inflation and Causing It." Robert J. Gordon presented perhaps the first *political* assessment of that deceptively simple government indicator of inflation. That is, of price movements, but by now it was assumed that prices overall always went up. There is an institutional history here. As Gordon notes, the CPI was first computed by the Bureau of Labor Statistics in 1919 to help set wage levels for workers in shipbuilding yards following the government mobilization of the economy during World War I. Which is to say an inflationary setting. President Nixon imposed peacetime wage and price controls, a measure Schumpeter had anticipated with great foreboding. As Gordon wrote a near decade later, "Inflation is widely believed to be the most important economic problem facing the United States and most other countries in the world." Hence, the CPI was closely watched, "probably the most quoted economic statistic in the world."

More to the point, the incomes or benefits of about half the American population was indexed by the CPI: Social Security recipients, federal retirees, food stamp recipients, and all manner of active workers with union or similar arrangements in the work contracts. These escalator clauses, in Gordon's view, created "a two-class society, separating those who are protected against inflation, legally or by contract, from those who are not." This was notable in itself, but more important yet was Gordon's judgment that the CPI *overstated* inflation by perhaps a third. (He does not specifically give that estimate, but his examples come out in that range. This was a period of high inflation. Later studies, at a time of low inflation, give much the same ratio.)

The sources for the overestimate are various but easily accessible, as matters in statistical economics go. First, the "substitution bias." The CPI measures price changes for a fixed "basket" of goods, updated every ten years or so to reflect changes in consumption patterns. During the relatively long run of the fixed basket, relative prices change. If consumers shift preferences, their cost of living does not rise, but the CPI does. Quality improvements are nigh impossible to capture by current methodology. Gordon estimated that "the quality-adjusted prices of refrigerators, washing machines, and air conditioners declined at about twice the rate registered by the CPI between 1950 and the mid-1960s." The huge decline in the cost of commercial computers never did show up, howsoever much benefit consumers derived. Innovations occur before they are recorded; the cellular phone has yet (as of 1996) to make it into the market basket, last revised in 1987. Again to cite Gordon, the gasoline tax dedicated to the Highway Trust Fund is recorded as a price increase; the benefits of the Interstate Highway System, measurable, are even so not measured.

Let us hasten to record that the Bureau of Labor Statistics insists that the CPI is *not* a cost of living index. A current pamphlet, "Understanding the Consumer Price Index: Answers to Some Questions," reads in part: "Is the CPI a cost-of-living index? No, although it frequently and mistakenly is called a cost-of-living index. *The CPI is an index of price change only.* It does not reflect the changes in buying or consumption *patterns* that consumers probably would make to adjust to relative price changes. For example, if the price of beef increases more rapidly than other meats, shoppers may shift their purchases away from beef to pork, poultry, or fish. If the charges for household energy increase more rapidly than for other items, households may buy more insulation and consume less fuel. The CPI does not reflect this substitution among items as a cost-of-living index would. Rather, the CPI assumes the purchase of the same market basket, in the same fixed proportion (or weight) month after month. About every 10 years the market basket is thoroughly updated to allow for the introduction of new products and services and to reflect more current spending patterns. In addition, the CPI does not reflect taxes that are not directly associated with the purchase of specific goods and services. In other words, the CPI excludes taxes such as income and Social Security taxes."

Disavowals to the contrary, the CPI is uniformly used as a cost-of-living index in federal practice. This begins with the Social Security Amendments of 1972, which provide for "cost-of-living increases in benefits" but stipulate that the Consumer Price Index will be used for this purpose. The identification was explicit in the Economic Recovery Tax Act of 1981. The serious inflation of the late 1970s, brought on by a succession of "oil shocks" and other developments produced in turn a pronounced "bracket creep" in the federal income tax. Wages and salaries rose in response to inflation so accordingly did tax *rates* as nominal incomes rose and taxpayers found themselves in higher brackets, paying higher rates of tax on income that was essentially unchanged, or likely as not lowered. Hence, the forecasts of budget surpluses for the early 1980s. There were grounds, in any event, to correct the tax inequity and doubly so, given the emerging conservative strategy of keeping federal revenues to a minimum. This view was pronounced in a newly Republican Senate, and so the first great tax bill of the Reagan years not only cut tax rates, but indexed them to the cost of living defined as CPI (to begin in 1984).

The two developments now interact. In 1979 wages—average hourly earnings—began to decline in constant dollars, whilst falling behind inflation in current dollars. This, together with considerable unemployment, slowed the growth in payroll taxes to the Social Security Trust Funds. Simultaneously, Social Security payments, now indexed, commenced a prodigious rise: 9.9 percent in 1979; 14.3 percent in 1980; 11.2 percent in 1981. At these rates, benefits double in five to seven years. This was not sustainable. The actuary gave as his professional opinion that the Trust Funds were in imminent danger of insolvency. In December 1981 President Reagan, by executive order, created a National Commission on Social Security Reform. A year's deliberation of a fine commission headed by Alan Greenspan came to nothing. Then, in a week at Blair House in January 1983, agreement was reached, much of it technical. The Trust Funds never touched bottom and now began to revive.

The 1980s moved on; Social Security was saved, but the actuarial forecasts became worrisome once more, and in any event, the federal debt accumulated. Now something happened both in accord and at odds with our theme of the professionalization of reform. Within the higher civil service and the attendant policy institutes by now flourishing in Washington, it came to be understood that the CPI overstated inflation and that the consequences were becoming horrendous. There was a defective chip—call it a "D" chip—in the political economy that was producing persistent deficits and in time promised paralysis. Moreover, various estimates all came out where Gordon had. The CPI overstates increases in the cost of living in a range that averages one-third. On October 3, 1994, just prior to the convulsive Congressional elections of the following month, Alice M. Rivlin, head of the Office of Management and Budget for President Clinton, prepared a memorandum ("for handout and retrieval in meeting") on the subject of "Big Choices." The Republican Congressional campaign "features empty promises about deficit reduction and unspecified spending cuts coupled with attractive sounding tax cuts." The administration, by contrast, should continue "our established policy of explicit and paid-for proposals." There followed, among others, a page of "Illustrative Entitlement Options." The first was: "COLA reduction: CPI minus 0.5 'technical' reform (CPI may be overstated by 0.4% to 1.5%); eliminate COLAs for one year; CPI minus 2 for five years."

A few months earlier, in August, a group of economists at the Division of Research and Statistics of the Federal Reserve Board had come to much the same conclusion: "Our calculations place measurement error in the consumer price index at between ¼ and 1 ¼ percent per year, although we recognize that these estimates are of necessity extremely rough." Even so, "we believe that zero inflation corresponds roughly to measured CPI inflation in the range of ½ to 1½ percent annually."[4]

The following June, Senator Packwood of Oregon, now chairman of the Finance Committee, and I appointed an explicitly "nonpartisan" Advisory Commission to Study the Consumer Price Index. The commission was chaired by Michael J. Boskin, former head of the Council of Economic Advisers under President Bush, now at Stanford. He was joined by Ellen R. Dulberger of IBM, Gordon of Northwestern, and Zvi Griliches and Dale Jorgenson of Harvard. On September 15 the Commission presented an Interim Report to the Committee: "The Commission's interim best estimate of the size of the upward bias looking forward is 1.0% per year. The range of plausible values is 0.7% to 2.0%. The range of uncertainty is not symmetric. It is more likely that changes in the CPI have a larger than a smaller bias."

Finally, in March 1996, Matthew D. Shapiro of the University of Michigan and David W. Wilcox of the staff of the Federal Reserve Board presented a paper to the 11th Annual Conference on Macro-Economics sponsored by the National Bureau of Economic Research. Entitled "An Evaluation of Mismeasurement in the Consumer Price Index," they suggest a range of 0.6 to 1.5 percentage points, with a midpoint estimate of 1.0 percentage point.

Note that with inflation at or about 3 percent, a 1 percentage overstatement amounts to one-third. The Interim Report of the Boskin Commission emphasized the power of these seemingly insignificant numbers: "If the change in the CPI overstated the change in the cost of living by an average of 1% per year over the next decade, this bias would contribute almost $140 billion to the deficit in 2005 and $634 billion to the national debt by then. The bias alone would be the fourth largest Federal program, after Social Security, health care, and defense." One percentage point over 12 years would produce $1 trillion, about 45 percent in corrected entitlement payments, about 35 percent in correct tax revenues; the remainder in foregone debt service. Finally, the Social Security retirement account would remain solvent until 2048 or 2049, as against the current forecast of insolvency by 2030.

The interim report shifted the agenda of the budget debate somewhat. Any who cared to know could now be shown there was a possible way out of a seemingly unforgiving and intractable environment. Not in itself a sufficient response; but surely a necessary precondition. Senator Bob Dole, Senate Majority Leader, was present in the Finance Committee when the one percentage point proposal was presented. Tony Snow of the *Detroit News* reported: "Dole embraced the idea quickly but warily. He announced that he would support the charge if Moynihan's colleagues (and Mr. Clinton) joined in."

The White House response was otherwise. As was his duty, Mike McCurry, the Press Secretary, gave out the shameless decree of the professionals in the Executive Office of the President: "This is a question that should be looked at from its technical aspects and should be looked at by experts." Snow was within his journalistic rights to have observed that the "experts" had already done so.

It happened that the Bureau of Labor Statistics was in the process of reformulating the CPI, as it has done every decade or so. This typically brings the index down a bit as the various biases are adjusted. Whereupon the overestimate of cost of living increases recommences. Economists in the administration hit upon this, arguing that the BLS was already making the corrections called for. Not so. The Commission *began* with the assumption that these corrections would be made. In the Budget of the United States Government for Fiscal Year 1997, the administration was candid to a point. The BLS would soon be about its periodic adjustments. These improvements in the CPI will go some way toward correcting its apparent tendency to overstate inflation. The largest potential biases—quality measurement and adjustments for new goods—will not be addressed by these changes. Continued research in these areas by BLS and outside experts is needed to improve this vital economic statistic. Not bad for a budget document.

Preferable, surely, to the remarks of Speaker Gingrich to a February 1996 meeting of the National Legislative Agenda Council of the American Association of Retired Persons (AARP): "We want an honest Consumer Price Index. We have rejected decisively, and the Republican Party in both the House and Senate has rejected, efforts by Senator Moynihan and other Democrats in both the House and Senate to go to a politically driven number that I think is ridiculous and that would represent an enormous out-year taking from the Social Security recipients."

Ours was becoming another "low dishonest decade." Even so, there was something new and promising on the agenda. It might take some years, might even require a reorganization of government data collection into a unified system such as Statistics Canada. Morgenstern spotted this also:

> We mention a serious organization difficulty in discussing and criti- cizing statistics. These are virtually always produced by large organi- zations, government or private; and these organizations are mutually dependent upon each other in order to function normally. Often one office cannot raise too many questions about the work of another, even when it suspects its quality, since this might adversely affect bureaucratic-diplomatic relations between the two. Otherwise, the flow of information from one office to another may be hampered. A marked *esprit de corps* prevails. All offices must try to impress the public with the quality of their work. Should too many doubts be aroused, the financial support from Congress or other monetary sources may not be forthcoming. More than once has it happened that Congressional appropriations were endangered when it was sus- pected that government statistics might not be 100 percent accurate. It is natural, therefore, that various offices will defend the quality of their work even to an unreasonable degree. Only when a truly scien- tific spirit prevails among those who produce and those who use the statistics can one expect a substantial change in the general situation.

That was written some 40 years ago; government statistics are much improved. Even so, the statistical agencies of the national government are scattered across the departmental system, with long histories—there was a Bureau of Labor Statistics well before there was a Department of Labor—and fierce constituencies. Redoubtable yes; but hopeless no. This is a problem that *can* be resolved. Indeed, on a single day of a budget debate in June 1996 some 53 Senators, about equally divided by party, voted for one or both of two amendments proposing to reduce the CPI by 0.5 percent for purposes of federal indexing. This done, fiscal balance and something like positive government can be had early in the next century. Absent this, expect instability. And deserve it.

– 3 –

Defining Deviancy Down

Sociology appeared in the United States and in Europe between the late nineteenth and the early twentieth century. In the United States it is reasonably associated with the long tenure of William Graham Sumner at Yale, culminating in *Folkways,* which appeared in 1907. A period of mounting confidence was followed by something of a crisis in confidence toward the close of the century.

Kai Erikson, chairman of the department at Yale, organized a Conference on Sociological Visions in the spring of 1992 in New Haven. I was invited to give a paper with some expectation that I might say "buck up." Which indeed I did. I began by acknowledging doubts, but insisting that the record was better than it might seem.

▼

Politics is almost always in some measure an argument about the future, and persons claiming to be knowledgeable in this regard will almost always find an audience among politicians. The recent collapse of Marxist-Leninist doctrine in Central and Eastern Europe and elsewhere, involving as it did the most audacious claim not only to know but to possess the future, is a useful reminder of how precarious such claims almost always are. But it also reminds us how much a demand—you could almost say need—there is for any seeming guide to the unknown.

Even as we observe the demise of the nineteenth-century vision of "scientific socialism," we do well to remind ourselves that in the eighteenth century the framers of the American Constitution were no less firmly advocates of what they called a "new science of politics." Given what Madison termed "the fugitive and turbulent existence of . . . ancient republics," they had a lot of convincing to do as they expounded the advantages of their proposed form of government. This they did in terms of a psychological realism adapted to Newtonian physics. Men were not angels, but they were *predictable*. In their selfishness. Hence, a system of government which allowed "opposite and rival interests" to offset one another would go far to make up for the "defect of better motives."

Thus, there began a tradition of pragmatic social inquiry—what Franklin called "useful knowledge"—which has flourished in the United States. At the turn of this century, much seemed possible. Thus, in 1908, writing in the *Columbia Law Review* on the subject of "Mechanical Jurisprudence," Roscoe Pound declared: "We have . . . the same task in jurisprudence that has been achieved in philosophy, in the natural sciences, and in politics. We have to attain a pragmatic, a sociological legal science."

By midcentury Peter Odegard, among others, was less buoyant, perhaps because more experienced. He lamented "the monumental accumulation of data and the meager crop of significant concepts." Edward Shils put it that "social research in the present century has been characterized by an extraordinary scattering of attention over a great variety of uncoordinated problems which were investigated at the very concrete level." Precious little, in Leonard Cottrell's phrase, being in any sense "additive."

And yet it may be argued that the tradition of psychological realism so evident in *The Federalist* has proved more than a little rewarding, and could have been of some service to the state had "they" but known it. An instance, verging on the prophetic, will be found in an obscure article, "Nationalism or Class?—Some Questions on the Potency of Political Symbols," which the then

28-year-old Daniel Bell published in 1947 in *The Student Zionist,* a journal based at the University of Chicago. He begins: "The basic political question in Palestine, apart from the immediate issue of immigration, is quite obviously the prospects of Arab-Jewish relations. The strategical policy of every Jewish political group is based on some perspective regarding the nature and direction of Arab thinking, ranging from the bi-nationalism of Hashomer Hatzair and Ichud to the violent Jewish particularism of the Irgun."

In the last analysis, each position is based on some estimation of the potency of certain symbols of identification. For the Hashomer, class consciousness in the Marxist sense is a strong enough cement to weld lower-class Arabs and working-class Jews into a common front. For the Ichud, the liberal utopianism of peace and fellowship is of sufficient appeal to unite all men of good will. For the other Zionist groups to a lesser extent, and for the Revisionists to a greater extent, the emotions of nationalism are the most potent in creating group solidarity.

The Hashomer Hatzair were, as Bell indicates, bi-nationalist Marxists; they looked to an Arab-Jewish worker state. The Ichud group, associated with Rabbi Judah Leon Magnes, chancellor and first president of the Hebrew University, were middle-class intellectuals and also bi-nationalists. What were the prospects of such a society? None, thought Bell. Not least because the Arabs were unlikely to "achieve that state of maturity which allows them to recognize a sense of class interest and rational cooperation with Jews." Whereupon? Whereupon the idea of a *Jewish* state would prevail, and that Jewish state would seek alliances abroad. "If nationalism is still the key to political action, then a policy of national alliances may be necessary for survival. This would involve an effort toward closer affiliation with Great Britain or the United States."

Which, I dare to think, meets William of Occam's, or for that matter James Tobin's, standard of parsimony.

Indeed, there is a succession of American social scientists going a long way back who have been remarkably acute in perceiving the sociological inadequacy of Marxism-Leninism as it confronted what was known as The National Question. In 1931 Carlton Hayes remarked on the paradox "that political nationalism should grow stronger and more virulent as economic internationalism increases." Paradoxical, that is to say, if you put much store in the Marxist prediction of the emergence of proletarian internationalism. In our time, that prediction was severely questioned by a school of ethnic studies which we associate with such scholars as Milton Esman, Milton Gordon, Nathan Glazer, Walker Connor, Donald Horowitz, and of course John Dollard of Yale.

To tarry a moment on the subject of social science and *foreign* policy, this line of inquiry made it possible in the late 1970s to forecast with some accuracy that the Soviet Union, that great Marxist-Leninist construct, would disintegrate in the late 1980s. I say this because I did. Thus, on the Senate floor, January 10, 1980: "The Soviet Union is a seriously troubled, even sick society. The indices of economic stagnation and even decline are extraordinary. The indices of social disorder—social pathology is not too strong a term—are even more so. The defining event of the decade might well be the break-up of the Soviet Empire. But that . . . could also be the defining danger of the decade."

This at a press meeting in Buffalo, New York, October 14, 1984: "There is a basic fact, so elemental, why do we have difficulty understanding it? The Cold War is over. The West won . . . The Soviet Union is a failed society and an unstable one . . . The place has collapsed. As a society, it just doesn't work. Nobody believes in it any more."

And so a case for sociological vision can be made. That no one listens is another matter. No one listened to the forecasts of what is an acknowledged crisis in portions of urban society.

▲

The association of welfare dependency both with urban violence and with race was a fixture of the 1992 campaign. In New Haven, a few days before the Connecticut presidential primary in March, the Reverend Jesse Jackson led the two remaining Democratic candidates, Governor Bill Clinton and former Governor Jerry Brown, in prayer at a Stop the Violence Rally which, according to the *New Haven Register*, "was organized by community activists alarmed by a recent acceleration of city violence, including six young black men shot to death between Feb. 27 and March 16. Much of the violence has centered around young people with guns." On the occasion, Reverend Jackson observed: "If this many blacks had been killed by whites, there would be riots . . . If this many whites had been shot by blacks, there would be portable electric chairs." On the subject of disparities between suburban and urban school expenditures, he continued, "One child is programmed for Yale, one programmed for jail."

Not much help there, but at least an acknowledgment of problems previously avoided. A month earlier, Bill Bradley had given a major speech in the Senate, which was received as a major speech. Fear, he said, now covered our city streets "like a sheet of ice." Not all cities, and not all streets. But enough to ask why it had been allowed to happen, and why so little of consequence was done about it. Bradley said what no one in politics had said since it all began: "In politics for the last 25 years, silence or distortion has shaped the issue of race and urban America. Both political parties have contributed to the problem. Republicans have played the race card in a divisive way to get votes—remember Willie Horton—and Democrats have suffocated discussion of a self-destructive behavior among the minority population in a cloak of silence and denial. The result is that yet another generation has been lost. We cannot afford to wait longer. It is time for candor, time for truth, and time for action."

In this paper at Yale I commented: "The speech was not only extraordinary in its explicitness, but also in its reception. It was the subject of a lead editorial in the *New York Times* the following Sunday, whilst the *Washington Post* reprinted part of the text the following Monday. The 'new crisis in race relations' of which I wrote a generation ago is now with us, and in a worse form than even we fully comprehended. And yet we seem no longer quite so willing to deny it." It was, I concluded, "no coincidence" that in 1992 James Q. Wilson was chosen president of the American Political Science Association and James S. Coleman president of the

American Sociological Association. This could not have happened fifteen years earlier.

Indeed, fifteen years earlier there had been an effort to *expel* Coleman from the Sociological Association. He had studied the effects of school busing, a bizarre form of court ordered social engineering based essentially on a misreading of his own work. He now found that in cities it induced white flight. This was politically incorrect, and he would have to go. Instead, he outlived the bastards and in the paradigmatic mode, a new generation came along which accepted his work as the best understanding so far.

Coleman asked me to address the Association on the occasion of his induction as president the following Labor Day weekend. Kai Erikson's earlier generosity in inviting me to address the Conference of Sociological Visions in April emboldened me to a larger thought.

▼

Defining Deviancy Down

In one of the founding texts of sociology, *The Rules of Sociological Method* (1895), Emile Durkheim set it down that "crime is normal." "It is," he wrote, "completely impossible for any society entirely free of it to exist." By defining what is deviant, we are enabled to know what is not, and hence to live by shared standards. This *aperçu* appears in a chapter entitled "Rules for the Distinction of the Normal from the Pathological." Durkheim relates: "From this viewpoint the fundamental facts of criminology appear to us in an entirely new light . . . The criminal no longer appears as an utterly unsociable creature, a sort of parasitic element, a foreign, inassimilable body introduced into the bosom of society. He plays a normal role in social life. For its part, crime must no longer be conceived of as an evil which cannot be circumscribed closely enough. Far from there being cause for congratulation when it drops too noticeably below the normal level, this apparent progress assuredly coincides with and is linked to some social disturbance."

He suggests, for example, that "in times of scarcity" crimes of assault drop off. He does not imply that we ought to approve of crime—"pain has likewise nothing desirable about it"—but we need to understand its function. He saw religion, in Randall Collins's terms, as "fundamentally a set of ceremonial actions, assembling the group, heightening its emotions, and focusing its members on symbols of their common belongingness." In this context "a punishment ceremony creates social solidarity." As on board an eighteenth-century man-of-war, or in a 1930s gangster movie, such ceremonies occur at fairly regular intervals.

The matter was pretty much left at that until 70 years later when, in 1965, Kai T. Erikson finished *Wayward Puritans,* a study of "crime rates" in the Massachusetts Bay colony. The design, as he put it, was "to test [Durkheim's] notion that the number of deviant offenders a community can afford to recognize is likely to remain stable over time." The notion proved out very well indeed. Despite occasional crime waves, as when itinerant Quakers refused to take off their hats in the presence of magistrates, the amount of deviance in this corner of seventeenth-century New England fitted nicely with the supply of stocks and whipping posts. Erikson continued:

> It is one of the arguments of the . . . study that the amount of deviation a community encounters is apt to remain fairly constant over time. To start at the beginning, it is a simple logistic fact that the number of deviancies which come to a community's attention are limited by the kinds of equipment it uses to detect and handle them, and to that extent the rate of deviation found in a community is at least in part a function of the size and complexity of its social control apparatus. A community's capacity for handling deviance, let us say, can be roughly estimated by counting its prison cells and hospital beds, its policemen and psychiatrists, its courts and clinics.
>
> Most communities, it would seem, operate with the expectation that a relatively constant number of control agents is necessary to cope with a relatively constant number of offenders. The amount of men, money, and material assigned by society to "do something" about deviant behavior does not vary appreciably over time, and the implicit logic which governs the community's efforts to man a police force or maintain suitable facilities for the mentally ill seems to be that there is a fairly stable quota of trouble which should be anticipated.
>
> In this sense, the agencies of control often seem to define their job as that of keeping deviance within bounds rather than that of oblit-

erating it altogether. Many judges, for example, assume that severe punishments are a greater deterrent to crime than moderate ones, and so it is important to note that many of them are apt to impose harder penalties when crime seems to be on the increase and more lenient ones when it does not, almost as if the power of the bench were being used to keep the crime rate from getting out of hand.

Erikson was taking issue with what he described as "a dominant strain in sociological thinking" that took for granted that a well-structured society "is somehow designed to prevent deviant behavior from occurring." In both authors there is an undertone which suggests that with deviancy, as with most social goods, there is the continuing problem of demand exceeding supply. Durkheim invites us to "imagine a society of saints, a perfect cloister of exemplary individuals. Crimes, properly so called, will there be unknown; but faults which appear venial to the layman will create there the same scandal that the ordinary offense does in ordinary consciousness. If, then, this society has the power to judge and punish, it will define these acts as criminal and will treat them as such." Recall the comment that there need be no cause for congratulations should the amount of crime drop "too noticeably below the normal level." It would not appear that Durkheim anywhere contemplates the possibility of *too much* crime. Clearly his theory would have required him to deplore such a development, but the possibility seems never to have occurred to him.

Erikson, writing much later in the twentieth century, contemplates both possibilities. "Deviant persons can be said to supply needed services to society." There is no doubt a tendency for the supply of any needed thing to run short. But he is consistent. There can be too much of a good thing. Hence "the number of deviant offenders a community can *afford* to recognize is likely to remain stable over time" (emphasis added).

Social scientists are said to be on the lookout for poor fellows—poor saints—getting a bum rap. But here is a theory that clearly implies there are circumstances in which society will choose *not* to notice behavior that would be otherwise controlled, or disapproved, or even punished.

It appears to me that this is in fact what we have been doing of late. I proffer the thesis that over the past generation, since the time Erikson wrote, the amount of deviant behavior in American society has increased beyond the levels the community can "afford to recognize" and that accordingly we have been redefining deviancy so as to exempt much conduct previously stigmatized, and also quietly raising the "normal" level in categories where behavior is now abnormal by any earlier standard. This redefining has evoked fierce resistance from defenders of "old" standards and accounts for much of the present cultural war such as proclaimed by many at the 1992 Republican National Convention.

Let me, then, offer three categories of redefinition: the *altruistic*, the *opportunistic*, and the *normalizing*. The first category may be illustrated by the deinstitutionalization movement within the mental health profession that appears in the 1950s. The second category is to be seen in the interest group rewards derived from the acceptance of "alternative" family structures. The third category is to be observed in the growing acceptance of unprecedented levels of violent crime.

Altruistic Redefinition

It happens I was present at the beginning of the deinstitutionalization movement. Early in 1955 Averell Harriman, the new governor of New York, met with his new Commissioner of Mental Hygiene, Paul Hoch, who described the development of a tranquilizer derived from *rauwolfia* at one of the state mental hospitals. The medication had been clinically tested and appeared to be an effective treatment of many severely psychotic patients, increasing the percentage of patients discharged. Dr. Hoch recommended that it be used systemwide; Harriman found the money.

That same year Congress created a Joint Commission on Mental Health and Illness with a view to formulating "comprehensive and realistic recommendations" in this area which was then a matter of considerable public concern. Year after year the population of mental institutions grew. Year after year, new facilities had to be built. Never mind the complexities—population growth and such like matters. There was a general unease. Durkheim's constant continued to be exceeded.[1]

The discovery of tranquilizers was adventitious. Physicians were seeking cures for disorders that were just beginning to be understood. Even a limited success made it possible to believe that the incidence of this particular range of disorders, which had seemingly required persons to be confined against their will or even awareness, could be greatly reduced. The Congressional Commission submitted its report in 1961; it was seen to propose a nationwide program of deinstitutionalization.

Late in 1961 President Kennedy appointed an interagency committee to prepare legislative recommendations based upon the report. I represented Secretary of Labor Arthur J. Goldberg on this committee and drafted its final submission. This included the recommendation of the National Institute of Mental Health that 2,000 community mental health centers (one per 100,000 of population) be built by 1980. A buoyant Presidential Message to Congress followed early in 1963. "If we apply our medical knowledge and social insights fully," President Kennedy stated, "all but a small portion of the mentally ill can eventually achieve a wholesome and a constructive social adjustment." A "concerted national attack on mental disorders [was] now possible and practical." The President signed the Community Mental Health Centers Construction Act on October 31, 1963, his last public bill signing ceremony. He gave me a pen.

The mental hospitals emptied out. At the time Governor Harriman met with Dr. Hoch in 1955, there were 93,314 adult residents of mental institutions maintained by New York State. As of August 1992, there were 11,363. However, the number of community mental health centers never came near the goal of 2,000 community centers. Only some 482 received federal construction funds in the period 1963–80. The next year, 1981, the program was folded into the Alcohol and Other Drug Abuse block grant and disappeared from view. Even when centers were built, the results were hardly as hoped for. David F. Musto of Yale writes that the planners had bet on improving national mental health "by improving the quality of general community life through expert knowledge, not merely by more effective treatment of the already ill." There was no such knowledge.

However, worse luck, the belief that there *was* such knowledge took hold within sectors of the profession, which saw it as an unacceptable mode of social control. These activists subscribed to a redefining mode of their own. Mental patients were said to have been "labeled," and were not to be drugged. Musto says of the battles that followed that they were "so intense and dramatic precisely because both sides shared the fantasy of an omnipotent and omniscient mental health technology which could thoroughly reform society; the prize seemed eminently worth fighting for." But even as the federal government turned to other matters, the mental institutions continued to turn out inmates. Professor Fred Siegel of Cooper Union observes that "in the great wave of moral deregulation that began in the mid-1960s, the poor and the insane were freed from the fetters of middle-class mores." They might henceforth sleep in doorways as often as they chose. The problem of the homeless appeared, characteristically defined as persons who lacked "affordable housing."

The *altruistic* mode of redefinition is just that. There is no reason to believe there was any real increase in mental illness at the time deinstitutionalization began. However, there was such a perception, and this enabled good people to try to do good, however unavailing in the end.[2]

Opportunistic Redefinition

Our second, or *opportunistic*, mode of redefinition reveals at most a nominal intent to do good. The true object is to do well, a well-established motivation among mortals. In this pattern, a growth in deviancy makes possible a transfer of resources, including prestige, to those who control the deviant population. This control would be jeopardized if any serious effort were made to reduce the deviancy in question. This leads to assorted strategies for redefining the behavior in question as not all that deviant really.

In the years 1963–65, the Policy Planning Staff of the U.S. Department of Labor picked up the first tremors of what Samuel H. Preston in the 1984 Presidential Address to the Population Association of America would call "the earthquake that shuddered through the American family in the past twenty years." The *New York Times* recently provided this succinct accounting. "Thirty years ago, 1 in every 40 white children was born to an unmarried mother; today it is 1 in 5, according to Federal data. Among blacks, 2 of 3 children are born to an unmarried mother; 30 years ago the figure was 1 in 5."

In 1991 Paul Offner and I published longitudinal data showing that of children born in the years 1967–69, some 22.1 percent were dependent on welfare, that is to say, Aid to Families of Dependent Children, before reaching age 18. This broke down as 15.7 percent for white children, 72.3 percent for black children. Projections for children born in 1980 gave rates of 22.2 percent and 82.9 percent respectively. A year later a *Times* series on welfare and poverty calls this a "startling finding . . . a symptom of vast social calamity."

And yet there is little evidence that this is regarded as a calamity in municipal government. To the contrary, there is general acceptance of the situation as normal. Of late, presidential candidates raise the subject, often to the point of dwelling on it. But while there is a good deal of demand for symbolic change, there is none of the marshalling of resources that is to be associated with significant social action. It is not for lack of evidence that there is a social problem here.

Richard T. Gill writes of "an accumulation of data showing that intact biological parent families offer children very large advantages compared to any other family or non-family structure one can imagine." Correspondingly, the disadvantages associated with single-parent families spill over into other areas of social policy which now attract great public concern. Leroy L. Schwarts, M.D., and Mark W. Stanton argue that the real quest regarding a government-run health system such as that of Canada or Germany is whether it would work "in a country that has social problems that countries like Canada and Germany don't share to the same extent." Health problems reflect lifestyles. The lifestyles associated with "such social pathologies as the breakdown of the family structure" lead to medical pathologies. They conclude: "The United States is paying dearly for its social and behavioral problems" that have now become medical problems as well.

To cite another example, there is at present no more vexing problem of social policy in the United States than that of education. A generation of ever more aspiring statutes and reforms have produced weak responses at best and a fair amount of what could be called dishonesty. ("Everyone knows that Head Start works." *Educational Goals for the Year 2000.*) None of this should surprise us. The 1966 report *Equality of Educational Opportunity* by James S. Coleman and his associates established that the family background of students played a much stronger role in student achievement relative to variations in the ten (and still standard) measures of school quality. In a 1992 study entitled *America's Smallest School: The Family,* Paul Barton came up with the elegant concept of the Parent-Pupil Ratio as a measure of school quality. Barton, who was on the Policy Planning Staff in Labor in 1965, noted the great increase in the proportion of children living in single-parent families since then. Further, he noted that the proportion "varies widely among the states" and is related to "variation in achievement" among them. The correlation between the percentage of eighth graders living in two-parent families and average mathematics proficiency is a solid .74. North Dakota, highest on the math test, is second highest on the family composition scale. The District of Columbia, lowest on the family scale, is second lowest in the test score.

A few months before Barton's study appeared I published an article showing that the correlation between eighth grade math scores and distance of state capitals from the Canadian border was .522, a respectable showing. By contrast, the correlation with per pupil expenditure was a derisory .203. I offered the policy proposal that states wishing to improve their schools should move closer to Canada. This would be difficult, of course, but so would it be to change the Parent-Pupil Ratio.

Indeed the 1990 Census found that for the District of Columbia, apart from Ward 3 west of Rock Creek Park, the percentage of children living in single-parent families in the seven remaining wards ranged from a low of 63.6 percent to a high of 75.7. This being a one-time measurement, *over* time the proportions become asymptotic. In the nation's capital. No demand for change comes from that community, or as near as makes no matter. For there is good money to be made out of bad schools. This is a statement that will no doubt please many a hard heart, and displease many genuinely concerned to bring about change. To the latter, a group in which I would like to include myself, I would only say that we are obliged to ask why things do not change.

For a period there was some speculation that if family structure got bad enough this mode of deviancy would have less punishing effects on children. In 1991 Deborah A. Dawson of the National Institutes of Health examined the thesis that "the psychological effects of divorce and single parenthood on children were strongly influenced by a sense of shame in being 'different' from the norm." If this were so, the effect should have fallen off in the 1980s. It did not. "The problems associated with task overload among single parents are more constant in nature," Dawson wrote, adding that since the adverse effects had not diminished, they were "not based on stigmatization but rather on inherent problems in alternative family structures," *alternative* here meaning other than two-parent families. We should take note of such candor. Writing in the *Journal of Marriage and the Family* in 1989, Sara McLanahan and Karen Booth noted: "Whereas a decade ago the prevailing view was that single motherhood had no harmful effects on children, recent research is less optimistic."

The year 1990 saw more of this lesson. In a paper prepared for the Progressive Policy Institute, Elaine Ciulla Kamarck and William A. Galston wrote that "if the economic effects of family breakdown are clear, the psychological effects are just now coming into focus." They cite Karl Zinsmeister: "There is a mountain of scientific evidence showing that when families disintegrate children often end up with intellectual, physical, and emotional scars that persist for life . . . We talk about the drug crisis, the education crisis, and the problems of teen pregnancy and juvenile crime. But all these ills trace back predominantly to one source: broken families."

As for juvenile crime, they cite Douglas Smith and G. Roger Jarjoura: "Neighborhoods with larger percentages of youth (those aged 12 to 20) and areas with higher percentages of single-parent households also have higher rates of violent crime." They add: "The relationship is so strong that controlling for family configuration erases the relationship between race and crime and between low income and crime. This conclusion shows up time and time again in the literature; poverty is far from the sole determinant of crime." But the large point is avoided. In a 1992 essay, "The Expert's Story of Marriage," Barbara Dafoe Whitehead examined "the story of marriage as it is conveyed in today's high school and college textbooks." Nothing amiss in this tale. It goes like this:

"The life course is full of exciting options. The lifestyle options available to individuals seeking a fulfilling personal relationship include living a heterosexual, homosexual, or bisexual single lifestyle; living in a commune; having a group marriage; being a single parent; or living together. Marriage is yet another lifestyle choice. However, before choosing marriage, individuals should weigh its costs and benefits against other lifestyle options and should consider what they want to get out of their intimate relationships. Even within marriage, different people want different things. For example, some people marry for companionship, some marry in order to have children, some marry for emotional and financial security. Though marriage can offer a rewarding path to personal growth, it is important to remember that it cannot provide a secure or permanent status. Many people will make the decision between marriage and singlehood many times throughout their life. Divorce represents part of the normal family life cycle. It should not be viewed as either deviant or tragic, as it has been in the past. Rather, it establishes a process for 'Uncoupling' and thereby serves as the foundation for individual renewal and 'new beginnings.'"

History commences to be rewritten. In 1992 the Select Committee on Children, Youth, and Families of the U.S. House of Representatives held a hearing on "Investing in Families: A Historical Perspective." A Fact Sheet prepared by Committee Staff began:

> Historical Shifts in Family Composition Challenge Conventional Wisdom
>   While in modern times the percentage of children living with one parent has increased, more children lived with just one parent in Colonial America.

The Fact Sheet proceeded to list program on program for which federal funds were allegedly reduced in the 1980s. We then come to a summary: "Between 1970 and 1991, the value of AFDC benefits decreased by 41%. In spite of proven success of Head Start, only 28% of eligible children are being served. As of 1990, more than $18 billion in child support went uncollected. At the same time, the poverty rate among single-parent families with children under 18 was 44%. Between 1980 and 1990, the rate of growth in the total federal budget was four times greater than the rate of growth in children's programs." In other words, benefits paid to mothers and children have gone down steadily, as indeed they have done. But no proposal is made to restore benefits to an earlier level, or even to maintain their value, as is the case with other "indexed" Social Security programs. Instead we go directly to the subject of education spending.

Nothing new. In 1969 President Nixon proposed a guaranteed income, the Family Assistance Plan. This was described as an "income strategy" as against a "services strategy." It may or may not have been a good idea, but it was a clear one, and the resistance of service providers was equally clear. In the end it was defeated, to the huzzahs of the advocates of "welfare rights." What is going on here is simply that a large increase in what once was seen as deviancy has provided opportunity to a wide spectrum of interest groups that benefit from redefining the problem as essentially normal and doing little to reduce it.

Normalizing Redefinition

Our *normalizing* category most directly corresponds to Erikson's proposition that "the number of defiant offenders a community can afford to recognize is likely to remain stable over time." We can further associate this with the popular notion of "denial." Again, I feel some association with the onset of the events we will discuss here. In 1965, having reached the conclusion that there would be a dramatic increase in single-parent families, I reached the further conclusion that this would in turn lead to a dramatic increase in crime.

In an article in *America* I put it this way: "From the wild Irish slums of the nineteenth century Eastern seaboard to the riot-torn suburbs of Los Angeles, there is one unmistakable lesson in American history: a community that allows a large number of young men to grow up in broken families, dominated by women, never acquiring any stable relationship to male authority, never acquiring any set of rational expectations about the future—that community asks for and gets chaos. Crime, violence, unrest, unrestrained lashing out at the whole social structure—that is not only to be expected; it is very near to inevitable."

The inevitable came to pass, but here again our response is curiously passive. Crime is a more or less continuous subject of political pronouncement, and from time to time will be at or near the top of opinion polls as a matter of public concern. But it never gets much further than that. In the words spoken from the bench, Judge Edwin Torres of the New York State Supreme Court, Twelfth Judicial District, described how "the slaughter of the innocent marches unabated: subway riders, bodega owners, cab drivers, babies; in laundromats, in cash machines, on elevators, in hallways." In personal communication, he writes: "This numbness, this near narcoleptic state can diminish the human condition to the level of combat infantrymen, who, in protracted campaigns, can eat their battlefield rations seated on the bodies of the fallen, friend and foe alike. A society that loses its sense of outrage is doomed to extinction." There is no expectation that this will change, nor any effica-

cious public insistence that it do so. The crime level has been
normalized.

Consider the St. Valentine's Day Massacre. In 1929 in Chicago
during Prohibition, four gangsters killed seven gangsters on February 14. The event became legend. It merits not one but two entries
in the *World Book Encyclopedia.* I leave it to others to judge, but it
would appear that the society in the 1920s was simply not willing
to put up with this degree of deviancy. In the end the Constitution
was amended, and Prohibition, which lay behind so much gangster
violence, ended.

In recent years, again in the context of illegal traffic in controlled
substances, this form of murder has returned. But at a level which
induces denial. James Q. Wilson comments that Los Angeles has a
St. Valentine's Day Massacre every weekend. Even the most ghastly
reenactments produce only moderate responses. On the morning
after the close of the Democratic National Convention in New York
City in July there was such an account in the second section of the
New York Times. It was not a big story; bottom of the page. But
with a headline that got your attention. "3 Slain in Bronx Apartment, but a Baby Is Saved." A subhead continued: "A mother's last
act was to hide her little girl under the bed." The article described
a drug execution; the now routine blindfolds made from duct tape;
a man and a woman and a teenager. "Each had been shot once in
the head." The police had found them a day later. They also found,
under a bed, a three-month-old baby, dehydrated but alive. A
lieutenant remarked of the mother, "In her last dying act she
protected her baby. She probably knew she was going to die, so she
stuffed the baby where she knew it would be safe." The matter was
left there. The police would do their best. But the event passed
quickly; it will never make the *World Book.*

Nor is it likely that any great heed will be paid to an uncanny
reenactment of the Prohibition drama a few months later, also in
the Bronx. The *Times* story, page B3, reported: "9 Men Posing as
Police Are Indicted in 3 Murders. Drug Dealers Were Kidnapped
for Ransom." The *Daily News* story, same day, page 17, made it
four murders, adding nice details about torture techniques. The

gang members posed as Federal Drug Enforcement Administration agents, real badges and all. The victims were drug dealers, whose families were uneasy about calling the police. Ransom seems generally to have been set in the $650,000 range. Some paid. Some got it in the back of the head. So it goes.

Yet, violent killings, often random, went on unabated. Peaks continue to attract some notice. But these are peaks above "average" levels that 30 years ago would have been thought epidemic.

Los Angeles, Aug. 24. (Reuters). Twenty-two people were killed in Los Angeles over the weekend, the worse period of violence in the city since it was ravaged by riots earlier this year, the police said today. Twenty-four others were wounded by gunfire or stabbings, including a 19-year-old woman in a wheelchair who was shot in the back when she failed to respond to a motorist who asked for directions in south Los Angeles. "The guy stuck a gun out of the window and just fired at her," said a police spokesman, Lieut. David Rock. The woman was later described as being in stable condition.

Among those who died was an off-duty officer, shot while investigating reports of a prowler in a neighbor's yard, and a Little League baseball coach who had argued with the father of a boy he was coaching. The police said at least nine of the deaths were gang-related, including that of a 14-year-old girl killed in a fight between rival gangs.

Fifty-one people were killed in three days of rioting that started April 29 after the acquittal of four police officers in the beating of Rodney G. King. Los Angeles usually has above-average violence during August, but the police were at a loss to explain the sudden rise. On an average weekend in August, 14 fatalities occur.

Not to be outdone, the South Bronx came up with a near record two days later, as reported in *New York Newsday:* "Armed with 9-mm. pistols, shotguns and M-16 rifles, a group of masked men and women poured out of two vehicles in the South Bronx early yesterday and sprayed a stretch of Longwood Avenue with a fusillade of bullets, injuring 12 people."

A Kai Erikson of the future will surely need to know that the Department of Justice in 1990 found that Americans reported only about 38 percent of all crimes and 48 percent of violent crimes.

This could be seen as a means of *normalizing* crime. In much the same way, the vocabulary of the crime reporting can be seen to move toward the normal-seeming. A teacher is shot on her way to class. The *Times* subhead reads: "Struck in the Shoulder in the Year's First Shooting Inside a School." First of the season.

It is too early, however, to know how to regard the arrival of the doctors on the scene declaring "public health emergency." The June 10, 1992, issue of the *Journal of the American Medical Association* was devoted entirely to papers on the subject of violence, principally violence associated with firearms. An editorial signed by former Surgeon General C. Everett Koop and Dr. George D. Lundberg is entitled "Violence in America: A Public Health Emergency." Their proposition is admirably succinct. "Regarding violence in our society as purely a sociological matter, or one of law enforcement, has led to unmitigated failure. It is time to test further whether violence can be amenable to medical/public health interventions. We believe violence in America to be a public health emergency, largely unresponsive to methods thus far used in its control. The solutions are very complex, but possible."

The authors cited the relative success of epidemiologists to gain some jurisdiction in the area of motor vehicle casualties by redefining what had been seen as a law enforcement issue into a public health issue. Again, this process began during the Harriman administration in New York in the 1950s. In the 1960s the morbidity and mortality associated with automobile crashes was arguably a major public health problem; the public health strategy arguably brought the problem under a measure of control. Not "in the 1970s and 1980s," as the *Journal of the American Medical Association* would have us think: the federal legislation involved was signed in 1965. Such a strategy would surely produce insights into the control of violence that elude law enforcement professionals.

For some years now I have had legislation in the Senate which would prohibit the manufacture of .25 and .32 caliber bullets. These are the two calibers most typically used with the guns known as Saturday Night Specials. "Guns don't kill people," I argue, "bullets do." Moreover, we have a two-century supply of handguns but only a four-year supply of ammunition. A public health official would right off see the logic of trying to control the supply of bullets rather than of guns.

Even so, now that the doctor has come, there is a real prospect that violence will be defined down by epidemiologists. Doctors Koop and Lundberg note that in 1990 in the state of Texas "deaths from firearms, for the first time in many decades, surpassed deaths from motor vehicles, 3,443 to 3,309." A good comparison. And yet keep in mind that the number of motor vehicle deaths, having leveled off since the 1960s, is now pretty well accepted as normal at somewhat less than 50,000 a year, which is somewhat less than the level of the 1960s—the "carnage," as it was once thought to be, is now accepted as normal. This is the price we pay for high-speed transportation; but there is no benefit associated with homicide, and no good of getting used to it. Epidemiologists have powerful insights that can contribute to lessening the medical trauma, but they must be wary of normalizing the social pathology that leads to such trauma.

The hope—if there be such—of this essay has been twofold. It is, first, to suggest that the Durkheim constant, as I put it, is maintained by a dynamic process which adjusts upward and *down-ward*. Liberals have traditionally been alert for upward redefining that does injustice to individuals. Conservatives have been correspondingly sensitive to downward redefining that weakens societal standards. Might it not help if we could all agree that there is a dynamic at work here? It is not revealed truth, nor yet a scientifically derived formula. It is simply a pattern we observe in ourselves. Nor is it rigid. There may once have been an unchanging supply of jail cells which more or less determined the number of prisoners. No longer. We are building new prisons at a prodigious rate.* Similarly, the executioner is back. There is something of a competition in Congress to think up new offenses for which the death penalty

*In a 1996 study for the Educational Testing Service, *Captive Students,* Paul E. Barton and Richard J. Coley record that the U.S. prison population tripled since 1980. If the trend continues the United States will soon have more people incarcerated than in four-year colleges. "One out of every three Black men in their 20s is under the supervision of the criminal justice system on any given day." Curfews have become commonplace; again, normalizing what was once an emergency measure.

seems the only available deterrent. Possibly also modes of execution, as in "fry the kingpins." Even so, we are getting used to a lot of behavior that is not good for us.

As noted earlier, Durkheim states that there is "nothing desirable" about pain. Surely what he meant was that there is nothing pleasurable. Pain, even so, is an indispensable warning signal. But societies under stress, much like individuals, will turn to pain killers of various kinds that end up concealing real damage. There is surely nothing desirable about *this*. If our analysis wins general acceptance—if, for example, more of us came to share Judge Torres's genuine alarm at "the trivialization of the lunatic crime rate" in his city (and mine)—we might surprise ourselves how well we respond to the manifest decline of the American civic order. Might.

▲

The lecture was cordially received by sociologists gathered for their 87th annual meeting, but no notice was taken outside the conference hall. In the 1970s great swarms of journalists used to attend the affair, seeking enlightenment. Alas, it hadn't paid off. At a press conference held just before the address, a sole reporter showed up from a local Pittsburgh radio station.

The following winter, however, the essay was published in the *American Scholar;* and comment, invariably favorable, resonated through all of 1993. There was a shock of recognition. *No one got mad.* Or, if some did, they didn't get into print. I have to assume that a great many persons didn't like it at all. But what was there to say: it was true. Mary McGrory agreed; William F. Buckley agreed with Mary McGrory. Buckley wrote that it was "nothing less than a cry from the heart" and it was heard.

More to the point, I was not alone. In his *Wall Street Journal* column "Capitol Journal," Gerald F. Seib noted this:

> It isn't just Sen. Moynihan sounding the alarm. From their widely divergent perspectives, William Galston, an assistant to President Clinton, and William Bennett, a conservative veteran of the Reagan and Bush administrations, have recently reached strikingly similar conclusions about the decline in the U.S. social order.

This troubling picture makes it clear that the oft-debated "social issues"—abortion rights, school prayer, gay rights and Murphy Brown plot lines—miss the wider calamities of life in the U.S. today. The powerful new writings of Messrs. Moynihan, Galston and Bennett are starting to cause ripples inside Washington, and in time are likely to transform the standard liberal-conservative debate over social policy.

Cold statistics they cite give the essence of the story: In the past three decades, the percentage of children born outside of marriage has risen fivefold, from 5% to 25%. Today, a stunning 63% of black children are born out of wedlock. At the same time, the divorce rate has tripled. The net result is that almost a third of U.S. families with children now are one-parent households.

And a lot of these children grow up poor. The poverty rate among female-headed families was nearly 45% in 1988, more than six times higher than in married-couple families. Deadbeat dads are a big reason; one Census Bureau report showed that only half the mothers entitled to child support payments got what they were owed, a quarter got partial payments and a quarter got nothing at all.

Mr. Bennett this week tried to illuminate these woes further by publishing what he calls an Index of Leading Cultural Indicators. His index tracks 19 different "social indicators," from crimes committed to child abuse, during the past 30 years. He found a 560% increase in violent crime, a jump of more than 200% in the teenage suicide rate, an 80-point drop in SAT scores.

But it is Sen. Moynihan who puts such statistics into a human context. A quarter-century ago, Mr. Moynihan warned that a large increase in single-parent families was coming, but found little support for his shocking forecast. Now, of course, he is vindicated. And in an obscure scholarly article that is fast becoming a cult classic in the Senate, he now argues that "deviant behavior" has become so common that society has chosen to stop recognizing it as such, and instead has redefined its standards.

A good many things were coming together. In his entry on SAT scores in Leading Cultural Indicators, Dr. Bennett offers a brief "Analysis": "SAT scores have dropped nearly 80 points in the past three decades while spending has increased significantly. In 1960, we spent (in constant 1990 dollars) an average of $2,035 per student. In 1990, we spent $5,247 per student. In addition, the way that the SAT is graded has changed. The same person taking the same test and getting the same answers would score between 18 and 30 points higher in 1992 than in 1960." A generation earlier, Coleman had explained all this. Outlays had all but tripled; scores had declined. Outlays did not *determine* scores. (In 1995 the College Board recalibrated its scoring such that the current average score of 424 on the verbals will henceforth be 500, which is what it was before the decline began.)[3]

The following summer, Amitai Etzioni published an article, "Restoring Our Moral Voice," in the context of communitarianism. He was having difficulty speaking to fellow liberals about the moral voice. It reminded them of the Moral Majority, a distinctly nonliberal group. And yet the public was ready for such talk: "The overwhelming majority of Americans, public opinion polls show, recognize that our moral fabric has worn rather thin. A typical finding is that while school teachers in the forties listed as their top problems talking out of turn, making noise, cutting in line, and littering, they now list drug abuse, alcohol abuse, pregnancy, and suicide. Wanton taking of life, often for a few bucks to buy a vial of crack or to gain a pair of sneakers, is much more common than it is in other civilized societies or than it used to be in America. Countless teenagers bring infants into the world to satisfy their ego needs, with little attention to the long-term consequences for the children, themselves, or society." I had argued "convincingly . . . that people have been so bombarded with evidence of social ills that they have developed moral calluses, which make them relatively inured to immorality." We had lost our moral voice, and increasingly were lost without it.

Withal, the more remarkable impress of the article occurred in the 1993 mayoral election in New York City. There was now to be a rematch, as the boxing imagery of the city goes, between Mayor David N. Dinkins and the former United States Attorney for the Southern District of New York, Rudolph W. Giuliani, Democrat and Republican, respectively. Early in the campaign, April 15, I was asked to a breakfast meeting of the Association for a Better New

York, a civic association, ably and irrepressibly convened by Lew Rudin, a realtor of large and deserved influence in the city. As near as makes no matter, everyone comes to his breakfasts—the Mayor, surely, the Speaker of the State Assembly, union leaders, business executives, educators, rabbis, priests, pentacostals.

New York Senators are assumed to represent the whole of the state, and try to do. And yet, I allow a special concern for the City of New York. Alexander Hamilton had agreed with Thomas Jefferson to move the capital from Manhattan to a malarial swamp on the banks of the Potomac. (In return the federal government assumed the state debt incurred during the Revolutionary War, and the credit of the United States was secured.) But if the capital moved south, the culture remained in the North, increasingly in New York. The culture of finance, manufacturing, trade. The culture of popular government and, from early on, a high culture of increasing consequence—and diversity. Not fifteen years after Jefferson and Hamilton reached their agreement, Lorenzo da Ponte, an Italian Jew born Emanuele Conegliano, Mozart's librettist—*Le Nozze di Figaro, Don Giovanni, Così fan tutte*—arrived in New York, became professor of Italian language and literature at Columbia University, and is buried at Old St. Patrick's. New York remained the nation's capital in all save government; at midcentury it had become the world capital, the United Nations firmly affixed to Manhattan's East Side.

Then a blight struck: an increasingly dysfunctional portion of the population began to consume ever more resources, not just of money but attention, energy, direction. By the 1990s, 40 percent of the children in New York City would be on one or another form of federal welfare at some point in the year. A clear majority would receive AFDC benefits before reaching eighteen—paupers. Moreover, in 1993 (the last year for which data are available) the percentage of children born out of wedlock in New York City rose to just above 50 percent for the first time. Things weren't working.

A. M. Rosenthal summed it up in the *New York Times:* "This is the world's most exciting and creative city; the others are vanilla. But it is suffering from a civil, moral and political disease that can kill it dead. It is called 'defining deviancy down.'" Crime was at once symbol and substance. "But when we barely bother to read about bystanders shot down in the street because so many are, when we know children kill, when we do not bother to report muggings and robberies, when we expect to be harassed by hustlers wherever we go, when we see people defecating in our streets, when cops are encouraged to pass by street drug deals—in other words, when crime is accepted as inescapable—then we are defining deviancy down, so down we are drowning in it. African-Americans, Latinos, Asians, whites, all." "It's safety, not race," Rosenthal insisted.

But an increasingly provincial liberalism—no longer an example to others, increasingly a symbol of decline—could not grasp this. David Dinkins, the first African American mayor, seemed to do so least of all. A wholly decent man, out of the honorable clubhouse tradition of J. Raymond Jones, he seemed, even so, lost in the New York of the '90s. Joe Klein in *Newsweek* got it together in one paragraph: "He may be the last of the big-time urban liberals, a straggler from the '60s. He has been slow to acknowledge the city's most profound problem—the changing nature of poverty, the growth of an underclass whose privation has *behavioral* as well as economic roots. He came to office, for example, believing that 'homelessness' was a housing problem. Most New Yorkers agree with liberal columnist Pete Hamill, writing in *New York Magazine,* that the presence of thousands of deranged, sometimes violent, beggars has more to do with drug abuse and mental illness than with a housing shortage." He got no help from his staff: stragglers themselves. The election looked lost.

When, of a sudden, something happened. His police commissioner, a cop's cop, read the *American Scholar,* and got it right off. George F. Will wrote about us both in a column, "The Worst Becomes the Norm": "Raymond Kelly, New York City's police commissioner, read Moynihan's article and wrote a splendid speech urging 'a new intolerance.' . . . Kelly said: 'The fight against crime in America, like that against Soviet domination, is now essentially a fight for freedom. Fearing crime, or being one of its victims, is to lose a fair measure of freedom . . . Society's increasing tolerance of

crime and antisocial behavior in general is abetting our own enslave-
ment. The erosion of freedom caused by crime is so pervasive that
we are in danger of failing to notice it at all."

I had also read Kelly's address; I had already endorsed the mayor
for reelection. I would now go before a great audience of New
Yorkers with a bank of television cameras watching, and declare that
David N. Dinkins was damned if *he* would surrender. We would get
our city back! To wit:

▼

Mr. Mayor, Mr. Speaker: I'm not going to ask you to look forward.
I'm going to ask you to look back and ask yourselves what in the
last 50 years, Lew Rudin apart, in New York City is now better than
it was.

I'm in such a mood, as you can see! It will be 50 years ago this
June that I graduated from Benjamin Franklin High School in East
Harlem, in the company of Joe Galiber, Senator Galiber, and a
number of other prominent New Yorkers. I find myself at this
half-century mark, thinking "How much better a city do we have?"
And wondering where so much went wrong. If you'll go back to
the newspapers then and look at the numbers, this reality just jumps
out at you. We were a city of the same size, about 150,000 more
persons then than now. The Depression was going on. Still, the city
was able to respond to what was happening. We had had half a
million people on relief in 1935. By 1943 we are down to 73,000,
of which the city reports 93 were claimed as employable.

Mayor LaGuardia, who was a wonderful man, got FDR to get
the Brooklyn Navy Yard going. We were building *Iowa* class battle-
ships at the Brooklyn Navy Yard, and soon thousands of people
were at work there. In time the city began that ascent to the
incomparable heights that followed just after the war. But we were
a city that already had a social structure . . . had an infrastructure
. . . the best subway system in the world, the finest housing stock
in the world . . . the best urban school system in the world and in
many ways, the best-behaved citizens.

Over on the West Side we made a business about Hell's Kitchen and a street warrior caste, but in truth the neighborhood was in a way idyllic. In 1943 there were exactly 44 homicides by gunshot in the city of New York. Forty-four. Last year there were 1,499.

Mayor LaGuardia was concerned about the condition of youth. He visited our school, our new school, up on 116th Street. I interviewed him and his message was this: "Take your lessons seriously but never forget how to have fun." I suppose he told that to every school newspaper reporter he ever saw, but he also told it to me. But he didn't mean too *much* fun.[4]

On January 4, 1943, in one of his radio talks, he told of a police officer, a patrolman he described as "a fellow-worker of mine," who had called in from the Yorkville section of the city, which was not far from Benjamin Franklin, and talked about young people who were hanging about "cider stubes" drinking soft drinks. The Mayor thought that we had had enough of that. He directed that they be closed down. The whole area of delinquency, while there was a lot of talk about it, scarcely existed. Police Commissioner Valentine was called in to make his annual report. He would describe with shock the paltry number of juvenile delinquency cases that made their way to the police blotter. The number of abandoned children seemed to have a sharp increase, perhaps owing to the drop in morale associated with wartime. There is a headline in the *New York Times*, "Abandoned Babies Increasing in City—74 Brought into Foundling Hospital This Year." Seventy-four.

The decline since then in our social institutions is really without equivalent. Most importantly, and absolutely essential, is the decline of family. The small platoons without which a society this large just cannot function. In 1943 the illegitimacy rate in New York City was 3 percent. Last year, it was 45 percent. This is not evenly distributed across the city. It is 80 percent in some health districts. There are parts of the city overwhelmed by the social chaos that comes in the aftermath of the inability to socialize young males. It grows worse by the year.

I have been having a correspondence with Judge Edwin Torres, who is a justice of the Supreme Court in New York State. He was raised in the *barrio*, the same area where Benjamin Franklin was in the first instance, on 108th Street. We have reason to believe we might have crossed paths in a pool room called Los Muchachos. I first began exchanging comments with him about the court system and what he can do with what he sees. He is in the Twelfth Judicial District, and he decries a civic acceptance of "the slaughter of the innocents," of persons in his courtroom, victims, who will say, "Well I suppose I shouldn't have been out at that hour of the night." Or, "It's probably my fault that I got in the way of the bullet."

This was a much poorer city 50 years ago, but a much more stable one. One that prepared you much better for the uses of prosperity when it came. I learned about Pearl Harbor from a man whose shoes I was shining on Central Park West, next to the Planetarium. On Sundays you shined uptown, around the Museum of Natural History, where people were. Saturdays were downtown. Five years later, I was an officer in the United States Navy. Benjamin Franklin High School did that for me. They thought it was routine. And it was. Joe Galiber went on to become what he is today. And others. Is that behind us? We had the finest urban housing stock in the world. Look what has happened. We could do things in no time at all. We could build the George Washington Bridge in four years and one month. And think far enough ahead to make it structurally capable of carrying a second deck when the traffic grew. [Also a third, as I learned.] Things happened quickly, easily. Mayor LaGuardia had a ticket, was flying in from Chicago, where the Mayors' headquarters were, and was going to land at Floyd Bennett Field. It was fogged-in so he landed in Newark. And he took out his ticket and said, "Mine says Floyd Bennett Field; what am I doing in a place called New Jersey?" And 24 months later, LaGuardia Airport opened. And we can do them again. But it seems to me that we dare not lose memory of what we have lost.

I was hugely encouraged by an address which Commissioner Kelly gave to the Second Annual National Symposium on Addressing Violent Crime Through Community Involvement. His address was entitled "Toward a New Intolerance." An intolerance of violence, an intolerance of the acceptance of violence. An intolerance of what Judge Torres describes as a "narcoleptic state" of acceptance: Here's what Commissioner Kelly had to say:

"There is an expectation of crime in our lives. We are in danger of becoming captive to that expectation. And to the new tolerance to criminal behavior, not only in regard to violent crime. A number of years ago there began to appear, I noticed this, I'm sure you did, in the windows of automobiles parked on the streets of American cities signs which read: 'No Radio.' Rather than express outrage, or even annoyance at the possibility of a car break-in, people tried to communicate with the potential thief in conciliatory terms. The translation of 'No Radio' is: 'Please break into someone else's car, there's nothing in mine.' These 'No Radio' signs are flags of urban surrender. They are hand-written capitulations. Instead of 'No Radio,' we need new signs that say 'No Surrender.'"[5]

▲

"Moynihan Speech Talk of Town" was the *Newsday* headline. The *Daily News* reported that Mayor Dinkins was "seething mad . . . frosty . . . really p——d off" and did not go up to shake hands. Later in the day, in a speech to a conference of black mayors, he stated, "In the good old days I wore the uniform of a U.S. Marine and I had to sit in the back [of the bus]." Which, indeed, he had done in Virginia. *Crain's New York Business* noted that "even Gov. Cuomo wagged an admonitory finger at good buddy Pat." But it wasn't quite the same this time around. The usual rabbis, ministers, and imams said the usual. But Peter Vallone, the Democratic Speaker of the City Council, countered, "If people get angry because he said he can't understand why there's not more outrage, that's a good wake-up call."

Rudolph Giuliani heard it. He said through a spokesman that the analysis "should be examined carefully and taken seriously." In time, he would state that Dinkins's response was the decisive event in the campaign. In October, in *Newsweek*, Joe Klein said Giuliani had taken "'Defining Deviancy Down' as a sacred text. He hasn't proposed any plausible solutions, but he *has* connected with the public fury." The next month, Giuliani won easily, perhaps the first assertedly conservative New York mayor of the century. Crime declined! Theory influenced practice, notably in the prosecution of minor offenses that were being redefined as acceptable behavior. He appointed a police commissioner who had read Wilson and Kelling's essay "Broken Windows: The Police and Neighborhood Safety." Small crimes ceased to be ignored; bigger crimes began to be solved. The city was safer and felt safer.

In the course of this campaign, Giuliani told a Greenwich Village crowd, "In English common law, assault is merely the act of threatening someone. Most of you are assaulted everyday on your way home from work." So was a Washington lady, Jessica Gavora, in the summer of 1995. She wrote to the *Washington Post:*

A few years ago, Sen. Daniel Patrick Moynihan (D-N.Y.) identified a syndrome with a potent message for the District. He called it "defining deviancy down," meaning that a society with rising levels of antisocial behavior copes by raising the threshold of what is considered deviant. Under this reformulation, only violent crime constitutes "real" crime—petty crime becomes merely one of the inevitable inconveniences of urban life.

As I drove home through the city one recent evening, I stopped at a traffic light and was confronted by a character straight out of the Moynihan scenario: the squeegee guy. In this case it was a woman who approached my car, unsolicited, and began washing its windshield. When I refused to "pay," she ran around to my open passenger window and gave me a few good squirts from her spray bottle. The liquid was blue, but it had a funny smell, like a public restroom.

I stopped the car, determined to make a point, and called the police. After waiting 45 minutes for the promised assistance, I came upon an officer, quite by accident, and asked for his help. As I stood talking to him, prostitutes openly plied their trade on 14th Street. A man ostensibly selling cassette tapes from a sidewalk table conducted what appeared to be a thriving drug business. The officer was polite but unhelpful. Eventually, the offending squeegee woman left her corner.

As I waited on the sidewalk for the police to come that night, I was not in search of vengeance, or even justice. I was merely waiting for a sign that Sen. Moynihan's warning had been heeded in the District—that the recipients of my tax dollars would take seriously the assault I had suffered and respond to it. My expectations were not high; a simple gesture would have done the trick.

It never came.

It remained for Charles Krauthammer in the *New Republic* to fill out the cycle. Not only have we come to consider deviant behavior normal, according to Krauthammer, but we are beginning to define a good deal of normal behavior as deviant. His particular concern as a psychiatrist is the expansion, as he sees it, of the concept of rape to include sexual activity previously seen to be acceptable if not especially admirable. Males are being defined as "rapists" who previously would have incurred no such animus. I would note that in the opposite direction, the charge of "statutory rape" has been disappearing despite evidence that pregnancy among minor females is disproportionately brought on by adult males.*

It seems clear enough that, in Mark Gerson's phrase, we are going through something of an "Orwellian nightmare" trying to retrieve old standards in what does indeed appear as a cultural conflict of large implication.

---

*In 1993, 86 percent of births to teenage girls in New York State were nonmarital, as the usage now is. Some 26,000 teenagers gave birth. There were a total of 307 indictments for statutory rape.

President Clinton addressed this issue in a news conference on June 13, 1996: "Statutory rape is still a crime in this country. The young women are victims, yet these laws are almost never enforced even in the most egregious of circumstances. It is time for them to be enforced so that older men who prey on underage women and bring children into the world they have no intention of taking responsibility for are held accountable."

— 4 —

America at Midnight?

In the course of thirty years, *The Public Interest* became skeptical, even apprehensive, about social policy. With time the citizenry overtook us. Following the 1994 elections, as one Democrat after another left the party or left the Congress, Michael Wines would write: "Unfortunately for Democrats, however, the numbers are more like digits on a thermometer, merely a way to gauge a worsening fever. The true collapse has occurred in the party's ideology, the core belief that government has a duty and the means to lift the oppressed and better the working man. It has guided the party for 60 years, and Democrats by and large still believe in it. But a deficit-hobbled government no longer has the means to deliver endless benefits. And voters, seeing the results of Democratic efforts to tame crime and eradicate poverty and its ills, are rejecting it outright." Democracy revived, but confidence was shaken all round.

The thought of a "deficit-hobbled government" would not have occurred to many in those earlier times, withal it might have been a glint in the eye of Milton Friedman, who in time would advocate policies to bring about just that. The question of "results" was different. Frederick Mosteller has observed that in the 1950s social science gathered a capacity to inform social policy. These findings, apprehensions, what you will, began to appear in the mid-1960s, just as *The Public Interest* appeared. There was trouble from the outset.

First came the Coleman Report. The Civil Rights Act of 1964 contained a section, little noticed at the time, which instructed the Commissioner of Education to carry out a survey "concerning the lack of availability of equal educational opportunities" by reason of race, religion or national origin, and to report to the President and Congress within two years. The legislative history is not clear, but it would appear the section was included in order to make the case against the dual school systems in the South when it did not yet appear that the final legislation would make such systems illegal. Coleman, then at Johns Hopkins, took on the task: perhaps the one mathematical sociologist in the nation who could have done.

Asked in the *Southern Education Report* why he was going to such a bother to prove what was obvious—that unequal schools made for unequal students—he replied, in effect, that it was obvious but not proved. Two years later, his study was ready—involving 600,000 children, in 4,000 schools, in 50 states. The findings were devastating to received understanding. The schools weren't that unequal, but in any event they didn't matter that much. Family did.

On July 1, 1966, the Commissioner issued a summary of the report. Curiously flat, as Coleman put it. If one read hard enough, long enough, the findings were there, but one had to search hard. I arranged with the editors for Coleman to write *his* summary for the fourth issue, Summer 1966, of *The Public Interest.* Nothing such had ever appeared in education literature.

Two points, then, are clear: (1) *These minority children have a serious educational deficiency at the start of school, which is obviously not a result of school;* and (2) *They have an even more serious deficiency at the end of school, which is obviously in part a result of school.*

Thus, by the criterion stated earlier—that the effectiveness of schools in creating equality of educational opportunity lies in making the conditional probabilities of success less conditional—the schools appear to fail. At the end of school, the conditional probabilities of high achievement are even *more* conditional upon racial or ethnic background than they are at the beginning of school.

There are a number of results from the survey which give further evidence on this matter. First, within each racial group, the strong relation of family economic and educational background to achievement does not diminish over the period of school, and may even increase over the elementary years. Second, most of the variation in student achievement lies within the same school, very little of it is between schools. The implication of these last two results is clear: family background differences account for much more variation in achievement than do school differences.

Even the school-to-school variation in achievement, though relatively small, is itself almost the educational backgrounds and attainments of the teachers in the school. *Per pupil expenditure, books in the library, and a host of other facilities and curricular measures show virtually no relation to achievement if the "social" environment of the school—the educational backgrounds of other students and teachers—is held constant.*

Few perhaps noticed, but at just this time Andrew Greeley and Peter Rossi published *The Education of American Catholics,* which demonstrated how extraordinarily weak was the effect of parochial school education on religious practices. When compared with the influence of family. No one liked any of this, least of all the authors. Liberals all, they would have wished nothing more than to settle once and for all that per pupil expenditure determined school achievement, and that school prayer induced a lifetime of churchgoing. But that is not what they found.

Such was the case with my investigation of the relation between employment and family structure. The work began in the most orthodox setting, the U.S. Department of Labor, to establish at some level of statistical conciseness what "everyone knew": that economic conditions determine social conditions. Whereupon, it turned out that what everyone knew was evidently not so. An enormous stir followed. The findings were denounced, rejected, seen as refuted. A period of calm followed—say a quarter century. Whereupon, a new generation came along, and the findings were accepted.

There is an uneasy parallel with Thomas Kuhn's *The Structure of Scientific Revolutions.* A new paradigm is offered; it is rejected by those holding to the established paradigm. Nothing is settled until a new generation comes along and, if it has held up, the new paradigm is accepted without further fuss. I speak of the parallel as "uneasy" for the simple reason that the social sciences are not that good, and I am not that good a social scientist. Still, it is an intriguing thought, if nothing more.

Thus, David Ellwood, in his treatise *Poor Support: Poverty in the American Family*, which appeared in 1988, in a chapter "The Transformation of America's Families," writes: "In 1965, Daniel Patrick Moynihan was one of the first to suggest that the structure of families is likely to be closely related to the fortunes of men. His then maligned and now hailed Moynihan Report suggested that high unemployment among men leads to an increase in the number of female-headed families—especially in the black community. Moynihan's thesis was dismissed as racist and sexist and received little attention until recently." Now this, from a scholar with the most generous intent, is even so entirely wrong, and equally revealing. What I had argued in the early 1960s was that a previously close relationship had suddenly seemingly vanished. To restate Wilson: "Moynihan's scissors." This thought was simply beyond the reach of the liberal imagination of that period.[1] It was left to a Republican president to break the silence.

On May 17, 1992, President George Bush gave the commencement address at the University of Notre Dame. It was a notable speech, and in due course addressed the subject an American President could no longer avoid. As I happened to be present, he included me with the consideration of an old friend.

> At the heart of the problems facing our country stands an institution under siege. That institution is the American family. Whatever form our most pressing problems may take, ultimately, all are related to the disintegration of the family.
>
> Let us look objectively at a few brief and sad facts. In comparison with other countries, the Census Bureau found that the United States has the highest divorce rate, the highest number of children involved in divorce, the highest teenage pregnancy rates, the highest abortion rates, the highest percentage of children living in a single-parent

household, and the highest percentage of violent deaths among our precious young. These are not the kind of records that we want to have as a great country.

In Philadelphia the other day, in the inner city in what they call the Hill area, I talked to a barber there, Mr. Buice, who is one of the leaders of the community there, and I said, "Do these kids come from broken families?" He said, "Sir, it's a question of babies having babies," tears coming into his eyes. We've got to do something about this. And unless we successfully reverse the breakdown of the American family, our nation is going to remain at risk.

Senator Moynihan, way back, way back, early in 1965, you gave us fair warning. You predicted with astonishing accuracy the terrible trends that would result from the breakdown of the family. And today, with respect, sir, you continue to sound the alarm. The Senator and I agree: If America is to solve her social problems, we must, first of all, restore our families.

He went on to state: "In addressing the problems associated with family breakdown, nothing is more critical than equipping each succeeding generation with a sound moral compass." Which is fair enough. But there was another matter to be attended to. The controversy had virtually closed down research in the field of family and social policy. Some university work continued, but it was scarcely encouraged. Brave names come to mind: Sara McLanahan, Larry Bumpass, Irwin Garfinkel, Peter Gottschalk, Richard Burhauser, Greg Duncan, Saul Hoffman, and others. As will be noted, Rainwater still. But the federal government would not go near the subject.

Then in his 1994 State of the Union address, President William J. Clinton had this unsettling news for the nation: "We cannot renew our country when, within a decade, more than half of our children will be born into families where there is no marriage." This would appear to be the first time an American President has mentioned the subject of illegitimacy in such a setting. Article II, Section 3 of the Constitution provides that the President "shall from time to time give to the Congress Information of the State of the Union, and to recommend to their Consideration such Measures as he shall judge necessary and expedient." The President depicted a perilous state indeed.

And just where was this "Information" obtained? The Bureau of the Census? The Bureau of Vital Statistics? The National Center for Health Statistics? Alas, no. The data derived from a chance conversation I had with the President. A year later, in *American Enterprise,* I recounted how this came about: "In 1993, John R. Fowle III, a scientist on leave to our Senate staff, analyzed trends in U.S. out-of-wedlock birth rates and found that they fit several curves, including an exponential curve which projected that the U.S. rate would reach 50 percent by the year 2004. I mentioned this, perhaps too casually, to President Clinton, who repeated it in his 1994 State of the Union Message" (see charts on page 174).

The American Enterprise Institute for Public Policy Research had chosen to devote much of an issue of its journal to "Blueprints for a New World of Welfare." It began with an article by William J. Bennett, "America at Midnight: On the 30th Anniversary of the Moynihan Report." I contributed an article on origins, "The Summer of '65." Referring again to President Clinton's address, I began:

▼

This presidential statement brought the very opposite reaction as had occurred 30 years previously. Whereas earlier there had been a huge response, much of it negative, but response withal, now there was none. I cannot imagine that the President's statement was completely ignored by the media but I know of none such.

Having examined our data, Professors Lee Rainwater and Reynolds Farley testified before the Senate Committee on Finance that by the year 2000, 40 percent of American babies would surely be born outside marriage. Now we have learned that the same worrisome circumstance of nonmarital births was taking place in Northern Europe. A curve developed by Fowle and Cynthia Rice, a Javits Fellow at the Finance Committee, shows a transformation in England and Wales nearly identical to our own (see chart on page 175).

Of note is the apparent influence in the early years of external events—in this case war and peace—after which the trend takes over and nothing affects, or appears to do, the out-of-wedlock birth rate.

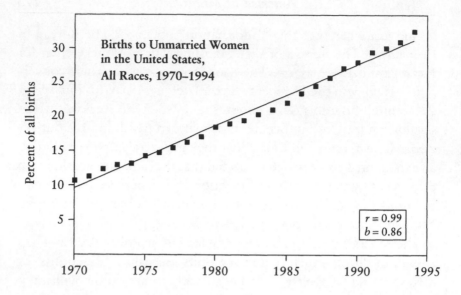

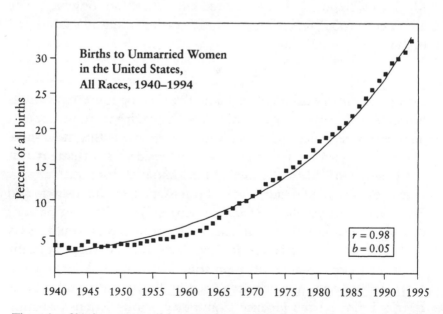

The ratio of births to unmarried women fits a straight line over the past two decades. This observation led our office to the question of the past half century. On further inquiry, the straight line from 1970 to 1994 turned out to be the upper reaches of an exponential curve going back to 1940. (The data fit an exponential regression $y = ae^{bx}$, where the constant $a = 2.59$. The correlation coefficient, r, indicates how closely a particular regression line fits the data; in both cases here we see an almost perfect fit. The slope, b, indicates how rapidly a line is rising or falling.)

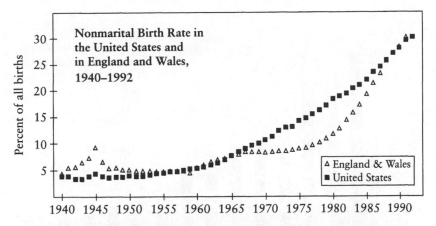

The rise of illegitimacy in England and Wales between 1940 and 1992 was nearly identical to our own. Note the apparent early influence of war and peace, after which the trend takes over and nothing appears to affect it.

We begin in 1940 with the United States and England and Wales at the "historic" 4-percent-plus-or-minus-a-bit ratio. Then war breaks out. Millions of young males leave the continental United States. The ratio goes down. Several million pass through the United Kingdom—by 1944 there were some 1.5 million American military personnel—where the ratio goes up. Whereupon things return to normal. Until the mid-1960s—when an unbroken ascent commences. In part, this growing proportion of all births coming out of wedlock may be ascribed to a decline in birth rates among married women. But that factor is not nearly sufficient to explain away this momentous change in social behavior.

This change was to be seen all across Northern Europe and Northern America (see chart on page 176). Canada trails just below the U.S. ratio, France just above. Italy and Switzerland are comparative laggards. We briefly entertained the hypothesis of distance from the Vatican as a determinant, but then we observed Japan: 1 percent born out of wedlock in 1960; 1 percent in 1990.

In his 1990 masterwork *Foundations of Social Policy,* and later in his 1992 presidential address to the American Sociological Association, James S. Coleman spoke of the "Great Transformation" of Western society in the eighteenth century, and of a similar transition

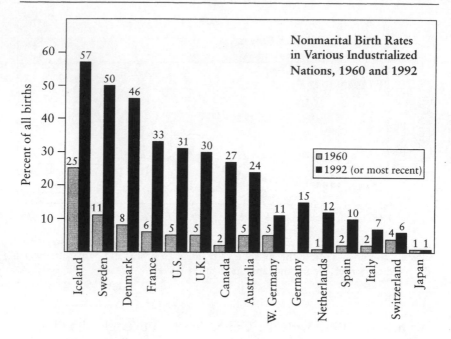

The explosion in out-of-wedlock births occurred all across Northern Europe and Northern America. The Canadian ratio is just below the U.S. ratio, the French ratio just above.

taking place today. "Modern societies are in the midst of a transformation in their very basis of organization. Brought on over the past two centuries, this is a change away from social organization derivative from the family and related primordial institutions, such as religious bodies . . . As the institutions of primordial social organization crumble it is the task of sociologists . . . to ensure that [the] reconstruction of society is not naive, but sophisticated." This is surely a political as well as a cultural and academic task. But the case that any of our political systems is equal to it is ambiguous at best.

▲

Establishing that the ratio of out-of-wedlock births has increased in neighboring countries of the North Atlantic much as our own has done has eased some of the racial taboo that has encumbered discussion until just now. (My own dear Delaware County, high in the Catskills, 98.8 percent white, notably Presbyterian, pre-eminently Scot, has seen the ratio go from 3.8 percent in 1963 to 32.2 percent in 1993.) But the federal government neither tracks the issue nor supports those who would do so. At least in any degree consonant with presidential exhortation. Thus, in July 1995, in the midst of a Senate debate on welfare, the Bureau of the Census issued its *Profile of the United States Population, 1995,* an annual source book of the widest circulation. Among the highlights, it reported: "Twenty-six percent of children born in 1994 were out-of-wedlock births." Called to account on the Senate floor, the chief of the Fertility Statistic Branch generously acknowledged that the ratio would be more like 32 percent, stating that the population profile "seriously undercounts the number of children born out of wedlock," being based on a small sample. But it is not a small matter, and the Census ought, by now, to have a better feel for the subject.

So ought scholars. Earlier I cited Ellwood's passage in *Poor Support.* I had been "one of the first" to suggest that "high unemployment among men leads to an increase in the number of female-headed families especially in the black community." That is precisely what I did *not* suggest. This had been the case but of a sudden had ceased to be. The possibility had to be entertained that something large was abroad that we did not understand. A generation later, we still do not understand. In 1992 I returned to the subject in a paper presented to the Committee on National Statistics of the Commission on Behavioral and Social Sciences and Education of the National Academy of Science.

▼

It would now be a generation since the Office of Policy Planning and Research of the United States Department of Labor, in 1965, produced "The Negro Family: The Case for National Action." It began with this proposition: "The United States is approaching a new crisis in race relations." It concluded with this policy recommendation: "The policy of the United States is to bring the Negro

American to full and equal sharing in the responsibilities and rewards of citizenship. To this end, the programs of the federal government bearing on this objective shall be designed to have the effect, directly or indirectly, of enhancing the stability and resources of the Negro American family."

I was then Assistant Secretary of Labor for Policy Planning and Research and was responsible for the document, which I also wrote. This was, even so, a collective effort, with notable contributions from Paul Barton, now at the Educational Testing Service, and Ellen Broderick. The paper reflected what we saw as a consensus among social scientists writing in that generation or the previous one. Thus, chapter 4 in the paper was entitled "The Tangle of Pathology," a term Kenneth Clark had used in his 1965 study *Dark Ghetto: Dilemmas of Social Power.* This was done without attribution, as none was needed. We had consulted at some length with Professor Clark and simply assumed that in the small circle that would read the document, the source would be routinely recognized.

The crisis we saw coming would arise from individual and group behavior in the inner city, as America's newest slums would in time be described. This behavior would be associated with the breakdown in family structure and the rise of welfare dependency. This would enforce a geographic isolation which "among Negro youth has already had the predictable outcome in a disastrous delinquency and crime rate," as well as narcotic offenses. Following John Dollard, we assumed a "caste and class" model with emphasis on adverse developments within the lower caste/lower class quadrant.

The paper became public in the aftermath of the urban riots in the Watts section of Los Angeles some three months later. On August 17, 1965, Bill Moyers, then presidential press secretary, gave out copies to a White House press corps demanding to know what was happening in California. The next day, August 18, Rowland Evans and Robert Novak recounted our findings in a column entitled "The Moynihan Report," albeit my name appears only in a furtive footnote referring to a book I'd written with Nathan Glazer a few years earlier. (Moyers had described the paper as mine, which, in terms of responsibility, it was.)

The "report" soon became available and evoked, for the most part, howling indignation and denial. Lee Rainwater, already emerging as one of the premier urban sociologists of our age, undertook to examine the ruckus along with a young colleague, William Y. Yancey. *The Moynihan Report and the Politics of Controversy* was published in 1967 by the MIT Press. It was and is a fascinating narrative—fascinating to me, at all events—which opens with this passage from Louis Wirth's Preface to Karl Mannheim's *Ideology and Utopia,* first published in 1929 and translated in 1936: "The distinctive character of social science discourse is to be sought in the fact that every assertion, no matter how objective it may be, has ramifications extending beyond the limits of science itself. Since every assertion of a 'fact' about the social world touches the interests of some individual or group, one cannot even call attention to the existence of certain 'facts' without courting the objections of those whose very *raison d'etre* in society rests upon a divergent interpretation of the 'factual' situation."

In feverish times—and those *were* feverish times—this normal disposition can become pathological in itself. One is reminded of Hannah Arendt's observation that the "superiority" of the totalitarian elites of the 1920s and 1930s in Europe lay in the ability to immediately dissolve every statement of fact into a declaration of purpose. I was everywhere attacked in this mode. And yet, one of the questions Rainwater and Yancey addressed was: Why all the fuss when what I had written was "nothing new"? The publisher featured this theme in the jacket copy: "The authors begin with two observations: first, the content of the Report was neither new nor startling; and second, it was instantly the focus of intense political debate, with presidential endorsement on one hand and important administration and academic objection on the other. How does 'nothing new' generate such heat?"

Just recently, I spoke with Professor Rainwater and he agreed that by "nothing new" they were referring to the standard statistics on AFDC caseloads and such like that I had cited. If no one else knew of them, he and his fellow researchers in the Pruitt-Igoe housing project in St. Louis knew them all too well. Rainwater agreed, however, that very soon after the report appeared "something happened." The indicators of difficulty swooped upwards. Thus, of the African American children born from 1967 to 1969, which is to say just after the report appeared, some 72 percent were recipients of AFDC benefits before reaching age 18. This is a devastating proportion if one considers that a child on AFDC is effectively a pauper. Family possessions are capped as low as $1,500. It would be helpful to know what the incidence of welfare dependency had been with earlier cohorts, but it cannot be anything such as we began to experience in the mid-to-late-1960s.

It is perhaps time I set down on paper just what we were getting at, or thought we were getting at, in the so-called Moynihan Report. The position of Assistant Secretary of Labor for Policy Planning and Research was new, part of the style of governing of the New Frontier. I had a small but exceptionally able staff, no more than half a dozen persons in all. But I also had supervision, nominal as it might be, of the Bureau of Labor Statistics, then as now an elite corps of American government statisticians, and wholly supportive of our fledgling enterprise.

In 1963 I had set about trying to develop correlations between economic data and indicators of social dysfunction. We began to find strong correlations between "manpower" data, as we would have said at that time, and family structures indexes of various kinds. Most striking was the relationship between the nonwhite male unemployment rate and the number of AFDC cases opened. Between 1948 (when our unemployment data series began) and 1961, we found a correlation of .91. Whereupon the correlation, having already weakened, went negative. The unemployment rate went down, the number of new AFDC cases went up. James Q. Wilson has called this split "Moynihan's scissors." As I later showed in a paper in the *Annals of the American Academy of Political and Social Science*,[2] the "scissors" appears in all manner of series relating unemployment data with various measures of marital arrangements and also with various conditions associated with poverty.

In 1984, twenty years later, William Julius Wilson and Kathryn Neckerman picked up those "scissors" and began to puzzle anew over the subject. In 1986 they published an analysis which showed that the crossover disappears when the number of AFDC cases is charted against the nonwhite male labor force *nonparticipation* rate. This and other work has led Wilson to fruitful insights into the role of male employment and earnings in the central city, issues which were at the heart of our research in the Department of Labor a generation ago. Rainwater's surmise that soon after the report appeared "something happened" needs to be revised. Whatever the something was *had already happened*. Our "lab" picked this up. No one understood it at the time; few since. But even so, we did it, and it speaks to the potential of quantitative analysis in social policy.

But then, of course, we ask just what was it that "happened"? I did not know then; I do not know now. After a point, we began to realize that illegitimacy ratios for whites had also begun to change at this time. In 1963, the last year for which we had data, the ratio was 3.0 percent for whites; 23.5 percent for nonwhites. Nearly 30 years later, in 1992, it was 22.5 and 58.2 percent, respectively. More recently, we learn that something such is happening abroad, and, indeed, in Canada to our north. But all this was in the future. All I had in 1965 was the scissors. Something was happening.

You would have needed to know a lot more statistics than I did or do to feel comfortable in telling the President of the United States that his nation was "approaching a new crisis in race relations." And yet I knew other things. I knew something of cities, for example. These other "things" reinforced the data. And so I bet. That is not a bad thing for government to do in moderation. I felt secure in doing so because the nation was then in a period of almost triumphalist self-congratulation at having presumptively resolved the ancient curse of caste barriers in American society. I saw class emerging as a surrogate—a convenient and comprehensible surrogate—for caste suspicion and fear.

I believe it is fair to say that just about everything I thought might happen did, in fact, happen. That "new crisis in race relations" has come upon us. It is everywhere in the symbolism of our politics just now. Consider President Bush's 1992 State of the Union address. As we learned in *Roll Call* of February 3, out in Arlington Heights, Illinois, Republican strategists assembled a focus group with hand-held Perception Analyzers, each with a dial hooked up to a computer. Viewers were told to turn up to 100 or down to 0 as they approved or disapproved parts of the speech. The address wasn't that much of a hit. The part about "The Cold War didn't end. It was won" left the focus group, well, cold. There were, however, two big scores. "This government is too big and spends too much" came in at 94. With "Welfare was never meant to be a lifestyle . . . passed from generation to generation like a legacy," President Bush hit 91. Had the President's speechwriters combined the themes in one sentence, "This Government is too big and spends too much on welfare," I dare to think the Perception Analyzers might have gone into meltdown.

Here is the full passage, as given out by the White House: "Ask American parents what they dislike about how things are in our country, and chances are good that pretty soon they'll get to welfare. Americans are the most generous people on earth. But we have to go back to the insight of Franklin Roosevelt who, when he spoke of what became the welfare program, warned that it must not become 'a narcotic' and a 'subtle destroyer' of the spirit. Welfare was never meant to be a lifestyle; it was never meant to be a habit; it was never supposed to be passed from generation to generation like a legacy. It's time to replace the assumptions of the welfare state, and help reform the welfare system."

There are two problems of fact here. The first has to do with the citations of President Roosevelt. These were from President Roosevelt's 1935 State of the Union Address. He was not talking about welfare, as we now understand the term, which is to say, aid to single-parent families, AFDC, under Title IV of the Social Security Act. He was talking about home relief, as it was generally termed, for the unemployed. He was calling for a public works program at a time when the unemployment rate was probably hovering at about one-quarter of the predominantly male workforce. As for the AFDC program, it did not exist. The Social Security Act had not yet been introduced in Congress. So much for the rigor with which American political speech now addresses this most painful and divisive issue.

The second problem is with the implied data. President Bush implied that "welfare" is somehow "passed from generation to generation like a legacy." The President did not outright declare this to be the case, but neither did he go out of his way to complexify matters by telling us that there are *no such data*. Or rather, such data as there are do not resolve the question.

In the most recent review (1990) of the literature on intergenerational welfare transmission, Robert Moffitt of Brown University finds that earlier studies which support the inference simply cannot be relied on. "Unfortunately, the reduced-form nature of most of the studies renders their findings essentially non-informative on the main issue at hand, which is whether AFDC receipt 'causes' later AFDC receipt or other behaviors. Since most studies do not attempt to control in any systematic fashion for the many omitted variables that may be responsible for the observed correlation—the human capital characteristics of the parental family, to name the most obvious—the interpretation of the observed correlations is highly ambiguous."[3]

I don't wish to be understood as rejecting the thesis. I surely do not want to get caught up with the Nothing Causes Anything school of data analysis. But can we not regret the tone? Consider those terms: lifestyle, habit, legacy. Governor Mario Cuomo of New York grew indignant when he discussed the issue in an address at the Kennedy School at Harvard University on February 12, 1992. "Making welfare the 'Willie Horton' of the '92 campaign would also appeal to and feed a sad, corrosive instinct for negativism and divisiveness that challenges this exquisitely balanced democracy in a fundamental way."

Not ten weeks earlier, Arkansas Governor Bill Clinton, now a candidate for the Democratic presidential nomination, spoke of the same subject at Georgetown University, his alma mater, also, of course, in Washington, D.C. This was billed as a major address, and it was. Moving from Abraham Lincoln and the Union to Franklin D. Roosevelt and the New Deal, skipping over intervening Democrats, Mr. Clinton came to the proposition of forging "a new covenant that will repair the damaged bond between the people and their government, restore our basic values embedded in the idea that a country has the responsibility to help people get ahead, but that citizens have not only the right, but the *responsibility,* to rise as far and as fast as their talents and determination can take them" [my emphasis]. This most emphatically extended to the matter of welfare. "The new covenant can break the cycle of welfare. Welfare should be a second chance, not a way of life. In my administration we're going to put an end to welfare as we have come to know it. I want to erase the stigma of welfare for good by restoring a simple, dignified principle: No one who can work can stay on welfare forever. We'll still help people to help themselves, and those who need education and training and child care and medical coverage for their kids—they'll get it. We'll give them all the help they need, and we'll keep them on public assistance for up to two years. But after that, people who are able to work, they'll have to go to work either in the private sector or through a community service job. No more permanent dependence on welfare as a way of life. We can then restore welfare for what it was always meant to be, a way of temporarily helping people who have fallen on hard times."

How are we to distinguish between these two pronouncements? The Republican President declares that "welfare was never meant to be a lifestyle." The Democratic challenger-to-be, and President-to-be, declares, "Welfare should be a second chance, not a way of life." Far more important, Clinton establishes a whole new agenda: time limits. "We'll keep them on public assistance for up to two years." "No more permanent dependence on welfare as a way of life." No previous Republican, much less Democratic President, had ever made any such proposal. Nor had Bush.

The concept originated with Ellwood's *Poor Support,* but Ellwood contemplates vastly greater federal outlays to provide for the transition from welfare to work, as the encapsulation went. It is fair, is it not, to suppose that the public heard the time limits part, not the extra welfare expenditure part? Not least that the latter was not mentioned, much less was a number attached.

And so we have come to the point where welfare, not as a consequence of unemployment but rather a baffling form of dependency which may be its *own* consequence, is a central issue of national politics. And yet at this time there were no national statistics that would tell us more about the subject. There is not even the mode of speculative analysis that arose in late nineteenth-century Britain in early attempts to account for "the business cycle." Let there be no doubt as to why this is so. Mannheim. The groups that had to be most concerned were fearful of what might be learned, and effectively suppressed any effort at systematic inquiry. In part, or in my view, this is because such information has been seen as threatening, even politically motivated. At least in part this perception arose in the aftermath of the outcry over our 1965 policy paper.

Contrast this with the history of labor statistics. From the first—the Bureau of Labor Statistics goes back to 1884, long before the establishment of a Department of Labor—labor organizations petitioned government, as an impartial observer, to compile statistics on wages and hours and conditions of work. The City Workers Family Budget was an early instance of government setting the parameters of a "living wage." It took a long time to develop the statistical techniques that would give us an unemployment rate. But they were developed first in the Works Progress Administration during the New Deal; our first survey dates from 1940. In 1948 our present series was begun and it continues to this day, continuously elaborated and improved.

An interest not unlike that expressed by the early labor movement was spelled out at this time by William Raspberry in the *Washington Post*. His subject was the seeming change in generational leadership in the National Association for the Advancement of Colored People. He suggested a change in the "direction" (his emphasis) of this renowned organization.

> Our children, particularly those with the bad luck to be born to poor parents, are too likely to become school dropouts, adolescent parents, drug peddlers or users, or criminals. The leading cause of death of young black men is not the Klan but young black men themselves. Our neighborhoods are terrorized not by whitesheeted nightriders but by drive-by gunmen who look like our own children.
>
> By announcing in February his intention to retire at the end of the

year, Ben Hooks has given black America's flagship organization the opportunity to set new priorities, to chart a new course. And what might the new direction be? For me, the answer is easy: Our children and our economic development. We are losing our children—our legacy and our future—and the pressing need is to rescue them and put them to useful work. It isn't necessary that Hooks's successor be someone who's figured out precisely how to accomplish that rescue. The fact is that Hooks and his predecessors took such good care of the organization's image and reputation that it would take only an invitation from the NAACP to assemble the best minds in black America to work out a rescue and economic development plan.

And not just black America. Top-flight sociologists of all colors would say yes to such an invitation. Major universities—historically black or not—would join in undertaking the necessary research. Philanthropists or philanthropic foundations would help with the funding if money turned out to be the critical barrier to what must be done. Not even a conservative administration could look the other way.

Raspberry's summons reminds us that something just as he described did happen back in 1965. The American Academy of Arts and Sciences, under the leadership of Stephen R. Graubard, had been thinking of a special issue of *Daedalus* directed to these issues. In May of 1965 a planning conference was held which attracted the widest participation. That fall, the first of two issues of *Daedalus* appeared, entitled "The Negro American." In the interval, in June, President Lyndon B. Johnson had given his address at Howard University in which he set out the themes of the report on "The Negro Family." I had written the first draft of the Howard address, the whole enterprise being carried off in a matter of days. It was now proposed that the President might write an introduction to the *Daedalus* volumes. I put this to Harry C. McPherson, Jr., counsel to the President. He much agreed, and so I prepared a first draft of this further presidential pronouncement. Not unexpectedly the draft, as edited, refers back to the Howard address.

Nothing is of greater significance to the welfare and vitality of this nation than the movement to secure equal rights for Negro Americans. This Administration is dedicated to that movement. It is also dedicated to helping Negro Americans grasp the opportunities that equal rights make possible. Much has been done—within government and without—to secure equal rights. Much remains to be done if a people enslaved by centuries of bigotry and want are to realize the opportunities of American life.

In June 1965 I spoke to the graduating class of Howard University about the condition of most Negroes in America. Before me were those for whom the future was illuminated with hope. My thoughts were of the others—those for whom equality is now but an abstraction. I said, "You do not take a person who for years has been hobbled by chains and liberate him, bring him up to the starting line of a race, and say, 'You are free to compete with all the others,' and still just believe that you have been completely fair." Thus it is not enough to open the gates of opportunity. All our citizens must have the ability to walk through those gates. This is the next and more profound stage of the battle for civil rights . . . the task is to give 20 million Negroes the same choice as every other American to learn and work and share in society, to develop their abilities—physical, mental, and spiritual—and to pursue their individual happiness.

No one who understands the complexity of this task is likely to promote simple means by which it may be accomplished. The papers that follow testify to the inter-locking effects of deprivation—in education, in housing, in employment, in citizenship, in the entire range of human endeavor by which personality is formed. It will not be enough to provide better schools for Negro children, to inspire them to excel in their studies, if there are no decent jobs waiting for them after graduation. It will not be enough to open up job opportunities, if the Negro must remain trapped in a jungle of tenements and shanties. If we are to have peace at home, if we are to speak with one honest voice in the world—indeed, if our country is to live with its conscience—we must affect every dimension of the Negro's life for the better.

We have begun to do that—sometimes haltingly and in great trepidation, sometimes boldly and with a high heart. The will of government and of the people has been committed to resolving the long, bitter trial of the Negro American in the only way that was ever really possible: by including him in our society. Some of these papers instruct us in the means by which that may be done. They are invaluable source materials for the White House Conference, which I have called "To Fulfill These Rights." For this contribution by the

American Academy of Arts and Sciences, the participants in that conference—and all those who work for a just society—are profoundly grateful.

In his Introduction to the published Academy papers, Talcott Parsons wrote: "The present project constitutes the most comprehensive survey of the problems and status of the Negro in American society since *An American Dilemma* written by Gunnar Myrdal and his associates nearly a generation ago." In *his* Introduction, Kenneth Clark was more cautious. Myrdal had put forward propositions which provided "a substantive basis for optimism for the resolution of the American racial dilemma." But we would see.

Supposing the optimism and commitment of that moment had continued. Supposing the federal government had undertaken a huge commitment of resources along lines indicated by scholarly inquiry. Would anything different have happened? Which is to say, would it have made any difference? The plain answer is that we do not know. There is no way of knowing; for we did not try.

The White House Conference "To Fulfill These Rights" met in Washington in June 1966. Martin Luther King, Jr., attended briefly. He thanked me for "your report" but said little in public.[4] The spirit of the occasion was captured by the statement of Berl Bernhard, a member of the White House staff who was serving as executive director of the Conference. In serious fun, as you might say, he told the opening session, "I want you to know that I have been reliably informed that no such person as Daniel Patrick Moynihan exists." In a paper especially prepared for the occasion, the U.S. Children's Bureau reliably informed the Conference that the Negro family was in fine shape and not to worry. The Conference agreed. Whereupon the Johnson administration stopped worrying, and an era pretty much came to a close.

Thus endeth that tale. It all happened a generation ago. Curiously, Rainwater and I are just about the only participants or observers who are still engaged with the subject. It was an event of the kind that, if I read history at all correctly, usually takes a half century or more to get over. Still, we may be ready sooner than that. Not least because the instability in the "dark ghettos" that we picked up on our radar now has spread to the majority community. Family stability and dependency are much more general issues, even if American politics is just now focusing on minorities.

We are clearly entering a period when state governments are going to be making changes in welfare programs designed to bring about changes in the behavior of welfare recipients. The Learnfare program in Wisconsin denies benefits for a minor who does not attend school. In New Jersey there is Wedfare, a program designed to encourage marriage, along with the denial of benefits to additional out-of-wedlock children. From Maine, literally, to California, this new enthusiasm for state intervention is sweeping the country. Will much of it work? We don't know, but I would hope we would try to keep track. Lest we forget.

Something like a century ago, William Graham Sumner pronounced the great wisdom of American conservatives: Stateways do not change Folkways. Are we now to understand otherwise? We shall see, but at all events, may we not resolve to start keeping track of what is happening? Statistics *do* change Stateways, whatever else happens. That is what the word means!

▲

Postscript

In the closing hours of my time as Chairman of Finance we enacted the Welfare Indicators Act of 1994 providing for an Annual Welfare Indicators Report, with the accompanying statement:

> The Congress hereby declares that
> (1) it is the policy and responsibility of the Federal Government to reduce the rate at which and the degree to which families depend on income from welfare programs and the duration of welfare receipt, consistent with other essential national goals;
> (2) it is the policy of the United States to strengthen families, to ensure that children grow up in families that are economically self-sufficient and that the life prospects of children are improved, and to underscore the responsibility of parents to support their children.

I had introduced the bill on the first legislative day of the 103rd Congress, January 21, 1993, making specific references to the Employment Act of 1946 and the annual Economic Report of the President that have since become the central assessment of our considerable progress in promoting "maximum employment, production, and purchasing power," as the statute—finally, after endless preface—provided. The President signed the bill without comment on October 31, 1994. In April 1996 he appointed four distinguished persons as members of an Advisory Board. The Senate and then the House followed. It may be an institution will develop here. It is needed, but the need is somehow not felt.

— 5 —

Drug Wars

James Q. Wilson has commented that the "liberal audience" of the 1960s rather approved of the urban violence of that period and certainly saw it as a stimulus to desirable social change. There was not much of this left by the 1990s; certainly not much left of the illusion that violence or the threat of violence does wonders for the social system.

Sam Roberts in the *New York Times*, reporting on my talk at the Association for a Better New York in April 1993 (see Chapter 3), noted that at the same time I was speaking, Bill Bradley was in Paterson, New Jersey, "gauging the depths of despair and the grounds for hope" in that ruined city in particular, and urban America in general. "I've gotten a lot of personal stories," he said, "that confirm the basic three problems of violence, joblessness and family disintegration." But the violence now was different. The visible urban violence of the 1960s was seen as something new, a form of minority protest not previously encountered; but in truth, it followed a well enough understood model.

Witness Mark A. R. Kleiman of the Kennedy School of Government on "the logical structure of rioting, whether the 'topic' of the riot is race, religion, famine, politics, or football." "It is surprising that many persons who would not find the material-plus-psychic rewards of breaking a shop window and stealing the contents an adequate inducement to endure the level of enforcement risk ordinarily associated with commercial burglary can be induced to participate in such activities once many others are doing so and thus competing for a limited supply of enforcement attention."

Riots run their course and order returns, especially when the shop windows are boarded up and the merchants depart. To the dismay of the "liberal audience," Wilson's colleague and collaborator Edward C. Banfield described the pattern in an essay, "Rioting Mostly for Fun and Profit." When the profit went out of it, the rioting stopped. It was, in any event, aversive behavior; not fun for long.

But now a different mode of violence descended on the cities. It began as a heroin epidemic in the mid-1960s. The social science literature uses that term, epidemic; for clearly the outbreaks in large populations exposed people to agents capable of doing injury to individual health and in a setting in which the agents become, effectively, contagious. The heroin epidemic of the 1960s subsides, only to be followed by the human immunodeficiency virus/acquired immune deficiency syndrome (HIV/AIDS) epidemic and an epidemic of crack cocaine.

New York City was an epicenter in both these latter instances. In 1986 a New York City detective, Charles Bennett, remarked to me that men were standing on street corners, gesturing with a raised right arm. A few months later he reported that men were snapping a whip, selling something called "crack." A mutant had arrived from the Caribbean of deadly potency. Within a year, "crack babies" had appeared in hospitals across the land, but again, most painfully in New York.

There is now some social science research in this field, much of it using economic models and econometric techniques. A paper in the *Annals of the American Academy of Political and Social Science* begins, "By several measures, the supply of heroin to the U.S. market has been increasing over the past several years, after more than a decade of relative stability. The frequency of large-scale seizures has risen substantially, and the sizes of individual seizures continue to set records. Wholesale (kilogram-level) prices are substantially below those of the early 1980s. Retail-level purity has soared; levels higher than 40 percent are now routine in many large urban markets. The average retail price per pure milligram for 1990 in the largest market, New York City, was estimated to be barely over $1, a figure comparable, in inflation-adjusted terms, to the price that prevailed at the beginning of the last great heroin epidemic, in the mid-1960s."[1] "Street ethnography" has developed. The paper suggested "a pilot study of a sample of young adults from high-HIV seroprevalence census tracts in New York City." A distinctive body of national statistics has been developed.

But to little avail. There are discernible rhythms in drug epidemiology. They appear to burn themselves out as the initial enthusiasts succumb to the effects of the drug, or to lateral afflictions (HIV/AIDS, in the case of the 1960s heroin cohort), or disappear into prison. Their behavior has become aversive; fewer recruits are attracted, and the episode subsides. No thanks, or little thanks, to the federal government, and here is the point. In most areas of social policy there is a legitimate question as to whether the federal government needs to be involved, or should be involved. Not so with drug abuse. The problem of drug abuse in the United States today—which is to say, the use of illicit drugs—is the direct, unambiguous consequence of federal law prohibiting their licit use. Prior to 1914 and the enactment of the Harrison Narcotics Act, heroin and cocaine were legal drugs, manufactured by reputable pharmaceutical firms, available without prescription. Heroin and Aspirin, copyrighted brand names, were introduced in the 1890s by the Bayer pharmaceutical firm, the former as a cough medicine. This government decision remains unexamined within a federal establishment that is equally indifferent to its epic failure.

As assistant to the President for urban affairs, I became involved with "the great heroin epidemic" of the 1960s. It is now largely forgotten, but it was terrifying at the time; that is to say, the crime associated with heroin use was terrifying. I attest that early in 1969 at a meeting of civic leaders in a boardroom of a bank across Pennsylvania Avenue from the White House—more precisely, the Treasury—I was asked to ask the President to garrison the capital.

Bring in the military! I replied that this could not be done but that we *could* break "the French connection." Which *was* done. This may have marginally contained the epidemic, but only marginally. It may even have made matters worse.

In the spring of 1993 I was invited to give the inaugural Norman E. Zinberg lecture at the John F. Kennedy School of Government. Zinberg had taught me all that I knew of the subject of drugs, even if we did not thereafter always agree. I called the lecture "Iatrogenic Government." The term is defined in the *American Heritage Dictionary* as "induced in a patient by a physician's activity, manner, or therapy. Used especially as an infection or other complication of treatment." It is from the Greek *iatros* for physician. Those who are concerned that government do good need to attend when government does bad. So ought professions, I contended: in this case the medical profession.[2]

▼

Writing in the *New England Journal of Medicine* in 1983, Armand M. Nicholi of the Department of Psychiatry at Massachusetts General Hospital and the Harvard Medical School commented: "When future historians study American culture, they may be most perplexed by the explosive increase in the nonmedical use of drugs that occurred during the seventh and eighth decades of this century. This widespread increase in the illicit use of psychoactive drugs began in the early 1960s, primarily in colleges and universities, during an era of unprecedented campus disorder and social upheaval. For the next 10 years studies were focused on patterns of drug use among college students—the late-adolescent and young-adult age groups. Perhaps because of the strong influence youth exerts in establishing the tone of our culture with respect to music, dress, and lifestyle, the nonmedical use of drugs spread rapidly to other age groups, and during the 1970s it reached epidemic proportions."

When these future historians set to work, one matter need not perplex them. If they should ask—and let us hope they do—did anyone in the medical profession, observing the onset of this epidemic, set out in a scientific manner to try to understand what was happening and to develop an appropriate medical response, the answer will be that there was one such person, Norman Zinberg, professor of psychiatry at the Harvard Medical School. He was, in the most profound sense, a healer, a life-enhancing man.

Although Zinberg's major work, *Drug, Set, and Setting,* was not published until 1984, his papers and lectures were well and widely known by the mid-1960s. At that time I was director of the Joint Center for Urban Studies of MIT and Harvard. We were neighbors and became friends, and I, in a legitimate sense, became his pupil. In 1969 I went to Washington as an adviser on urban affairs to President Nixon. The urban crisis, as it was known at that time, was very much a drug crisis, chiefly entailing heroin. Early on it fell to me to try to fashion a response by the federal government. This was perhaps the first time the federal government had attempted to establish a relationship between social policy and drug policy. This is also the subject of the final chapter in *Drug, Set, and Setting.*

My first foray into the field came in August 1969, after the President had sent to Congress a considerable legislative program that addressed urban matters. The welfare system was to be replaced by a guaranteed income, known as the Family Assistance Plan. The federal government would share its revenue with state and city governments. A new job training program was to begin. Now was the time for drugs. At that time most of the heroin consumed in the United States was coming in from Marseilles, where it was refined from Turkish opium. I set out for those countries to tell their officials and our own embassies (which seem never to have heard of the issue) that the United States could not accept "the French connection."

After a scattering of heroin-related deaths among French youths during this period, *Le Monde* published an article ascribing drug addiction to broken homes, and the National Assembly had a day-long debate on the subject. The French took us seriously, and before long Marseilles was clean, as the argot has it. Having reached tentative agreements in Turkey also, I found myself in a helicopter flying up to Camp David to report on this seeming success. The only other passenger was George P. Shultz, who was busy with official-looking papers. Even so, I related our triumph. He looked up. "Good," said he, and returned to his tables and charts. "No, really," said I, "this is a *big* event." My cabinet colleague looked up once more, restated his perfunctory "Good," and once more returned to his paperwork. Crestfallen, I pondered, then said, "I suppose you think that so long as there is a demand, there will continue to be a supply." Shultz, sometime professor of economics at the University of Chicago, looked up with an air of genuine interest. "You know," he said, "there's hope for you yet!"

As indeed there was: both for me individually and for the federal government as it once again engaged itself with the matter of drugs. Early in December 1969 a governors' conference was convened to address the issue. At a luncheon at the Department of State I was the principal speaker. I do not suggest that my views were held uniformly throughout the administration, but there I was, Counselor to the President, telling the governors what *I* thought—a point of view that they had reason to believe was close to what others like me thought. The truth in either event is that we were mostly asserting what we did not know and would need to learn.

I called my address "The Whiskey Culture and the Drug Culture." I had a simple theme:

> Drug use—and abuse—represents simply one more instance of the impact of technology on society. This is the central experience of modern society. At one or two removes, most of the ills we suffer are the consequences of technology. That is to say, the *bad* results that accompany the *good* ones—good results which led to the adoption of the technology in the first place. A commonplace observation, but truly an important one, and one which will I think be recognized by governors who struggle daily with waters polluted by technology, underprivileged populations displaced by technology, drivers and pedestrians maimed by technology, cities choked with technology, and air fouled by it. Not to mention urban populations near to terrorized by crime brought about by the need to obtain money to purchase certain drugs which are yet another product of technology. From nuclear weapons to cyclamates, this is what is so unsettling about modern life. The effort to master and somehow transcend technology is central to the concerns of the great philosophical historians and sociologists of the age, men such as Jacques Ellul,

Lewis Mumford, David Riesman, Michael Young. But for the moment one of the tasks of government is to keep technology from rending the fabric of society. That is what this conference is about, the specifics of which I would like now to consider.

I discussed in some detail the extraordinary destructiveness of distilled alcohol when it first became readily available in the eighteenth century as a combined result of the invention of distillation and an agricultural revolution that produced a relative abundance of grain. The species had no experience with an intoxicant of this power. In his fine study *Town Planning in London: The Eighteenth and Nineteenth Centuries* Donald J. Olsen identified the onset of distilled spirits as a form of social pathology: "Cheap gin helped to keep the population of London stable from 1700 to 1750."

In truth, the numbers are astonishing. M. C. Bauer estimated the population in 1700 to have been 674,000 and 50 years later to be no more than 676,000. By contrast the population of London tripled in the first half of the *following* century, going from 864,845 in the census of 1801 to 2,363,236 in 1851. Ought we not to think that a form of social learning was taking place—at a time of robust laissez-faire government—and that the population was coming to terms with this new product of technology?

W. J. Rorabaugh's *The Alcoholic Republic: An American Tradition* would not appear for another decade, but enough of the American experience was available to provide some useful generalizations. The first law enacted by the first Congress established the oath of office required by Article VI of the Constitution. To wit: "I, A.B., do solemnly swear or affirm (as the case may be) that I will support the Constitution of the United States." The second law imposed a ten-cents-per-gallon tariff on Jamaican rum—to encourage consumption of American whiskey. This was a general tariff bill, but it is noteworthy that each of the first seven items concern drink.

On all distilled spirits of Jamaica proof, imported from any kingdom or country whatsoever, per gallon, ten cents.
On all other distilled spirits, per gallon, eight cents.

> On molasses, per gallon, two and a half cents.
>
> On Madeira wine, per gallon, eighteen cents.
>
> On all other wines, per gallon, ten cents.
>
> On every gallon of beer, ale or porter in casks, five cents.
>
> On all cider, beer, ale or porter in bottles, per dozen, twenty cents.

(Molasses, in the current jargon, is a precursor basis of rum.) Distilled spirits in early America appeared as a font of national unity, easy money, manly strength, and all-round good cheer. It was at first irresistible. It felt good and was thought to be good for you. The more the better. It became routine to drink whiskey at breakfast—in the case of Harry Truman, just before—and to go on drinking all day. (Laborers digging the Erie Canal were allotted a quart of Monongahela whiskey a day, issued in eight four-ounce portions commencing at six o'clock in the morning.) Only slowly did it sink in that such a regimen was ruinous to health and a risk to society. When it did, society responded.

Apart only from the movement to abolish slavery, the most popular and influential social movement of nineteenth-century America concerned the effort to limit or indeed prohibit the use of alcohol. The former brought about three amendments to the Constitution; the latter, two. In *Thinking about Crime* (1983), James Q. Wilson estimates that by the end of the nineteenth century the temperance movement had reduced per capital alcohol consumption by two-thirds. Alcohol abuse continues to be a major health problem—and a murderous one in combination with that other technological wonder, the automobile. But at least the dangers of alcohol are far better understood than in the past.

The use of what might be termed high-proof drugs appears roughly a century later than the use of high-proof alcoholic drink. Just as beer and wine are naturally fermented products of grain and grapes, narcotics and stimulants appear in nature as attributes of the poppy and coca plant. The crucial technological event here was the development of organic chemistry in German universities in the middle of the nineteenth century.

First, morphine was produced from opium. In combination with the hypodermic needle, morphine was widely used in Civil War medicine, giving rise to a form of addiction that was popularly called soldier's disease. (Morphine was also used in childbirth and, when prolonged, led to similar forms of addiction.) A generation later, heroin, a "distillation" of morphine, was developed by the Bayer Pharmaceutical firm in Germany. (Employees on whom it was tested found that it made them feel *heroisch*—hence, its trade name.) It appears to have been thought useful as a treatment for morphine addiction.

In like manner, cocaine, the active ingredient of the coca leaf, was isolated before 1880. Its early use was medical, again in association with the hypodermic needle. Freud used it to treat a friend suffering from morphine addiction. As he increased the doses, he induced an episode of cocaine psychosis and, as reported by Oakley Stern Ray in *Drugs, Society, and Human Behavior* (1978), "thereafter was bitterly against drugs." On the other hand, in 1885 the Parke-Davis Pharmaceutical Company asserted that cocaine "can supply the place of food, make the coward brave, and the silent eloquent" and declared it a "wonder drug."[3]

Along with alcohol, these substances came under federal prohibition early in this century. Alcohol prohibition was a convulsive event that, among other things, led to the creation of a criminal underworld of exceptional influence and durability. There was always a certain amount of drug trafficking within this underworld, and this continued at modest levels until the epidemic outbreak of heroin use in the 1960s. It thereupon provided the model on which the large-scale import and distribution of drugs commenced.

Rereading my little-noticed and long-forgotten 1969 governors' conference address is rewarding—to me, at any rate—in the way it reveals the incompatibilities that beset anyone who tries, however tentatively, to derive drug policy from drug research, and for that matter social science. Here I would invoke the wonderfully allusive remark of Rudolph Virchow, the eminent nineteenth-century pathologist. "Medicine," he said, "is a social science, and politics is nothing but medicine on a grand scale." As I developed first this argument, then that analogy, I kept running up against the fact that our society has made a political choice between two almost equally undesirable outcomes. As Kleiman spells out in his fine new study *Against Excess: Drug Policy for Results,* in dealing with drugs we are required to choose between a crime problem and a public health problem. In choosing to prohibit drugs, we choose to have a more or less localized—but ultimately devastating—crime problem rather than a general health problem.

Kleiman writes: "The case for heroin prohibition is simply that a number, probably a large number, of persons who now lead reasonably satisfying, dignified, and useful lives would, if heroin were legal, find themselves leading, and regretting, lives with a narrowed range of satisfactions, impaired dignity and self-command, and reduced usefulness to their families, friends, neighbors, coworkers, and fellow citizens. To prevent this we pay a price in a form of increased misery for those who become heavy heroin users despite prohibition, and increased external costs: the spread of disease, user crime, black-market crime, neighborhood disruption from open dealing, and the expenditure of law enforcement resources that could instead be used to suppress predatory crime."

While I surely opposed legalization, or decriminalization, of drugs, I took the technological ascent seriously. In his *Letters from an American Farmer,* published in 1782, J. Hector St. John de Crèvecoeur notes his surprise at a "singular custom" among the good, and presumably Quaker, ladies of Nantucket: "They have adopted these many years, the Asiatic custom of taking a dose of opium every morning . . . This is much more prevalent among the women than the men." But opium is one thing; heroin another. My 1969 address concluded: "There are those who will and do propose a social policy of complete and free availability of almost all chemical substances that are or can be ingested in one form or another. In its most popular form today, this takes the form of advocating the free use of cannabis, and somewhat less frequently, the free, or mildly regulated, use of heroin. I believe this to be a very mistaken position. It is a form of hiding behind the principle of individual freedom to avoid the reality of individual danger and individual harm. It is almost a form of indifference to pain: and I say that in full knowledge of the generosity of spirit and the effort to be understanding that often motivates such proposals. Our object must be higher. We must learn to use fewer drugs, not more. The question of course is how?"

That was almost a quarter century ago; we were just entering our current federal preoccupation with illicit drugs—or rather, with drugs the federal government has declared illicit. I had put it to the governors: "We have had drug prohibition for 55 years now. And here we are at this conference. Not exactly a record of success. What are we to learn? The first thing, obviously, is that this is not an easy problem. Men as good as us or better have struggled, and by all outward indices, they have failed." There was not going to be any cheap way out of this. Technology has unleashed an enormous social agent that threatened us in the most serious way. This problem now involves "the structure of authority and governmental legitimacy in America." Are the laws obeyed? Does the state maintain a monopoly on violence? If not, what kind of state have we?

This is where Norman Zinberg entered my calculations. Here is one last passage from the State Department address. "Dr. Norman Zinberg has, it seems to me, most helpfully described the drug phenomenon in terms of a triangle of 'Drug, Set, and Setting.' That is to say, we need to know so much more about the interaction of a particular chemical, a particular individual, and the social (or antisocial) context in which the two come together. This is very like the epidemiological triad, and deserves the most careful attention and serious research. Until very recently most drug users have been treated in terms of medical or criminal categories. Drug users were treated as deviants. Benignly so in the case of the Civil War opium addicts swilling away at patent medicines to cure what was known as 'soldier illness,' or punitively so as in the case of the heroin addict of the slum, supporting his habit by thievery or worse, and in agonizing numbers ending his life by what society prefers to diagnose as an 'overdose' of whatever it is that ailed him."

A near quarter century has passed. Nothing much has happened. There has been precious little research, with as yet precious little by way of result on that epidemiological triad. Thanks to Vincent Dole and Marie Nyswander we have methadone treatment, but that was already in place when the federal government entered its current "war on drugs."

At the risk of propounding what I cannot prove, let me suggest that in considerable measure this is the result of a disinclination within the medical profession to engage itself with drug research. In the preface to *Drug, Set, and Setting,* Zinberg notes that the train of thought that led him to his subject began in 1962 in Beth Israel Hospital in Boston, where, making rounds with nonpsychiatric physicians, he "began to puzzle over the extreme reluctance these sensible physicians felt about prescribing doses of opiates to relieve pain." Concern about iatrogenic addiction established the social setting that Zinberg would go on to elaborate. He noted "the strength of Puritan moralism in American culture which frowns on the pleasure and recreation provided by intoxicants." Whatever the causes, and they are surely multiple, it is clear to this observer that the medical profession finds drug research aversive behavior.

As an example of our most recent affliction, take "crack" cocaine. This is typical of an ascent on the technological ladder: beer to whiskey; opium to morphine to heroin; coca to cocaine; and now to this most potent possible form of "free-base" cocaine. Crack differs only in being the product of folk science rather than the work of bearded professors in German laboratories. (Although, come to think of it, Highland single malt was probably a similar, if more welcome, discovery.) Crack first appears in the Bahamas. By 1985 a Bahamian physician warned that an epidemic was stirring. This item appeared in the *Atlanta Journal* of December 31, 1985: "Nassau, Bahamas. A highly addictive practice of smoking cocaine 'rocks' has swept this chain of islands off the coast of Florida. In a country of 230,000 people, the number of cocaine users treated at mental health clinics has zoomed from zero in 1982 to 209 in 1984, according to Dr. David Allen, a Harvard-trained psychiatrist who heads the National Drug Council. 'What we have [Dr. Allen said] is the world's first free-basing epidemic [which] could be preceding an epidemic in the industrialized states. Anywhere there is readily available high-quality cocaine, there is this potential.'"

Here was a psychiatrically trained epidemiologist telling us that an epidemic was coming our way. But such is the low status of drug research that, so far as I have been able to learn, apart from a single sentence of a 1982 issue of the Centers for Disease Control publication *Morbidity and Mortality Weekly Report,* there was no official response anywhere in the vast organizational network that was by now carrying out the war on drugs. The first medical report appeared in the British journal the *Lancet* in a 1986 article by Dr. Allen and others entitled "Epidemic Free-Base Cocaine Abuse: Case Study from the Bahamas."

This was the situation when Congress returned to the subject of drugs in 1988. Society had had two bad breaks during that decade: the sudden onset of AIDS and the appearance of crack in settings of lethal proximity. The public demanded action, or at least the appearance of action, or so at least loud political voices declared. In May 1988 Senate Majority Leader Robert S. Byrd established a working group on substance abuse, to be co-chaired by Senator Sam Nunn of Georgia and me. Interdiction and crackdown were then all the rage. (A law providing the death penalty for "kingpins" reached the President's desk months before ours did. It was promptly signed.)

My role on the working group was to assert—quietly, so as not to disturb the public peace—that, other than to raise the price of drugs somewhat, interdiction was not going to have the slightest effect on supply. This George Shultz had taught me. Accordingly, any comprehensive legislation should place at least equal emphasis on demand. The lesson Norman Zinberg taught me, the idea that controlled use was possible, even common, led directly to the proposition that treatment could be developed that could move drug users across the line toward abstinence, or as near to abstinence as possible.

I consulted Zinberg. I asked him to coach me on how to make this case. In the end it worked. After an unusually compressed six months of congressional debate, ending with a 65–29 vote in the Senate, the Anti-Drug Abuse Act of 1988 became law on November 18 of that year.

Section 2012 sets out the purposes of the law. These include: "To increase to the greatest extent possible the availability and quality of treatment services so that treatment on request may be provided to all individuals desiring to rid themselves of their substance abuse problem." The legislation established an Office of National Drug Control Policy in the executive office of the President. It was headed by a so-called czar and included a deputy director for supply and a deputy director for demand. And so the attempt to get drug problems under control began again. And once more it failed to thrive. Czars resigned, which czars are not supposed to do. Deputies departed. Silence fell.

Even so, knowledge edged on. Richard Millstein of the National Institute on Drug Abuse (NIDA) notes that scientists have for some time known that by manipulating the opiate molecule it is possible to develop compounds that block or reverse the effects of drugs such as morphine and heroin. For example, naloxone was approved for use in 1971 and is now part of the Emergency Medical Service protocol. A longer-acting narcotic antagonist, naltrexone, was approved for use in 1984. And a time-released "depot" dosage has been found to block the effects of opiate challenges, as doctors say, for up to seven weeks in rhesus monkeys. However, as an internal paper of the Institute states, while there is an agonist treatment (methadone) and an antagonist treatment (naltrexone) for opiates, no approved medication for the treatment of addiction to cocaine (including crack) currently exists. And crack cocaine is where the problem is centered. Withal that heroin returns.

Having said that, a social scientist is honor-bound to add that the power of government *or* science to influence behavior is limited. People do or do not get on with their lives. Most do. Here, as an example, is an excerpt from *Tales Out of School,* the autobiography of Joseph A. Fernandez, who until recently was the New York City School Chancellor; this excerpt describes his years as a drug-dependent teenager.

> The beginning of my own fateful turnabout came in one night of horror on 135th Street when I was still enrolled at Commerce High. Jimmy Conn (not his name) had become my closest friend during that time, partly because of the experimenting we were doing with

heroin. Jimmy was a Scotch-Irish kid from a poor family, with no father at home. Actually, he lived outside the neighborhood, up in the 1930's, but we were very close, to the point of swapping clothes to wear.

This particular night we were at somebody's house and got tied into some really potent heroin. I got sick almost immediately, a scary new kind of sickness. I remember saying to Jimmy, "Something's wrong. We gotta get outta here."

By the time we got downstairs to the street, we were both reeling. I can barely remember my friends walking us up and down the sidewalk, trying to keep us from fading out. They probably saved our lives. I was half in and half out for hours. Jimmy came to first. When I finally did, I was scared enough to realize it was time to make a change.

I dropped out of Commerce the following week and enrolled at Textile High, down in Hell's Kitchen, where I didn't know anybody. I could tell immediately it wasn't going to work. I was there only a week and dropped out again.

Norman Zinberg would have thought young Fernandez a pretty hard case. But he would not have been the least surprised that the kid got hold of himself, joined the Air Force, married a strong woman, got an education, and went on to do serious work. His *setting* changed.

As for our 1988 legislation, it had a brief half-life. William Bennett, the forceful first director of the Office of National Drug Control Policy, was followed by a political appointee with no apparent views on the subject. Dr. Herbert D. Kleber left after two years, and his position was not soon filled. Nor has support for treatment been as forthcoming as the legislation indicated it ought to be.

Kleber wrote: "Funding for treatment of substance abuse has been a bipartisan failure. Our Republican President has requested substantially less money than is needed; and the Democratic Congress gave him only one-third of what he asked for. The situation in research is not much better, in spite of the desperate need to develop medications to treat cocaine abuse. The House gave the President $17 million less for research at NIDA than he had requested. In fact, the overall increase for NIDA was slightly over 1 percent, one of the lowest if not the lowest of the NIH [National Institutes of Health]. Both government leaders and the general public need to be made aware of the potential promise that can occur by adequately funding treatment and research, and of the many harms to society that will occur if it does not happen."

The 1992 presidential campaign was only marginally encouraging. The Republican platform was straight out. Ignoring treatment altogether, the GOP chose instead to fry the kingpins, as the battle cry goes. "We oppose legalizing or decriminalizing drugs. That is a morally abhorrent idea, the last vestige of an ill-conceived philosophy that counseled the legitimacy of permissiveness. Today, a similarly dysfunctional morality explains away drug-dealing as an escape, and drive-by shootings as an act of political violence. There is no excuse for the wanton destruction of human life. We therefore support the stiffest penalties, including the death penalty, for major drug traffickers."

The Democratic position called for "treatment on demand," which was mildly disappointing since no one seemed to remember that we have already legislated "treatment on request." ("Request" was my term; I thought "demand" sounded too imperious.) The platform read: "*Drug treatment on demand:* Thousands of addicts have volunteered to take themselves off the streets, only to hear the government tell them that they have to wait six months. In a Clinton administration, federal assistance will help communities dramatically increase their ability to offer drug treatment to everyone who needs help."

Our hope must be that the political generation now coming into its own will be able to recall that drug use first became conspicuous in *this* cycle among educated and relatively affluent young persons on college campuses. It is so no longer. Drug use—and in notably destructive forms—is now concentrated in the weakest and least affluent segments of the population. It is essential that we understand that by choosing prohibition we are choosing to have an intense crime problem concentrated among minorities. It is no different from Prohibition in the 1920s. Al Capone and Legs Diamond were recognizable urban slum types of that era. Much of the crime in our day is of the same order, down to formal executions. And sometimes the innocent are slaughtered. This from the press: "A falling-out between drug gangs claimed a pregnant 22-year-old woman yesterday when she was caught in the crossfire and shot to death while on her way to a store in the Bronx, the police said. The police said the victim, Brenda Garcia, was in the first three months of pregnancy, and had left her two small children at home when she was shot in the East Tremont section. The police said their initial investigation indicated that Ms. Garcia was an unintended victim of gang warfare. The shooting came just four days after a 4-year-old girl skating in front of a housing project in Brooklyn was shot to death when one rival drug gang sought revenge against another and instead shot several children. Soon after Ms. Garcia was shot, a woman who was identified as her grandmother arrived at the victim's apartment and silently took her two children away."

Always the grandmother. The two drug gangs comprised, shall we say, seven men. Three will themselves be shot. One will make it back to, say, the Dominican Republic. One will go straight. Two will be in prison for life. The grandchildren do not have better prospects. The 4 year old girl killed while skating in front of a housing project in Brooklyn was in one sense spared. The killings occurred on the day New York State reinstated the death penalty. Another cost not calculated by the confident advocates of alternative lifestyles.

Clearly federal drug policy is responsible for a degree of social regression for which there does not appear to be any equivalent in our history. The number of inmates imprisoned for drug offenses now exceeds those in prison for property crimes. And, to say once more, the medical profession is mostly mute.

One more once more. We must recognize that our choice of policy—legalization or prohibition—involves a choice of outcomes. An enormous public health problem on the one hand, an enormous crime problem on the other. The latter clearly requires more by way of public policy than the death penalty for people who kill each other in any event. Surely, drug policy should be a central concern

for those who deal with issues involving race in our society. Interdiction and "drug busts" are probably necessary symbolic acts, but
nothing more. Only the development of a blocking or neutralizing
agent will have any real effect, given the setting in which our drug
problem now occurs.

That setting—an independent variable, as Norman Zinberg insisted—is the near collapse of family structure in our central cities.
Without this, drug abuse would present a real but, even so, manageable problem of behavior by marginal individuals. With it, the
problem is no longer manageable. To use an epidemiological analogy, we have a famine-weakened population attacked by a fierce
new virus.

▲

The *American Scholar* published the Zinberg lecture in its summer
1993 issue, six months after my "Deviancy" article appeared. This
time, the reaction was quite different. There was none. I had
expected at least some response from the medical schools; they were
mostly silent, although a few letters were supportive enough. The
aversion Zinberg had observed 30 years earlier in Beth Israel Hospital, with exceptions, seems still in place. (Consider, by contrast,
the enormous effort to crack the AIDS puzzle. *Think* of the Nobel
prizes!) Ominously, there was no response whatever from within
the federal government.

The one cheering exception was a letter from Kleiman, Associate
Professor of Public Policy at the Kennedy School, who has followed
and been involved with government policy for a considerable time.
Was it possible, he asked, that the Nantucket "Quaker 'testimony'
against intoxicating liquors led to the substitution of opiates?" The
troubles of this proud and angry flesh. He had a mild "quibble with
the potential value of enforcement." "In reaching the unassailable
conclusion that interdiction must fail, you may be unduly slighting
the possible contribution of well-designed retail-level enforcement.
The capacity of demand to call forth supply works more reliably in
the market for kilograms than it does in the market for dime bags.
As Mark Moore pointed out years ago, and as some of my col-

leagues have now demonstrated empirically, search time may be more important than price in determining the number of new users." Then this powerful proposition:

> More substantively, I am less hopeful than you are that the development of a cocaine blocker would be an important event. Who would take it? The experience with opiate blockers is not encouraging. (A long-acting blocker, like the 30-day Naltretone now awaiting approval, would be a different matter, especially for the criminal-justice population which could be required to take it.)
>   On the other hand, without any technological innovation beyond the urine screen for drug metabolites developed twenty years ago, we could, through the agency of probation and parole departments, reduce the demand for heroin and cocaine by between a third and a half, at a gross cost of about $5 billion per year. (The net cost, after subtracting the savings from not having to imprison people who would otherwise continue to use drugs and commit crimes, would be much less; possibly there would even be a net saving.) The required innovations are not technological, but conceptual, legal, and organizational. This is Mr. Clinton's one chance to make a serious impact on the crime rate within his first term. Pray God he can be persuaded to take it.

He did not, having no seeming interest in the subject. Any more than his predecessors, that is; yet the intense interest in health and medical issues in the early years of his administration might have made a difference here. That it did not is further evidence that the 1988 legislation had changed nothing at the federal level. A serious effort was made at exhortation; not to be dismissed. But of medication, nearly none. I have yet to encounter a "czar" who was aware that heroin began as a cough medicine.

And so, after an interval, law enforcement was once more the mode of drug control. More and more, federal offenses have been put on the statute books, such that the federal courts are clogged and not getting on with their other business. I have yet to meet a federal district *judge* who knew that heroin is a trade name. Few, if any, are trained to this form of criminal adjudication. Even so, the jails fill up. By 1994 the number of inmates in federal, state, and local prisons was three times that of 1980.

About three-quarters of federal outlays goes to interdiction—when the 1988 statute was drafted, Congress clearly intended that demand reduction equal supply reduction, but that was not to be. Clearly, the United States cannot be indifferent to the violation of its borders, but just as clearly it can do little about it. Looking back, I do think the experience with the French connection was misread. Turkey and France are members of the North Atlantic Treaty Organization, thoroughly accustomed to cooperating with the United States, disposed to do so on matters marginal to their own interests, and used to enforcing decisions and maintaining the authority of the state. (Wilson once visited Marseilles. He was taken to a street with one house missing. The site of a heroin laboratory which had not chosen to close down and so was blown up. To this day, Turkey harvests its poppy crop by baling, such that the ingredients are available for pharmaceuticals but not for opium.) But the world in main is made up of soft states and poor people. That heroin or cocaine is cultivated in Latin America or Asia and consumed in Europe or the United States matters nothing to Nigerian couriers, who—quite literally stuffed with swallowed condoms full of drugs—pass through Lagos airport with the full knowledge and cooperation of well-rewarded customs officials. A growing trade on its way. Nigeria's farmers may not have mastered the agrarian dimensions of coca or poppy. But its entrepreneurs recognize a commercial opportunity when they see it. There is no business as profitable as dealing the contraband of others.

Worse by far, in the Western Hemisphere it is not much of a Good Neighbor that supports a drug habit that would appear to be devastating the political and social structure of Colombia, a nation that had seemed to be recovering from the internal violence of the mid-twentieth century. Similarly, a modernizing Mexico could readily enough lapse into instability if the drug traffic becomes sufficiently lucrative and violent. Apart from the People's Republic of China and Cuba, it is the last surviving Leninist state, with one party, the Institutional Revolutionary Party (PRI), in power since 1929. Should the central government lose control of its police through the corruption endemic to drug trafficking, the possibility of chaos is formidable.

Thus, it may be that drug addiction is one of the problems government simply cannot solve. In 1993 a book was published in New York describing the experience in foster care of a young woman named Crystal whose parents had drifted into drugs in the 1970s, who began using drugs herself at age twelve, gave birth at fourteen, and so through all manner of hell. The book was reviewed in the *Wall Street Journal* by an adviser on social policy to an unimpeachably liberal New York elected official. The publisher had thought to condemn "the system"; this was not the reviewer's perspective:

> The publisher's jacket copy for this book tells us that it "charts a terrifying legacy of institutional abuse and neglect [and] shows the damage that has been inflicted on three generations of one inner-city family." This is certainly a wrong reading. There is little in [the] narrative to suggest that either racism or the economic "system" caused this family's disintegration. Whatever the author's intention, this book turns out to be less about institutional failure and much more about personal moral failure and its consequence for our social order.
>
> It should more properly be read as a powerful case study confirming Senator Daniel Patrick Moynihan's recent warning that urban society is increasingly accommodating individual destructive behavior, and that to avoid confronting the social chaos caused by that behavior, the tendency of the prevailing culture is to keep "defining deviancy down."
>
> Through the 23 years covered in this book, Crystal's family probably cost the taxpayers in the neighborhood of $1 million in outlays for foster care and welfare. But the government that was doling out these funds was incapable of demanding minimal standards of responsible behavior from the adult family members. Ultimately Crystal and her family—and all of us—were victimized. Not because there was a hole in the social safety net, but because during the past two decades the social contract has been torn up.

— 6 —

The Coming of Age of
American Social Policy

By 1989, it seemed to me to be reasonably clear that the discontents
roiling through the land over the seeming incapacity of government
to get anything right might be eased if it were understood that
government was dealing with something new. Which is to say, social
policy in a postindustrial age.

Ronald Reagan would say, with emphasis but without anger, that
the United States had declared war on poverty and "poverty won."
Not so. The poverty we know how to deal with—which is to say,
lack of resources in an otherwise competent population, as, for
example, the aged—had all but disappeared. But new issues had
emerged which old remedies seemingly could not resolve. The
United States would not cut loose from its long European tutelage.
Bismarck introduced health insurance in the late nineteenth century; Churchill introduced unemployment insurance in the early
twentieth century. We had learned from Europe; now it was time
for us to teach, for we were first on the scene of a new set of social
issues. This, it seemed to me, was a challenge, and accordingly
cheering. Not until four years later, in 1993, would we discover the
extraordinary parallel rise of illegitimacy ratios in other North Atlantic nations.

It would surely be wrong to think of our circumstances as entirely new; nothing ever is. It helps to keep in mental touch with earlier periods of perceived crisis. In 1853 Charles Loring Brace founded the Children's Aid Society and some years later published *The Dangerous Classes of New York*. His account resonates:

> Though the crime and pauperism of New York are not so deeply stamped in the blood of the population, they are even more danger-ous . . . The intensity of the American temperament is felt in every fiber of these children of poverty and vice. Their crimes have the unrestrained and sanguinary character of a race accustomed to over-come all obstacles. They rifle a bank, where English thieves pick a pocket. They murder, where European proletariat cajole or fight with fists. In a riot they begin what seems to be the sacking of a city, where English rioters would merely batter policemen or smash lamps. The dangerous classes of New York are mainly American born, but the children of Irish and German immigrants. They are as ignorant as London flashmen or corten mongers. They are far more brutal than the peasantry from whom they descend, and they are much banded together in association such as the Dead Rabbit, Plug Ugly, and various target companies, when *enfants ont perdu* grow up to young manhood. The murder of an unoffending man is nothing to them. They are ready for any offense or crime, however degraded or bloody. New York has never experienced the full effect of the nurture of these young ruffians as she will one day.

As it had in the Draft Riots of July 1863, when the Negro Orphan Asylum was burned to the ground and Brooks Brothers looted; violence ebbed, until by the early part of the twentieth century the homicide rate in New York City was below the national average. Eric Monkkonen, a historian at the University of Califor-nia, Los Angeles, has shown that it remained there for the first half of the twentieth century until, of a sudden, it broke out, and as the end of the century approached was three times the national average. Monkkonen has found yet another "scissors," a phenomenon I surely don't understand, but there it is in the data (see chart). As for the increase in homicides, it was *probably* owing to the reappear-ance of heroin, but this area of demography is only beginning to be developed. We shall see.

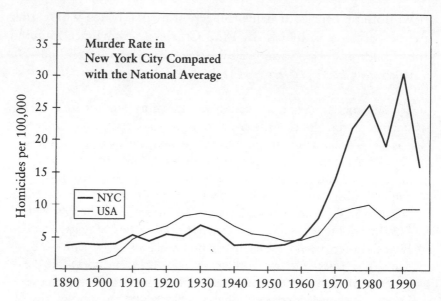

In the early part of the twentieth century the homicide rate in New York City was below the national average, where it remained until around 1960. Then, of a sudden, it crossed over in the manner of "Moynihan's scissors." (Data from Eric Monkkonen, "New York City Homicides: A Research Note," *Social Science History*, Summer 1995, pp. 201–204.)

In the course of a lecture I gave at a Conference on the Changing American Family at Brown University in the spring of 1989, which follows, I mentioned the Family Support Act of 1988, with its redefinition of welfare, and the Anti-Drug Abuse Act of 1988, with its emphasis on demand reduction, including treatment on request. This was then brand-new legislation. Note the comment that "there does not now exist within the executive branch of government the institutional capacity to put either of these new laws into effect." Which is exactly what proved to be the case, along with the lack of any enthusiasm from groups whose support was needed. The professionalization of reform, indeed! A great challenge of social policy in the new era will be to summon sufficient conviction from the polity, the people, to change the society in desired ways. Gertrude Himmelfarb has spent a lifetime of scholarship demonstrating how the Victorians did this: the hard way, without government. This is my reading of her work, not necessarily hers. But we have had sufficient failure *with* government as to raise a question that really hasn't been asked much in this century. The Children's Aid Society of the 1850s is still around; whatever happened to Model Cities of the 1960s?

▼

We are just three days short of a quarter century from the time I sat alongside Sargent Shriver in the hearing room of the House Committee on Education and Labor as he presented the opening testimony on what was to become the Economic Opportunity Act of 1964. Whereupon began the War on Poverty.

In recent years this effort has been judged a failure. At least by many, and not least by former President Reagan. I would offer a radically different view. If one sees the 1960s and early 1970s as the culmination of a long effort, beginning in the Progressive era, to eliminate the particular kinds of poverty and distress associated with industrialism, these were hugely successful years. The effort was not, however, successful in dealing with an emergent form of dependency and difficulty which I associate with postindustrial society. Whether such an effort *could* have succeeded is not something we can know, for we did not try. Instead, there was a massive denial that any such problems existed.

Many people have written a great deal about this subject. I have contributed my share, and would as leave allow the matter rest, awaiting the judgment of historians. Still, there needs to be some prologue to the era of social policy which may now be in prospect.

The century-long effort to which I have referred sorts itself out, roughly, as three periods of notable energy, as much as enactment. Using presidential terms as a kind of shorthand, we see the Progressive era, Roosevelt to Wilson; the New Deal, Roosevelt and Truman; and lastly, Kennedy to Nixon. Some will note that this does not leave many Presidents out, and that is correct. This was more a continuous exercise than otherwise; but some periods saw particular bursts of energy.

This is key to understanding that third period. The essential social legislation of the twelve-year period 1961–1973 basically extended and concluded the initiatives of the previous ones. Medicaid and Medicare (1965) provided the health insurance that Truman had called for; the indexation of Social Security benefits (1972) insured the stability of Roosevelt's retirement benefits; while Supplemental Security Income (1972) rounded out such benefits for the indigent aged, blind, and disabled.

Each of these programs provided for cash transfers or for services in kind—health care—which would otherwise have had to be purchased or foregone. Each has parallels in the social legislation of Europe, where industrialization created new social problems, such as unemployment, and simultaneously the collective resources with which to address them.

It is helpful to think of this final period in which a new set of problems also appeared, call them postindustrial, which engaged the period but produced no very conclusive results. This was termed the problem of poverty, but is better understood in the common formulation poverty-amidst-plenty. This is to say, as against more or less readily comprehended problems, the anomaly of poverty amidst the evident riches of the age.[1]

This anomaly was graphically set forth in the report of the President's Task Force on Manpower Conservation entitled "One-Third of a Nation: A Report on Young Men Found Unqualified for Military Service," which as much as anything served as the data base on which we fashioned the Economic Opportunity Act of 1964. (The title, of course, harkened back to the second Roosevelt.) It was a project I had conceived in the summer of 1963 as Assistant Secretary of Labor for Policy Planning and Research. At that time, half the young men called up for military service failed either the mental or the physical test, or both. It occurred to me that a closer inquiry might provide support for the enactment of our Youth Employment Act, S.1, then languishing. (It became Title I of the Economic Opportunity Act.)

A survey and analysis of 2,500 young men who had failed to pass the Armed Forces Qualification Test was undertaken, enabling us to "correct," as the statisticians say, for the fact that only a portion of all the eligible males were actually tested or examined. Some were in college, some had enlisted, and so on. We established that if everyone were "called up," the rejection rate would be one-third.

The report was finished January 1, 1964, whereupon the Secretary of Labor flew off in a military plane to the LBJ ranch, where it was presented to President Johnson. We had a considerable sense of having learned some things of consequence. On January 5 the President issued a statement which I recall drafting, but which in any event reflects my understanding at the time. The statement begins:

> I am releasing today the report of the Task Force on Manpower Conservation, appointed by President Kennedy on September 30, 1963. I regard with utmost concern the two principal findings of that report.
>
> First, that one-third of the Nation's youth would, on examination, be found unqualified on the basis of standards set up for military service and, second, that poverty is the principal reason why these young men fail to meet those physical and mental standards.
>
> The findings of the Task Force are dramatic evidence that poverty is still with us, still exacting its price in spoiled lives and failed expectations. For entirely too many Americans the promise of American life is not being kept. In a Nation as rich and productive as ours this is an intolerable situation.
>
> I shall shortly present to the Congress a program designed to attack the roots of poverty in our cities and rural areas. I wish to see an America in which no young persons, whatever the circumstances, shall reach the age of twenty-one without the health, education, and skills that will give him an opportunity to be an effective citizen and a self-supporting individual. This opportunity is too often denied to those who grow up in a background of poverty.

Looking back, I do not have the confidence I then had as to the second finding. Indeed, it now seems to me that the data could lead to quite different conclusions. It comes to this. The overall number, one-third, was a composite of hugely varied rates of mental and health failure as between subgroups in the population and between political jurisdictions. And it is the *latter* differences which are the most pronounced. Thus, the population of 1962 draftees who failed the mental test in Rhode Island was 14.3 percent, whereas for neighboring New York (we have a boundary in Long Island Sound) the rate was 34.2 percent. In another New York neighbor, Vermont, only 6.4 percent of draftees failed the mental test. Why did I write that this was the result of poverty? Why did I not write that poverty was the result of *this*?

Ignorance, as Dr. Johnson observed. I don't know how to describe my "understanding" of social structure that long ago, save that it was not especially formed. I was surely no Marxist. What Ralf Dahrendorf was to call the "concealed romanticism of a revolutionary Utopia *à la* . . . Marx" had never in the least appealed to or persuaded me. Yet I did think, as a proper Madisonian, that "the various and unequal distribution of property" accounted for a lot of behavior, political and otherwise. What I had not thought through was the degree to which these unequal distributions of property were in turn dependent variables of a yet more powerful agent, which is to say, behavior.

Two years earlier Dahrendorf had given his lecture "On the Origin of Inequality among Men" at the University of Tübingen. I came upon it shortly after it appeared in English, in 1968, and may have begun for the first time to think to some purpose about this subject. The essay is readily available, and I will only summarize it: All societies establish norms of behavior to which some individuals adapt better than others. Hence, inequality is inevitable. Nations that believed the abolition of private property would end inequality, for example, were romantic and naive. Consider the Soviet "experiment." Social expectations exist, and those who most fulfill them will have a higher status than those who least fulfill them. "The hard core of social inequality can always be found in the fact that men as the incumbents of social roles are subject, according to how their roles relate to the dominant expectational principles of society, to sanctions designed to enforce these principles."

It needs to be emphasized (I suppose) that Dahrendorf's model of social stratification is value-free. The normative orders that different societies reward can be vastly disparate, ranging from that of St. Francis of Assisi to that of Vlad the Impaler. No matter. Some will excel at charity, some at brutality. Inequality ensues. Thus, the economist John Kenneth Galbraith, 6 feet 9 inches tall, has perfected a brief discourse on "Why Tall Men Are Best Suited to Govern." From a Scots Presbyterian point of view, the logic is inescapable. Tall men, being more conspicuous, are more readily observed by their neighbors. Being more readily observed, of necessity they behave better. Behaving better, they are Best Suited to Govern. At a reception following the funeral of President Kennedy, Dr. Galbraith recounted this theorem to General de Gaulle. *Le Grand Charles* commented that the reasoning was sound but omitted an essential correlative. Which was to say that "tall men should show small men . . . no mercy."

Rereading "One-Third of a Nation," I am struck by how prominently we pointed to the variation among the different states. "The state with the highest proportion of persons failing the mental examination had a rate 19 times as great as the state with the lowest." The lowest was Minnesota, with a failure rate of 2.7 percent. This is scarcely above the incidence of mental retardation in a large population. South Carolina, with 51.8 percent was, well, insanely out of line. What was going on down there? Or over there?

The answer, surely, was the people were behaving differently. Rewarding different things, punishing different things. This was, after all, the United States of America in the seventh decade of the twentieth century. We lived under the same Constitution, shared essentially the same material culture. Yet some jurisdictions were turning out citizens who were going to be poor and others who were not. Economics could not account for that much of the difference. Surely not between jurisdictions as comparable as Rhode Island and New York. There is no more elemental form of wealth than a well-educated, healthy cohort of young people. In some parts of the United States this "wealth" was being produced in abundance. To cite the charter of Brown University, young people were coming along able to lead "lives of usefulness and reputation." Other parts of the nation were producing the social infrastructure of poverty.

Hence, this period of social reform was most successful—was hugely successful—where we simply transferred income and services to the elderly, a stable, settled population group. It had little success—if you like, it failed—where poverty had its origin in social behavior. More. It could not have succeeded because of a massive denial that there was any real problem. This period is already receding in our history, and the memory may be difficult to retrieve. But that is about what happened. In a series of policy papers prepared for President Johnson and then President Nixon, I commenced to argue, for example, that family structure was an emerging problem. Class, not race, is the way I would state it. Both Presidents were receptive. However, their initiatives in this direction never survived the hostility they evoked, and after a period the subject was more or less banished from public discourse.

In a recent effort to improve poverty statistics by counting income and government tax and transfer (both cash and in-kind) benefits, the Census Bureau has just now summarized the quarter-century aftermath: "The data show clearly that the effect of government transfers on the poverty status of persons 65 years and over is very large compared to the effect of such transfers on the poverty status of young persons. The percent of older persons (65 years and over) in poverty was 47.5 percent before government transfers were added to the income definition. The addition of no means-tested cash transfers (primarily Social Security) reduced the rate to 14.0 percent, and the addition of other government transfers brought the rate to 9.0 percent. The total effect of adding government transfers was to *reduce the poverty rate of older persons by 81.1 percent*. Among those under 18 years of age, the before-transfer poverty rate was 24.0 percent and the addition of all government transfers brought the rate to 17.1 percent. The effect of government transfers was to *reduce the poverty rate of young persons by 28.8 percent*" (emphasis added).

It begins to appear that family structure is now a principal correlate of poverty in the United States. This in turn has revived an *age* category of poverty. The poorest group in our population are children, at last count 23 percent of those under 6 years of age. They live, overwhelmingly, in single-parent families. In 1988 a quarter—24 percent—of our 63 million children lived with only one parent. That was double the proportion of 1970 and a yet higher multiple of the ratio a quarter century ago. Children in female-headed households have a poverty rate of 55 percent. This is five times the rate of children in families that are not headed by single mothers.

Single-parent, female-headed families have become the norm. The Bureau of the Census estimates that only 39 percent of all children born last year will live with both their parents through their eighteenth birthday. Put the other way, over 60 percent of children will live with only one parent for a period of time before reaching maturity. The vast majority of them will live with just their mothers, and over half of them will be poor (46 percent of whites, 68 percent of blacks, and 70 percent of Hispanics).

From a Census study, "Household Wealth and Asset Ownership: 1984," we know that median net worth for all households was $32,677. Median net worth for all households with incomes under $11,000 was $5,080. By contrast, households headed by black females with incomes under $11,000 have a median net worth of −$18, according to unpublished information supplied by Gordon Green of the Bureau.

I have speculated that family structure may now prove to be the principal conduit of social class status. Family structure will prove, I suspect, to be the primary setting in which social capital, as James S. Coleman uses the term, is amassed or dissipated. Social capital makes for education, access, mobility, ensuring that talent is rewarded.

Dahrendorf's is a dynamic model. Nothing stays still for long. His essay continues: "The system of social stratification is only a measure of conformity in the behavior of social groups; inequality becomes the dynamic impulse that serves to keep social structures alive. Inequality always implies the gain of one group at the expense of others; thus every system of social stratification generates protest against its principles and bears the seeds of its own suppression. Since human society without inequality is not realistically possible and the complete abolition of inequality is therefore ruled out, the intrinsic explosiveness of every system of social stratification confirms the general view that there cannot be an ideal, perfectly just, and therefore non-historical human society." It is difficult to work out the sequence, but it is not difficult to conceive a society in which social norms are reversed and the more achieving modes of behavior are discredited. This could happen.

At all events, one matter would already seem clear. We have entered a new social condition, which is clearly postindustrial. Here we are in a state of full or overfull employment, enjoying the longest unbroken peacetime economic expansion in our history, while in many if not most of our major cities we are facing something like social regression.

Moreover, we are facing it first. For most of the twentieth century, the social problems of the United States—always excluding that of race—had first appeared in Europe, as had the first responses. With a one or two generation lag, we adopted them here: Workman's Compensation, Unemployment Insurance, Social Security, Medical care, and such like. But now we have a new set of problems and there is no European "solution" at hand.

That is why I speak of the coming of age of American social policy. We are going to have to work our own way through these issues. It doesn't follow that we will, but I don't know that we won't. We are not entirely alone. The Luxembourg Income Study data indicate that, like the United States, Canada and Sweden also have more children than elderly in poverty. However, Sweden has no poverty among the aged and virtually none among children. Still, we must entertain the thought that a more universal, post-industrial pattern is emerging. Mature social insurance systems gradually eliminate poverty among the aged. At the same time, marital instability and tenuous labor markets will leave a fair number of children poor even in prosperous countries.

Even so, there is no industrial democracy with as much social dysfunction as the United States today. The normative order of American society still very much rewards "traditional" family patterns and punishes those which previously would have been openly labeled as deviant. What is not at all obvious is why this is obscure to so many. The matter may not be left to rest: We must either change our norms, or change our behavior. Recent trends are dysfunctional in the extreme. As are recent trends of substance abuse, although these have been with us—at intervals—for a longer period in our history.

I would note that the 100th Congress enacted two major bills addressed to these issues. The Family Support Act of 1988 was the first redefinition of the purposes and expectations of the welfare system since it began as a temporary widows' pension in 1935. And, for the first time since Theodore Roosevelt declared war on drugs in 1907, the Anti-Drug Abuse Act of 1988 addressed this issue from the perspective of treatment and demand reduction.

Our difficulty is that there does not now exist within the executive branch of government the institutional capacity to put either of these new laws into effect. Worse, there is no great enthusiasm for them. Editorial comment was restrained at best. Subsequent commentary has generally been negative, while advocacy groups have on the whole been hostile or indifferent. Still, the Congress found the energy and, I believe, the insight to enact them. If we *want* to believe that "nothing happened," then nothing will. Another generation will pass before we try again. But that need not be the outcome.

Mind, these are not the only aspects of American society that aren't working as they ought. The 1980s saw a period of wildly irresponsible fiscal policies on the part of the national government. In eight years of peace we increased the national debt by an amount nearly that which was incurred in World War II. In the course of doing so, we ended up a debtor nation, with nothing like our post-1945 capacity to retire the debt and resume a strong path of saving and investment directed to future growth—which would presumably provide resources that a new era of social policy will require.

In the 1988 Taubman Lecture at Brown, Frank Levy observed that there are all too many parallels between the level of national savings and the current condition of children—our provisions for the future. We will need, he insisted, values to guide behavior. Simple benefit/cost calculations at the individual level, with the classic free-rider phenomenon, won't get us there. Still, we are surely a nation in which such values can be found. And summoned. In the context of a tough-minded approach to postindustrial social issues, we may yet see the coming of age of American social policy.

▲

It may just be that this had, in fact, already begun with the administration of George Bush. It was now his time to speak as President; and as none before him, he spoke of the breakdown of family as a central fact of the American condition. This to the National League of Cities in 1992: "The urgency is clear. We all know the statistics, perhaps you know them better than most Americans, the dreary drumbeat that tells of family breakdown. Today, one out of every four American children is born out of wedlock. In some areas, the illegitimacy rate tops 80 percent. A quarter of our children grow up in households headed by a single parent. More than 2 million are called latchkey kids who come home from school each afternoon to an empty house. And a large number of our children grow up without the love of parents at all, with nobody knowing their name."

In 1992, in an article in *The Public Interest,* Richard T. Gill, sometime of the department of economics of Harvard University, pointed to an "accumulation of data showing that intact biological-parent families offer children very large advantages compared to any other family or nonfamily structure one can imagine. Not only are these advantages indisputable in economic terms, they are equally hard to contest where children's emotional development, behavior, health, and school performance are concerned. If one had to select the single most important factor responsible for the disturbing condition of many of today's younger generation—a condition that almost everyone now views with alarm—the breakdown of the intact biological-parent family would almost certainly be at or near the top of the list." We have just entered this period in social history, and it could well take another half century to sort things out.

Economists Richard Freeman and Paul Osterman have looked

into the natural experiment of the 1980s, when employment rose dramatically. They found that a tight labor market sharply lowered the official unemployment rate but did nothing to reverse "the trend toward single-parenthood, to lower the inner-city crime rate or to appreciably reduce the proportion of men who had stopped working." The lesson, according to Freeman, is that full employment "is necessary but not sufficient." All this is consistent, or so I would think, with Wilson and Neckerman's 1986 analysis. The problem then as now is that no one has a clue as to what it would take for public policy to be *sufficient*.

Here we come to the crux of the issue of social science and social policy. We are at the point of knowing a fair amount about what we don't know. The past quarter-century has been on the whole productive in this regard. On the other hand, our social situation is considerably worse.

Epilogue

Government, to cite Alfred Marshal, "is the most precious of human institutions; and no care can be too great to be spent on enabling it to do its work in the best way. A chief condition to that end is that it should not be set to work for which it is not specifically qualified, under the conditions of time and place." A century after the appearance of *Principles of Economics* (1890), we can agree that some governments have proved wholly unqualified to manage their economic affairs, while others have proved adept indeed.

We may count the United States in this latter group. Tentatively, for one supposes that nothing is ever finally settled. Still, by 1996 the American economy was in its fifth year of uninterrupted growth. There was full employment, as generally understood. Ten states had unemployment rates below 4.0 percent; Nebraska checked in at 2.9 percent, a number scarcely known to labor statistics. For four years the Consumer Price Index had risen by less than 3 percent. Economists would adjust this index downward, giving an inflation rate more like 2 percent, which is as close to price stability as one could wish. All of this comes in a setting of one social science, economics, informing social policy in the pursuit of generally agreed goals.

Thirty years earlier it was possible to observe that this form of social learning was essentially in place and could very well produce prodigious results. It was also possible to spot other emergent problems for which there was little social science and no ready response, a condition that continues to this day. Nonmarital births would seem the best leading indicator for whatever it is that is going on. In 1994 this ratio reached one-third (32.6 percent) of all births. The overall ratio follows the exponential curve depicted earlier (see chapter 4), having all but doubled in fifteen years. For the fifty largest cities, the 1994 ratio reached one-half (48.0 percent), with St. Louis at 69.0 percent, Baltimore at 67.8 percent, New York at 52.3 percent, Minneapolis at 45.9 percent. *The Monthly Vital Statistics Report* of the National Center for Health Statistics of June 1996 describes the limitations of the currently available data:

The proportion of all births that were to unmarried women rose in 1994 to 32.6 percent. Twenty-five percent of white births, 70 percent of black births, and 43 percent of Hispanic births were nonmarital. The proportion of nonmarital births is affected not only by the birth rate for unmarried women, but also by the birth rate for married women. This rate . . . has fallen sharply in recent years to unprecedented low levels—83.8 per 1,000 in 1994, down 10 percent compared with 1990 (93.2). This rapid decline in marital fertility—measured for both white and black women—is the principal factor in the continued increase in the *proportion* of nonmarital births in the last few years. Although the proportion of nonmarital births (the nonmarital birth ratio) clearly has important analytic limitations, it is often the only measure that is available in addition to the number of births . . . The proportions of nonmarital births vary widely by race and Hispanic origin. At least 41 percent of births to American Indian, Hawaiian, Mexican, Puerto Rican, Central and South American, and non-Hispanic black women were nonmarital in 1994 (range of 41–71 percent). Proportions were lowest for Chinese and Japanese births (7–11 percent). The range for other groups was 16–23 percent (Filipino, "other" Asian, Cuban, and non-Hispanic white) . . . Over the next several years, the principal area of population change will be an increase in the number of teenagers while the number of women in their thirties starts to decline. Thus the number of unmarried women can be expected to grow faster because the overwhelming majority of teenagers are unmarried. This population growth in turn will likely contribute to further increases in nonmarital births unless birth rates for unmarried women begin to fall.

The 1990s brought prosperity, but also a rising debate about income inequality. Are the rich getting richer and the poor getting poorer? Daniel Weinberg of the Census Bureau has analyzed the change in household income equality over the postwar period. He finds a decline (using the Gini index of income concentration) of 7.4 percent from 1947 to 1968. Thereafter an increase of 22.4 percent, 1968 to 1994. Great and growing disparities of wealth and income are certainly unlovely, but need not be unendurable if most incomes are rising and most households are self-sufficient. But neither is now the case. Weinberg asks, "Why are these changes in inequality happening?" His answer: "Changes in the Nation's labor market and its household composition." In the former category we find "shifts in labor demand away from less-educated workers." This is a pattern that has been in place for a long while. Hence school-children are being provided laptop computers. It is a familiar pattern of economic change for which there are a range of economic responses: trade unions, minimum wage, tax credits, training programs, the like. But what of the second category, changes in household composition? It is a two-part phenomenon of striking contrast. "The increasing tendency . . . for men with higher-than-average earnings to marry women with higher-than-average earnings has contributed to widening the gap between high-income and low-income households." Nothing the matter with that, or at least nothing to be done about it. But then this: "Divorces and separations, births out of wedlock, and the increasing age at first marriage have led to a shift away from married-couple households and toward single-parent and non-family households, which typically have lower incomes."

In 1994, in the highest fifth of income distribution, 94.9 percent of households were married-couple families. (In the top 5 percent the ratio was 96.8 percent.) By contrast, in the lowest fifth of income distribution, just over half (50.7 percent) of households were "male householder, no wife present" or "female householder, no husband present."* This data series goes back only to 1987, but a pattern is surely present. In that year single-parent households made up 45.6 percent of the lowest quintile. The proportion of single-parent families at the bottom of income distribution has grown and will continue to grow.

What is to be done? Are we witnessing Marx's revenge? Substitute human for physical capital, and observe the inexorable process of concentration at the top and immiserization at the bottom? Possibly. But Robert K. Merton in his 1936 essay "The Unanticipated Consequences of Purposive Social Action" showed how the predictions of social scientists can interfere with the course of events, often with welcome results. Merton suggested that Marxist analysis had encouraged the development of trade unionism, which in turn headed off the misery Marx predicted. So it may yet prove with the dilemmas of our time. Something is going on which we do not yet understand. But it has only taken a generation to get onto the fact that something *is* going on. Another generation of hard and complex analysis may give us insights that may yet change outcomes. Call that facile if you like, but surely now we recognize the power of explanatory models to influence behavior at one or two or three removes.

Expect little of government, especially national government. Good-hearted persons who might be put off by that forecast would do well to study the history of the debate over "welfare reform" in the 104th Congress. A "liberal" executive and a "conservative" Congress were quite prepared to enact legislation that verged on vengeance against children whose existence is seen as an affront to the values of a threatened society. When fear takes hold, even so piteous a fear as that of losing an election, expect no mercy. There was none. Nor is this the fault of the democratic process: it is the nature of the problems we confront. They are about values.

---

*Of these, 43.5 were female-headed; 7.2 percent were male-headed. Source: Unpublished data, Current Population Survey, 1996.

In the summer of 1996, in a second round of welfare legislation, a second letter was pried out of the Executive Office of a Democratic President as to the impact on children of the Republican bill. Back came "a magnificently fuzzy reply," as the *Washington Post* commented, which said, in effect, that one study of child poverty was plenty. The *Post* continued: "Among much else, the reply observed that studies are chancy things, dependent on all kinds of assumptions—guesses really—and who would want to base policy on so weak a reed as that? The response also noted that cash income, meaning the number of children likely to end up in poverty, ought not to be the only test of a welfare reform plan. Factors like the moral value of work and the 'crushing burden of welfare dependency' need to be taken into account as well. The reply did little to reassure the bill's critics, who also believe in the value of work but don't want to dismantle a system on which an eighth of the children of the country depend without having a better idea of where those children can expect to turn next for sustenance." It is the nature of children to be dependent. The behavior of adults is another matter; but if the two are to be conflated in Washington, it is time, surely, to look elsewhere.

Even were governments specifically qualified for such work, which is to say the restoration of individual character and moral instruction in everyday life, the national government has entered a time of chronic, even disabling, fiscal stricture. For all the good work done in 1993 at deficit reduction, nothing could delay the onset of insolvency in the Social Security "Trust Funds." Here demography *is* destiny, and we are destined to be fighting about *this* subject for a generation. The present situation is unsustainable; it can be made so, but this will require a degree of concentration of energy and resources that will leave room for little else. Which may be just as well, for if things are bad it is possible even so to make them very much the worse. It is time for small platoons; a time possibly to be welcomed for such can move quickly, and there are miles to go.

Notes

Introduction

1. Remarks of Professor Jack F. Matlock, Jr., "Introduction of Senator Daniel Patrick Moynihan" (The Lionel Trilling Lecture, Columbia University: February 19, 1996).
2. In 1992, preparation of the annual report, previously known as "New York State and the Federal Fisc," was taken over by Herman B. Leonard and Monica E. Friar of the John F. Kennedy School of Government of Harvard University and is now titled "The Federal Budget and the States."
3. See Jordan A. Schwarz, *The New Dealers* (New York: Alfred A. Knopf, 1993).
4. See Daniel Patrick Moynihan, *Politics of a Guaranteed Income* (New York: Random House, 1973).
5. See David A. Stockman, *The Triumph of Politics* (New York: Harper & Row, 1986).
6. See Daniel Patrick Moynihan, *Maximum Feasible Misunderstanding* (New York: Free Press, 1969).
7. Jonathan Mahler, "Sharpton's Image as New Moderate Dimmed by Video," *Forward* (formerly *The Jewish Daily Forward*), December 22, 1995.
8. Lewis Thomas, *The Medusa and the Snail* (New York: Viking Press, 1979).
9. AFDC is not an entitlement to individuals but rather to states. The federal government matches spending at varying rates.
10. The analytic method known as "meta-analysis," first used in medical research and associated with Dr. Thomas C. Chalmers, has begun to challenge this earlier pattern of findings. Pooling data, the analysis of large numbers of separate analyses, appears to increase the degree of statistically valid results. Christopher Jencks writes that the starting premise that nothing works—the

null hypothesis—is being replaced by the premise that "everything works." (Letter: Christopher Jencks to DPM, March 26, 1996.) Rossi does not disagree. (Letter: Peter Rossi to DPM, March 14, 1996.) Others are much more cautious, and the debate will go on. In the end it is conceivable that the judgment will be made that it is just as well the social science of the 1960s and thereafter had so little influence on social policy! Conceivable but not likely, or so I would think at present.

11. Greg J. Duncan and Wei-Jun J. Yeung, "Extent and Consequences of Welfare Dependence among America's Children" in *Children and Youth Services Review,* vol. 17, nos. 1–2 (1995), pp. 157–182.

12. "Welfare Overhaul Leaves Dole with Campaign Dilemma," *Congressional Quarterly,* April 20, 1996.

13. David Remnick in "Dr. Wilson's Neighborhood," *New Yorker,* April 29 and May 6, 1996, p. 107, reports: "Wilson is furious because the Republicans in Congress support a welfare reform proposal without guaranteed jobs, one that would adopt the idea of time limits but would then make welfare the business of the states, with the states, in turn, allocating, or not allocating, benefits, as they saw fit."

1. Three Decades of *The Public Interest*

"The Professionalization of Reform" and "The Professionalization of Reform II" first appeared in *The Public Interest* in Fall 1965 and Fall 1995, respectively.

1. The manuscript was accepted at the *New Yorker* but not immediately printed. At midyear I became U.S. Permanent Representative to the United Nations and, in the circumstances, asked that it be withdrawn. The *New Yorker* graciously agreed.

2. At the Policy Planning staff of the Department of Labor we had indeed picked up the first tremors of "a rising measure of social disorganization among poor families and poor communities." Thirty years later this would be a subject at or near to the center of domestic politics. If there is a better case for professionalization, none comes readily to mind. On the other hand, there was at the time almost no popular perception of anything amiss, and the proposition received a decidedly mixed reception. I leave it to my betters to judge, but we may have an instance here of what Joseph A. Schumpeter termed the "decomposition" of bourgeois society attendant on its very successes. The relentless rationality of capitalism will, he conjectured, "eventually kill its roots." Which is to say, in Eugene D. Genovese's words, the "pre-capitalist institutions and values necessary for social and political stability." Thus, Chapter 14 of *Capitalism, Socialism and Democracy:* "Still more important however is another 'internal cause,' the disintegration of the bourgeois family. The facts to which I am referring are too well known to need explicit statement. To men and women in modern capitalist societies, family

life and parenthood mean less than they meant before and hence are less powerful molders of behavior; the rebellious son or daughter who professes contempt for "Victorian" standards is, however incorrectly, expressing an undeniable truth. The weight of these facts is not impaired by our inability to measure them statistically." To anticipate, we had begun to get a statistical fix on the subject.

In *The Public Interest,* Winter 1968, I would publish an article, "The Crises in Welfare," which included this passage: "In general, many persons active in the civil-rights movements, as in most social-reform efforts in recent American history, bring to the undertaking a considerable disenchantment with the traditional 'middle-class' values of the society. Although they are likely to be—or because they are—the products of quite successful families, ideas of family stability and morality tend to be seen by such persons as part of the bourgeois *apparat.* And they say to hell with it. Thus, a recent article on Harlem in *The Urban Review,* published by the Center for Urban Education in New York City, spoke with scorn of 'Victorian notions about broken homes.' Somehow or other, the idea that sexual repression is bad has gotten mixed up with the idea that illegitimacy, or whatever, is good. In a curious way the more liberated youth of the present seem to be affected by a culture lag of sorts: The newest and best thinking about such matters is considerably more respectful of the 'nuclear family' than they seem to know. Or care to know."

3. The five Congressional committees with jurisdiction over health care reform reported legislation with the following provisions limiting the total number of medical school graduates permitted to enter resident training: House Ways and Means Committee—a cap determined by the Secretary of Health and Human Services; House Education and Labor Committee—residency slots limited to 110 percent of U.S. medical graduates; House Energy and Commerce Committee did not report legislation; Senate Labor and Human Resources Committee—a cap determined by a council; and Senate Finance Committee—no provision. The leadership bill debated on the floor of the Senate initially included a provision to cap the number of residency positions at 110 percent of U.S. medical graduates (unless modified by the Secretary of Health and Human Services). Senator Mitchell later modified his bill so that the cap was determined by a council.

4. In March 1996 the National Resident Matching Program, the route through which most U.S. medical school seniors secure residency programs, announced: "For the second year in a row, more than half of graduating U.S. medical school seniors will pursue training in one of the generalist disciplines, while the number of students entering specialities such as anesthesiology and diagnostic radiology dropped significantly." A *Washington Post* editorial of March 30, 1996, observed: "As recently as the great debate over the Clinton health care proposals, it was an unquestioned assumption that doctors needed to be steered in the direction of primary care—the only question was how

aggressively. What a difference a few years of bad news make. From the familiar concern about doctor shortages in the primary care areas that need them most, the pendulum has swung to more generalized fears of a doctor 'glut' and a general pinch of joblessness across all sorts of practices."

2. Repealing Economics

1. See Claus Mueller, *The Politics of Communication: A Study in the Political Sociology of Language, Socialization, and Legitimation* (New York: Oxford University Press, 1973), Chapter 4, "The Crisis of Governmental Authority."
2. See Daniel Patrick Moynihan, *Maximum Feasible Misunderstanding* (New York: Free Press, 1969); *The Politics of a Guaranteed Income* (New York: Random House, 1973).
3. On February 3rd, at a press conference held in the Mike Mansfield Room of the Senate, Robert M. Solow presented a letter from himself, Paul Samuelson, Herbert A. Simon, James Tobin, and other economists stating further: "Frustration with the reckless fiscal policies of the past decade is understandable. Indeed, many of the signatories to this letter have been among the foremost critics of policies that have contributed to high budget deficits and large increases in the national debt. But the proposed balanced budget amendment is not a solution. Indeed, it would worsen the nation's economic prospects."
4. David E. Lebow, John M. Roberts, and David J. Stockman, "Monetary Policy and 'The Price Level'" (Division of Research and Statistics, Board of Governors of the Federal Reserve System: August 1994).

3. Defining Deviancy Down

"Defining Deviancy Down" first appeared in *The American Scholar* in Winter 1993. Reprinted by permission.

1. In *Spanning the Century: The Life of W. Averell Harriman* (New York: William Morrow, 1992), Rudy Abramson writes: "New York's mental hospitals in 1955 were overflowing warehouses, and new patients were being admitted faster than space could be found for them. When he was inaugurated, 94,000 New Yorkers were confined to state hospitals. Admissions were running at more than 2,500 a year and rising, making the Department of Mental Hygiene the fastest-growing, most-expensive, most-hopeless department in state government."
2. Note that in 1965 (see Chapter 1) I exulted that "the vast Mental Retardation Facilities and Community Mental Health Centers Construction Act had just become law." Note also that I garbled the title of the statute.
3. Charles Krauthammer, *Washington Post*, "Inflation Hits the SATs," June 17, 1994, p. A25: "Now, turning every silver SAT medal into gold is hardly the worst instance of the assault on excellence now taking place in our educational

institutions—pass/fail deserves that honor—but it is highly symbolic. Indeed, the recentering of SAT scores is yet another instance of the recentering of our entire society. As Daniel Patrick Moynihan has noted, today we accept as the norm levels of crime, illegitimacy, homelessness and various other social pathologies that in the past would have been considered intolerable."

4. Nathan Glazer has noted that in a recent "massive" biography *Fiorello LaGuardia and the Making of Modern New York* (New York: McGraw Hill, 1991), by Thomas Kessner, the subject of the school system never appears. "There was simply no problem about New York City's Schools, nothing for even that enormously energetic Mayor to concern himself with." Well, he did visit our new building!

5. There was no text. This is a hurried transcript from tape.

4. America at Midnight?

1. Two years later, in the Fall 1990 issue of *Journal of Economic Perspectives,* Ellwood, with Jonathan Crane, published a paper "Family Change among Black Americans: What Do We Know?"

"Economists and models have not been very successful in explaining the changes in black or white families. Further research is desperately needed, and we hope it will offer new insights. Still, our work has led us to be increasingly pessimistic that economic factors and traditional incentive-based models can explain much of the change in family patterns. Our fear is that the dramatic changes were generated by a complex interaction of social, cultural, legal, and economic factors that will be extremely difficult to disentangle.

"We are even more skeptical about the potential for traditional economic policies ranging from macroeconomic changes to altered public assistance incentives to reverse current trends. We should not ignore the potential incentives of economic policies for the family, but they ought not to drive too many economic policy decisions.

"On the other hand, the consequences of the changing family structures are increasingly apparent. A majority of black children are now virtually assured of growing in poverty, in large part, because of their family status. Families are changing the white community as well. According to several estimates, the majority of children born today will spend some time in a single-parent home. The economic well-being of many of our children probably will be far more influenced by changing family patterns and how the country responds to them than by any of the myriad of forces which traditionally command so much attention in economics. And we are convinced that a great deal can be done in the form of altered social policies to encourage work and independence while reducing poverty in single-parent homes for examples of discussions along these lines."

I trust it will be recognized that this is precisely what we had "discovered" a quarter century earlier. Social science will be of little help to social policy if it takes this long to catch up.

2. "Urban Conditions: General" in the *Annals of the American Academy of Political and Social Science: Social Goals and Indicators for American Society,* vol. 1, May 1967, p. 159.

3. Real life situations can often be represented by a set of equations involving multiple variables. Frequently, however, in the interest of simplicity, the set is reduced to a single equation with a limited number of variables which can lead to quite misleading results. One example of this problem cited by Moffitt is "AFDC Participation across Generations" by Peter Gottschalk, in the *American Economic Review,* May 1990.

4. Dr. King understood the need for facts, and we kept in touch. In an address delivered at Abbott House in Westchester County, New York, on October 29, 1965, he succinctly imparted his reaction to the subject: "As public awareness [of the breakdown of the Negro family] increases there will be dangers and opportunities. The opportunity will be to deal fully rather than haphazardly with the problem as a whole—to see it as a social catastrophe and meet it as other disasters are met with an adequacy of resources. The danger will be that problems will be attributed to innate Negro weaknesses and used to justify neglect and rationalize oppression."

5. Drug Wars

"Iatrogenic Government: Social Policy and Drug Research" first appeared in *The American Scholar* in Summer 1993. Reprinted by permission.

1. Mark A. R. Kleiman and Jonathan P. Caulkins, "Heroin Policy for the Next Decade," *Annals of the American Academy of Political and Social Science,* vol. 521 (May 1992), pp. 163–174.

2. The medical profession does indeed offer hope for success. The cover of a recent issue of *Nature* contains the auspicious query, "Vaccination against Cocaine?" A group of scientists at the Scripps Research Institute of LaJolla, California, may have made a great discovery. In experiments with immuno-chemistry they have created a stable cocaine analogue which caused rats to produce antibodies that "prevented the accumulation of cocaine in the brain and made the rats resistant to the behavioural effects of the drug."

3. A second opinion may be found in an article in the *New York Times Magazine* of August 2, 1908, on "The Growing Menace of the Use of Cocaine": "'The coke-peddler,' said an expert on the drug, 'is a familiar figure in the back rooms of saloon dives throughout the country and every red-light district has a drug store which caters especially to the coke is probably much more widely spread among Negroes than among whites. Heaven dust they call it.' Young men and girls got hold of it, first in a spirit of investigation and curiosity, then

to find themselves bound fast to the wheels of the chariot. Father James B. Curry, pastor of St. James's Church, was one of the first men in the city to become interested in the evil. From his vantage point just off the Bowery he early saw the hold the habit was getting upon the denizens of the district. When it commenced to reach out toward 'his boys,' as the Father calls the young men of his parish, he arose to combat it. The matter was taken to the Department of Health and an investigation started . . . A terrible state of affairs was uncovered. 'Sniff parties' were found to be as frequent and informal in the Tenderloin and along the Bowery . . . Dr. Graeme Monroe Hammond, the neurologist, says that it is absolutely impossible to cure the cocaine fiend once the habit has become fixed upon him. 'There is nothing that we can do for the confirmed user of the drug,' says he. 'The best thing for the cocaine fiend is to let him die.'"

6. The Coming of Age of American Social Policy

1. These distinctions are not simple. Obviously it was the general rise in living standards that in turn gave rise to the notion of social insurance. Nor was sympathy unalloyed. We recall the celebrated passage from Beatrice Webb's *Our Partnership* (London: Longman's, 1948), p. 479: "To us, the compulsory insurance with automatically distributed money, allowances during illness or worklessness, with free choice of doctor under the panel system, would not and could not prevent the occurrence of sickness or unemployment. Indeed, the fact that sick and unemployed persons were entitled to money incomes without any corresponding obligation to get well and keep well, or to seek and keep employment, seemed to us likely to encourage malingering and a disinclination to work for their livelihood."

Index